SALUTE
OF GUNS

To
N.B.,
died of wounds, 1917,
S.B.,
died of gas poisoning, 1926,
C.R.G.,
C.B.T.,
R.K.C.

SALUTE
OF GUNS

DONALD BOYD

Pen & Sword
MILITARY

First published in Great Britain in 1930 by Jonathan Cape
This edition published in 2012 by
PEN AND SWORD MILITARY
an imprint of
Pen and Sword Books Ltd
47 Church Street
Barnsley
South Yorkshire S70 2AS

Copyright © Estate of Donald Boyd and Clare Ajenusi, 2012

ISBN 978 1 84884 850 4

The right of Donald Boyd to be identified
as the author of this work has been asserted by Clare Ajenusi
in accordance with the Copyright, Designs and Patents Act 1988.

A CIP record for this book is available from the British Library.

Printed and bound in England by
CPI Group (UK) Ltd, Croydon, CR0 4YY

Typeset in Times by CHIC GRAPHICS

Pen & Sword Books Ltd incorporates the imprints of
Pen & Sword Aviation, Pen & Sword Family History, Pen & Sword Maritime,
Pen & Sword Military, Pen & Sword Discovery, Wharncliffe Local History,
Wharncliffe True Crime, Wharncliffe Transport, Pen & Sword Select,
Pen & Sword Military Classics, Leo Cooper, Remember When,
The Praetorian Press, Seaforth Publishing and Frontline Publishing

For a complete list of Pen and Sword titles please contact
Pen and Sword Books Limited
47 Church Street, Barnsley, South Yorkshire, S70 2AS, England
E-mail: enquiries@pen-and-sword.co.uk
Website: www.pen-and-sword.co.uk

Contents

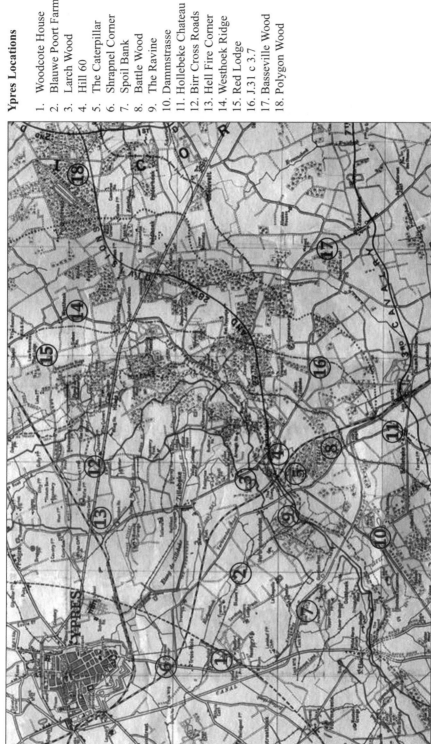

Ypres Locations

1. Woodcote House
2. Blauwe Poort Farm
3. Larch Wood
4. Hill 60
5. The Caterpillar
6. Shrapnel Corner
7. Spoil Bank
8. Battle Wood
9. The Ravine
10. Dammstrasse
11. Hollebeke Chateau
12. Birr Cross Roads
13. Hell Fire Corner
14. Westhoek Ridge
15. Red Lodge
16. J.31 c 3.7
17. Basseville Wood
18. Polygon Wood

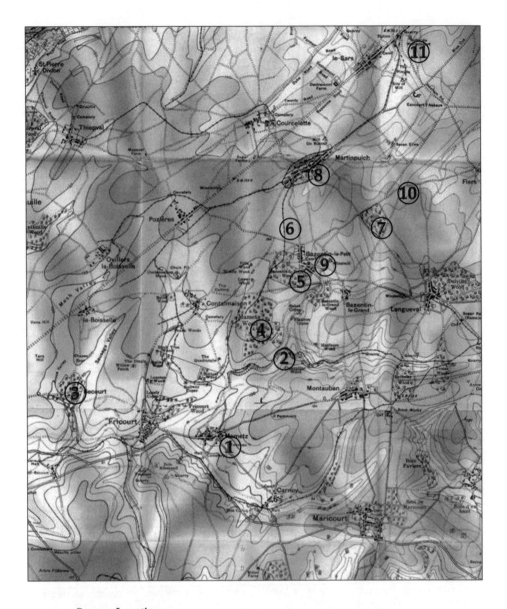

Somme Locations

1. Mametz
2. Caterpillar Valley
3. Becourt Wood
4. Mametz Wood
5. Bazentin Wood
6. 70th Avenue/Welch Alley
7. High Wood
8. Martinpuich
9. Bazentin
10. The Starfish
11. Butte de Warlencourt

Introduction to the
2012 Edition

Most historians would agree that the First World War was an artillery war, at least on land: 58 per cent of British casualties were produced by artillery or mortar shells, compared to 38 per cent caused by rifle or machine-gun fire. Artillery was the decisive weapon, playing the major role initially in creating the stalemate on the Western Front and finally in breaking that deadlock and bringing victory. Yet the literary history of the war is dominated by the infantry and because literary sources dominate the public memory of the war a very significant element is over-looked.[1] The re-publication of Donald Boyd's *Salute of Guns* is a welcome opportunity to correct the neglect of the gunner's war.

In 1931 Robert Graves called *Salute of Guns* 'the best record of Western Front fighting' and there is no doubt about its literary merit. Boyd was after all a professional journalist working in the newsroom of the *Manchester Guardian* alongside Neville Cardus, Howard Spring and other well-known writers. It would be hard to find more compelling descriptions of what it felt like to endure gas or shell bombardments than those in Chapter 5. In addition, the historian can observe how the artillery war developed, as new concepts such as creeping barrages and barrage maps were introduced. Boyd's service record survives in the National Archives, along with the War Diaries of the units in which he served.[2] They confirm the chronology and geography of *Salute of Guns* and, most importantly, the narrative of events. Although Boyd disguises the names of his fellow gunners, they can often be identified without much difficulty. For example, Major Nankivell seems to be Major H. M. Nornabell, Captain H. Jacoby became Captain Michaels and Captain Pilditch appeared as Captain Beecham.

Donald Boyd was born in Chapel Allerton, Yorkshire, on 11 April 1895.[3] His father was a well-regarded wool merchant and nonconformist lay preacher. The family moved to Ilkley where Boyd attended the local grammar school. By August 1914 he was a trainee reporter with the *Leeds*

Mercury but when he decided to enlist in September he returned to Ilkley to join the local Territorial Force unit, 11 Battery of the West Riding Howitzer Brigade, Royal Field Artillery (RFA). Chapter 1 portrays the frustration experienced by new recruits in 1914, training with obsolete equipment (the 5-inch BL howitzer) and with little prospect of seeing early action. In Boyd's case, he had to master horsemanship as well as gunnery. It is not surprising that life as a gunner recruit soon bored him and by the end of the year he had applied for a commission which was gazetted on 18 January. After training in Edinburgh and Sheerness he was posted to France in May 1915.

Chapters 2 and 3 follow Boyd's career once he arrived in France and joined XVIII Brigade RFA of the Lahore Division. Two Indian Divisions had been sent to France in 1914 and they had been heavily involved in the spring battles of 1915; replacements were required and wartime commissioned officers had to be accepted. For both the long-serving Regulars of the Indian Army's artillery and their eager volunteers this was a painful culture shock. Boyd's experience in the Festubert sector has many parallels with Robert Graves' account of life in the 2nd Battalion Royal Welch Fusiliers nearby at Laventie during the same period. 'The peacetime custom of taking no notice of newly-joined officers is still more or less kept up.' It is relevant that 2nd RWF had returned from India not long before the outbreak of war.

In December 1915 the Indian troops were withdrawn from France but they left their artillery behind. The Lahore Division's artillery was attached to the newly raised 3rd Canadian Division and moved north to the Mont des Cats, on the southern side of the Ypres Salient but as more artillery, shells and gunners became available, the BEF's artillery was expanded and re-organized. Boyd's battery, 93 RFA, was divided into two and he found himself serving with a new commander in the new battery. Captain Conrad is the most vividly drawn character in the book and the chapters in which he appears are a very instructive study in leadership. Although a pre-war regular officer with the same Indian Army background as Boyd's tormentors he was young enough to relate to his wartime subalterns. While rigorously maintaining the highest professional standards he was capable of joining, or indeed initiating, their horseplay in the evenings in the Battery Mess. He was just as sceptical about the higher command as his young officers and far more effective in evading their bureaucratic prescriptions.

The figure of Conrad was based on Captain Raymond Cotter who was twenty-six when he joined the Battery and therefore ten or fifteen years younger than a peacetime battery commander and only five years older than Boyd. Cotter had been commissioned from Woolwich in 1909 and had served in India until war broke out. As Boyd describes, his health broke down in late 1916. Cotter returned to England and was trained as an Ordnance specialist. However his health recovered sufficiently by 1918 for him to be posted abroad again, to another Territorial unit, 240 Brigade RFA of 48th Division in Italy, where he was awarded a Military Cross. After the war he remained in the Army and served in the Ordnance Branch in India as a major. It is impossible to tell how accurate Boyd's portrayal of Cotter/Conrad is but it carries conviction and suggests the pre-war British officer corps was a less stereotyped organization than it sometimes appears. In addition, it is worth noting that one of the great strengths of *Salute of Guns* is the description of personal relationships within a small group such as a battery officers' mess and their impact on individual and sub-unit morale and efficiency. Shortly after Cotter was invalided back to England, Boyd suffered his first nervous breakdown. One suspects that he would have lasted longer if Cotter had still been in command and that Cotter would have found ways of easing the strain on his junior officers.

Chapters 4, 5 and 6 follow the Battery as it completes its training on the coast near Boulogne and is then sent to join a Territorial division, which although never named was in fact 47th (2nd London) Division. The battery became C Battery of 235th Brigade, RFA. The 47th Division had been in France for nearly a year and had taken part in several of the 1915 battles and had played a significant part in the Battle of Loos. It was now holding the Notre Dame de Lorette sector, facing Vimy Ridge. Boyd refers to the German spoiling attack on 21 May 1916 although he was on leave at the time. Shortly afterwards the Battle of the Somme began and 47th Division was moved south to prepare for the major offensive on 15 September, the Battle of Flers-Courcellette, which saw the first use of tanks. But the artillery went into action a month before the infantry, and remained in the line when the infantry were rested after the capture of High Wood. Initially the artillery supported 15th (Scottish) Division, hence Boyd's references to Scottish infantry. In Chapter 5 Boyd brings home the stress of an artillery subaltern's routine during the Battle of the Somme. His infantry counterpart faced the more acute risks of 'an attack over the top' but if he survived would be rested after a few days. The gunner could expect to be rotated between duty as a forward observer in the front line, sharing the infantry's risks, or serving on the gun lines, exposed to German counter-battery fire. 'Rest' would mean a few days at the horse lines but even then more shells had to be brought up to the gun lines every night. These were the strains that brought Donald Boyd to the point of collapse, though the breakdown did not occur until December 1916 when the division had left the Somme and was holding a supposedly 'quiet' sector in the southern part of the Ypres Salient.

The 'Confidential Report on Case of 2/Lt. BOYD' of 4 December 1916 which survives with Boyd's records, substantiates the account in Chapter 6 and is worth quoting in full.

This officer was perfectly fit and well up to 17th September 1916, on which date he was acting as FOO for 24 hours in a very exposed position N. of HIGH WOOD. Enemy fire was very heavy, and several shells burst close to him, one in fact within about 6 feet. On relief he was so obviously affected that his Battery Commander, Captain V. NICKALLS, ordered him to report sick, which he did. I was then prepared to send him to Field Ambulance, but as he thought he was improving I did not do so.

Since then he has carried out all his duties, but obviously with increasing difficulty. He is very easily tired physically and does not seem able to concentrate his attention long on any point. His reflexes are normal. He is troubled by a certain amount (not very marked) of Insomnia, and by terrifying dreams, usually dealing with fighting, which occasionally lead to his waking with a scream.

In my opinion he is suffering from a mild degree of TRAUMATIC NEURASTHENIA dating definitely from a shell burst which half buried him (17/9/16). The difference in him before and after that date was very marked to all who knew him. He has since never shirked his duties, though his battery commander has been careful to spare him as much as possible. This is, therefore, certainly not a case of an officer seeking to cover neglect or cowardice by a claim to be suffering from shell shock.

The diagnosis was changed to anaemia and by the end of the year Boyd had been sent back home on sick leave. His gradual recovery is monitored in the medical reports where he is marked 'Fit for light duties', 'Fit for Home Service' and finally, in July 1917, 'Fit for General Service'. A month later Boyd was back in France with 47th Division and now posted to B Battery, 235th Brigade RFA.

The Third Battle of Ypres was in progress and Chapter 7 provides a valuable account of the three aspects of an artillery subaltern's role in the battle. Re-ammunitioning the battery at night, when the tracks might be searched at any time by German shellfire, illustrates how the famous 'Shrapnel Corner' got its name. The practicalities of firing a creeping barrage off a 'Barrage Map' are illustrated by the account of the night before the opening of the Battle of the Menin Road. This was the first offensive in which General Plumer was in charge and the detailed preparation for which Plumer was famous is obvious. Finally came the stress of spells as FOO in an observation post in the front line.

The contrast of a tour in a quiet sector, near Gavrelle, is described in Chapter 8[4] but in November, despite well-founded rumours that the division was to move to Italy, it was drawn into the fighting at Cambrai. The infantry were committed at Bourlon Wood with the support of the artillery in line: 47th Divisional Artillery was therefore available when the Germans counter-attacked on 30 November. Boyd vividly describes his Brigade's advance through rear area chaos to support the Guards Division's attack on Gonnelieu. The exchange of traditional military courtesies between an Army Service Corps column and the gunners as they trot into action was precisely the sort of incident which sticks in the memory even on such a confused day.

The shock of 30 November was mild compared to the impact of the German offensive which opened on 21 March 1918. Once again the infantry of the division were being supported in the line by another divisional artillery and 47th Division's gunners formed part of the Corps Mobile Reserve. They were soon separated from their parent division and operated independently until the beginning of May. The 235th Brigade War Diary records that in the withdrawal on the afternoon of 22 March 'it was found that Brigade had lost 3 guns and 2 wagons but were later able to recover 2 of the guns'. This incident is described in Chapter 10 and Boyd was responsible for the recovery of the guns. He was awarded the Military Cross for this action but does not mention the award in his book.

When the German offensive was finally halted a period of stalemate followed, at least in the Somme sector where 47th Division was located. Chapter 11 describes this period during which the artillery supported the Australian-American attack on Hamel on 4 July which was considered the model for the offensives of the final Hundred Days' campaign which began on 8 August. Boyd missed the beginning of the campaign because he was on leave and then on a course at Fourth Army Artillery School. When he rejoined the Brigade the division had moved north and was advancing towards Lille. Boyd's old nervous problems returned, triggered perhaps by the arrival of a new and apparently less than competent battery commander in July. Even a transfer to a new battery in September did not improve things and by October the strain was overwhelming. In Chapter 12 the effect of the night-time harrassing fire of a German long-range gun is vividly described. The 47th Divisional artillery intelligence summaries confirm this pattern of operations, noting that 'The enemy keeps fairly quiet during the day; but wakes up at night and shoots at roads and tracks'. Eventually, on 10 October, Boyd was forced to report sick. The medical reports describe his condition some days later when he reached a Base Hospital at Harfleur. 'Any nervous exertion causes feelings of extreme weakness.' He 'now finds that he cannot sleep and that he becomes easily depressed and worried.' 'He looks ill. His facial expression is strained ... He needs a rest out of the line.' Fortunately the war was about to end and 11 November found Donald Boyd carrying out light duties at le Havre.

Boyd claimed that *Salute of Guns* was 'as plain and truthful an account as I could manage' and the documents seem to bear out his claim. It is hard to know why the book was so quickly submerged in the flood of 'war books' which saw the light in the 1930s and has had to wait so long for a second edition. The re-publication of *Salute of Guns* will be welcomed. Military historians will gain new insights into some of the most significant passages in the history of the Western Front. General readers will enjoy a book which depicts the reality of warfare as vividly as the well-worn favourites on their shelves with a freshness created by its unjustified neglect.

Michael Orr
May 2012

Notes

1 It is, of course, not true that there have been no artillery memoirs at all but their number does not match the infantry memoirs. Among those worth reading, N. Fraser-Tytler *Field Guns in France* (1922) and *The War Diary of the Master of Belhaven* (1924) are interesting accounts by battery commanders but not literary. *Blasting & Bombardiering* by Wyndham Lewis (1937) is possibly too literary. A. Wade *The War of the Guns* (1936) describes a ranker's view of the artillery war.

2 Donald Boyd's personal file may be found in The National Archives (TNA): Public Record Office (PRO) WO 339/22401.

Relevant unit War Diaries are: XVIII Brigade RFA, TNA: PRO WO 95/3918; 235 Brigade RFA, TNA: PRO WO 95/2717; 238 Brigade RFA, TNA: PRO WO 95/2718; 47th Division Commander Royal Artillery, TNA: PRO WO 95/2710, 2711 & 2712

3 I am grateful to Donald Boyd's grand-daughter, Clare Ajenusi, for providing biographical details of her father and the loan of his unpublished memoir of his life before and after the First World War.

4 Boyd mentions meeting his uncle while marching from the Ypres Salient to the Arras area and notes that his uncle was serving with the Canadian Corps and was killed near Vimy Ridge shortly afterwards. The Commonwealth War Graves Commission lists Private Norman Boyd, 2nd Canadian Infantry Battalion and the son of Eldad Boyd of Burley-in-Wharfedale, Yorkshire, as being killed on 12 October 1917. He is buried in Aix-Noulette Communal Cemetery Extension.

Chapter 1

Riding to Persepolis

England – August 1914

W e trotted round and round, so empty that the sight of the coarse grass was almost enough to turn one sick. 'My boots' Sam gasped, and shook his head and fell out on the grass inside the circle, looking white. My boots hurt too. They were my father's boots, heavy nailed boots that swung through the grass and made my legs feel like thin coiled springs. The black leather had a dull blue shine on it, like cast iron, and the soles were so heavy that they would not bend. The sergeant paid no attention to Sam. He said it was his boots, but that was not all. There were several others lying there, one on his stomach, the others looking up at the morning sky. We jogged on. Every time the sergeant shouted 'About turn!' somebody stumbled on somebody else, and somebody was so tired he never heard the order and went on. Then the sergeant started again. 'You cod-fish, you with a chest like a ninepenny rabbit, you've got a back like a half-shut knife.'

When he finished we dropped and threw our arms out, and let ourselves sink into emptiness. A bugle sounded for breakfast. We picked up the casualties and went to the cooks' tent for bits of cold bacon, dry bread, and scalding tea.

The sun was hot upon us that first day. We were dragging a gun over the tussocks of grass. Most of us had scarcely seen such a thing before. It was like a piece of sculpture snuffing the sky. The name of the piece was deeply incised over the burnished breech. '5-in B.L. Howitzer' it said. The heat radiated in wavering streams from the metal, the spokes rattled dryly in felloes and axle-box and the grease trickled along the grey-green paint. As we threw our weight on the wheels the hard indifferent smell of her filled our noses. She would move and then subside with a jar into the rutted grass. Even in our shirt sleeves the sweat poured out of us, and each time 'Detachments Rear!' brought us to a halt about the short trail of the piece we made a chorus of heavy breathing to which the instructor paid no heed. Sam gritted his teeth as we chased to limber up. The howitzer settled heavily in each hollow and snubbed its way out, sometimes swinging the pole men off their feet. 'Halt! Action right!' More running, the limber grumbling off, the gun team carrying the trail round a quarter circle to the left, Number 4 securing his sight. But even before he had clamped we were off again, hauling on the wheels, our boots tripping wearily in the grass, the sweat running into our eyes, our throats glued up with thirst.

At last our two hours was over. At a little distance there was a man sitting on a cask and banging it with an enamelled mug. Sam and I ran to him. 'What is it?' we asked. 'Bitter,' he said. We accepted 'bitter' in an innocent adjectival sense. 'How much is it?' It was three half-pence. We bought mugs and spat the stuff out on the grass. The farrier was horrified and agreed to drink it for us. After that we had tea and marmalade and bread dished out to us on our own plates. We had no other. We were too exhausted to think of washing, but lay on the grass in the tent and sipped the thin hot tea. Sam slept, and shortly a corporal came to warn him for picket duty. We were jealous he should be chosen first to do duty. 'What do you do if the horses kick, Corporal?' he asked.

'Swear like hell,' the corporal said, and then added kindly, 'you don't want to worry, it's an easy job.'

'Come for a walk, Starchy?' I asked.

'Do you think we can?'

'Why not?'

We pulled on our civilian jackets and wiped our boots on our socks. On our way we leaned over a rope fence to talk to Sam, who was sitting on a pyramid of hay. In the distance over the white tents we pointed out to him a broad belt of trees now in the full foliage of late summer. The wind ruffled the trees into silver flecks, and disclosed the cool green depths within, as though we looked into water.

'You're lucky,' Sam said. 'If one of those big brutes hits out,' he added, grinning like a rising sun, 'I shall be dead before breakfast. Aceldama, the field of blood.'

We walked on till we came to the edge of the camp. There were two or three soldiers at the gate. One of them put a riding whip across my chest.

'Got a pass?'

We explained that we were going for a walk.

'Well, where's your pass?'

Surely, we could go out into the wood, there? We were not going to run away – No, not without a pass.

'If this is the British Army, I don't think much of it,' I said.

'You clear off sharp, or you'll find yourself in the guardroom.'

Starchy said, as we turned back, 'I tell you what it is, once the army has got you, you can't even have a soul of your own, much less a walk. I wonder what the chap that made the speech at the drill-hall, Lord Charles Beresford, would say if he got stopped going out of his office for a walk. He said we were gallant fellows.' Starchy giggled.

We had to take two horses apiece to water after grooming them in the lines. They seemed enormous and terrifying. Sam was a lightweight, and they carried him clean across the trough and trod on his feet. His bursts of laughter caught the attention of the lieutenant, who came round to show us how to control the horses with a hitch of rope round the nose. That night we were warned that one of the tent must be ready next morning for a medical inspection on behalf of all of us. We suspected that it concerned something improper, so we chose the boy whom we called 'the holy clerk' to offer himself. We argued that a divinity student must be all right. In the morning we left him standing at attention in front of the tent pole wearing a pair of grey flannel trousers, an army shirt and a straw hat. He waited about three-quarters of an hour before the doctor came, and complained afterwards that the doctor tickled him.

I wrote home—'The great tent of the YMCA is a splendid place, absolutely crowded, and, of course, only selling aerating drinks which cost a penny. Our equipment has not arrived, but the small kit amply satisfies all other needs, two shirts, two pairs of excellent socks, hussif, hold-all, razor, brush and hair-comb, spoon, knife and fork, jack-knife are all included free. Even this paper and envelope are free at the YMCA. The drill movements are very intricate but adequate and interesting. I had the job of fixing the sight. I must add a word of praise for the sergeants, who are a splendid and equable set of men. I am having a good time.'

The phrase covered many unwritten thoughts. I had seen a number of recruits falling from horses as tall as houses. I had learned for the first time the habit of a field latrine; its powerful smell of raw wood, sacking and chloride of lime. There was trouble in the latrine because some used the trench one way, some another, and Sam nearly got his eye blacked by a shoeing-smith because he stopped at the exit bellowing with laughter at the confusion. Instructions were issued; thereafter we conversed amiably, squatting in rows. It was most companionable to go with friends.

A week or so later we marched to Doncaster in our civilian garments. We carried spades, mallets and buckets, and the officer in charge rode a mile or more in front or behind us. We thought he was ashamed of us. On the high road a woman came out with a pitcher of milk for us, but everybody agreed we couldn't expect much more of that. The war was over a month old.

At Doncaster the violence of training increased. The war was slipping past too quickly, and still we were not ready. We rose at 5.30 for stables and worked for a couple of hours before breakfast. After battery parade we went for drill on the howitzers. The afternoon was as bad. We ran in circles for miles with eyes fixed in front, by order of Sergeant José, a Devonshire man, who cried, 'No, lard, you'll not trip, keep them eyes up.'

'Death's door!' Sam said through his teeth.

'Next in!' I answered.

Gun drill was upon a tongue of tussocky grass bounded by a tiny ditch. Sometimes José would stop us, and with one foot on the trail, and his eyes wrinkled against the sun, would talk about war as he had seen it in South Africa. 'Remember, lards,' he said, 'the moral effect of the first shell is more than what ten thousand million bullets will do.' His long-necked burnished spurs clinked as he walked back to his position of command. We admired him enormously. 'Detachments rear!' We stood like images while he walked up and down detailing the gun drill, stopping suddenly with a finger on Sam's chest or another's to hear him continue. 'Numbers Seven, Eight and Nine remain at the wagon line to replace casualties as ordered,' I said. The words were sinister. A casualty seemed some accidental wounding; a splinter off its course interrupting the business of war. 'And always make sure,' José's voice droned on, 'you have your field dressing intact. It may save your life.' At the end of gun drill one of the rich recruits went up to José and offered him a cigarette from a gold case. 'Thank you, I prefer my own,' he said and took a Woodbine packet from his tunic. The squad laughed. Then we joined our drivers for stables again. At the end of the afternoon there were orders for a night battery action to begin at 9 p.m. and end probably at midnight, five and a half hours before reveille.

Our room in the grandstand was a long one with blankets rolled down on the floor. At nine o'clock at night a corporal's party brought round a bucket of cocoa and sometimes a large lump of sausage meat. The night-latrine buckets sometimes stood inside, but usually outside, the door, and every Saturday they overflowed on to the wood, and round about the walls were splashed with vomit. But on ordinary nights, exhausted to the point at which the hardest palliasse becomes luxury, we lay and watched the fire flickering on the low roof. There were story-tellers. Starchy was a favourite, but others preferred their tales more strongly flavoured. Occasionally an undersized driver named Lob went off into monkeyish tricks. Dressed only in long pants, he leaped about the room howling and scratching. He clambered up the windows and hung on the transoms with scraping nails, mopping and mowing above our heads in the red firelight, breaking wind and belching at will. Most of the drivers were grooms and coachmen, gamekeepers and farm hands and butcher boys. They delighted to tease their own weaker friends about their amorous adventures or upon sexual weakness of a common kind. Reveille always came too early. Even to get half-dressed was difficult. Sleep was solid gold. We woke Scaife, a mining engineer, one night at a quarter to ten and told him to hurry for early morning parade. He rolled on to the floor groaning loudly and dressed himself before he saw we were undressing. Now we were awakened at 5.15 and came reeling down the staircase, a collection of animated carcases. The mornings were bitter cold in November. If we could get down in time we could buy a cup of imitation coffee and a parkin cake for two pence at a small shop whose incandescent light was our morning star. Guard duty increased the desire for sleep.

The guardroom had been a police office. Its oily walls had now accumulated a thick grime and its old-fashioned grate spread ashes all over the floor. Upon this fire were cooked odd meals of cheese and cocoa and tea, at all times of the night, and their fragments also worked into the boards on which we slept. When the time for guard came the sergeant rocked our shoulders on the boards till we woke. Then we would half rise and blink at the black figures silhouetted against the fire, the steam from the mess tins rising in rosy clouds till it met the throbbing green glimmer of the gas mantle. Sam came back horrified to tell us how he had been relieved by the sergeant early in the morning and how upon their return the sergeant called him to look under the counter at another of the guard who was apparently in the throes of a sexual nightmare. When we were actually on the beat round the gun-park it was almost impossible to keep from collapsing on the concrete from want of sleep. Eyes closed of themselves, a hypnotic desire for sleep spread illusion over the stormy sky. Again and again I found I had

5

hitched myself on to the corner of a wagon and was already dozing and must tear myself away. A loud clatter woke me; I had dropped my rifle, and the colonel was coming across the square! Once again the heavens seemed to have fallen. I jumped into the air; an old horse had slept standing and lost his balance. He was now weaving with his melancholy head and shifting his feet about, while the flying moon dappled the water in the horse trough. The soft gnawing of the crib-biters and the shuddering breaths of the windsuckers were strange sounds in a sleeping world.

The weather got worse, and those who objected to be marched out on an Anglican church-parade were employed, like Mrs Partington, in brushing back the flood of dung and mud from the lines on the racecourse. The church parade was irksome and it seemed impossible to induce a spiritual fervour upon a regimental occasion in which the voice of the sergeant major was not silenced until the service actually began. My religious views were revolted at the idea of marching to their exercise in column of fours. At last I found a 'Free Christian Church' whose services began at eleven. No longer had I to be marched off with gangs regimentally to church. Nobody else knew of my church and I had a church parade of my own under the winking eye of the orderly sergeant, and upon his dismissal conducted my own march into the town.

We were always very hungry. Often we could not swallow the food provided. Every week we spent our 9s 7½d (49.5p) pay in two or three days at the café which bears the name of Parkinson's Celebrated Butterscotch. There was a smoke-room in which we could talk at ease with some infantrymen from Sheffield University. But in the end some officers came, and so we had to go. The drinkers of the battery did better. They safeguarded their smoke-room by springing officiously to attention whenever an officer came in. This device was successful after a few glasses had been broken. Everywhere we went we smelled strongly of horse dung and ammonia. This was very embarrassing. One of our genteel companions rented a room in town to which he retired every evening he could. There he changed and sat until roll call. He also had a soldier's uniform made by his own tailor.

We had nicknamed our driver's horses Romulus and Remus in honour of their Roman noses, and the drivers, finding in Sam rich-sounding unfamiliar names, came to him for help. Casseopeia was another, and Bellerophon, a beast with no manners and feet as big as dinner plates.

Sam suddenly became tired of the filth and the uncooked gobbets of meat we had to eat. He got an infantry commission almost straightway. We celebrated Christmas in the long room as a farewell feast, with bottles of home-brewed elderberry wine contributed by one of the two jovial butchers who were members of the septette. I was on guard the night he went. The dead weight upon my eyelids, the loss of a friend and the dislike of the guardroom, where we still slept among fragments of cinders, spittle, and decaying meat, resolved me also to seek a commission. So I too deserted the septette. The corporal who had baulked me of my leave because I never stood him drinks called me by my Christian name. Starchy stood and looked at me with his long arms at his side, his head thrust forward and a wry smile on his moon face. 'You'll be wun of the nobs neeoo,' he said, 'and you wun't know the likes of us low common fellows.' He put his horsebrush, glistening palely with grease, into the other hand, wiped his palm on his trousers' seat and shook hands. I shouldered my kit bag and turned away from the racecourse, waving to the row of booths as I went.

I left Doncaster with a fair knowledge of gun drill. I had another accomplishment. I could ride a horse bareback at exercise, lead another and light a pipe. My seat had been skinned till it bled. Now it was hardened, and more nimble in its efforts to coincide with the horse's trot. It was not a substantial equipment for war, but it seemed much then.

The real business of the Scottish barracks to which I was sent in my new stiff uniform seemed to be an introduction to regimental customs and to the raffish world. Its mess, a repository of formalities, was filled with a mixture of younger sons from overseas, and accidental arrivals from the professions. Connellan was an Irishman with a flat nose in a flat face, whose grey eyes looked peculiarly unusual in his grey skin. He was drunk most nights and occasionally brought a woman into the barracks with him, she lying on the floor of the taxi-cab to evade the guard. The taxi waited outside his staircase till he had finished with her, and she then departed as she had come. Connellan had acquired a captaincy by some chance and was in a position to touch money. Early in the New Year he departed for France with thirty pounds, the value of three worthless cheques which he left behind. A telegram was despatched offering him the alternatives of returning at once or being arrested at le Havre. He returned. Connellan was a relic of the early nineteenth century. He was wholehearted in drinking and gambling. He rejoiced to bait the captain of my battery, a pale-faced Scot who suffered from an interesting disease. Whenever his name was about to appear on the draft list the sickness made itself evident and confined him to bed. Its nature was otherwise uncertain. When Connellan finally left us we all turned out, in accordance with custom, to see him off. The drafts all left at night. The station glimmered ghostly under the arc lamps as though the air were thick with mist. A crowd of civilians pressed behind the raw wood barrier, crying out mock-hearty farewells to their men. The officers in their own group laughed and talked higher up the platform. The train was due to leave when Connellan appeared, supported by two friends. He was hauled into a carriage and locked in, but immediately started to climb out of the window. As the whistle blew a girl rushed up the platform and flung herself into his arms. She was dragged away by a porter, and departed smiling vaguely through her powder at the group left behind. We returned in a fleet of taxis. Amongst us was Laverick who kept a stud farm in the east of England, a handsome figure wearing uniform liberally inlaid with buckskin, and Miller, a mining engineer from South America, whose revolver butt was nicked twice to record men he had shot dead with a cold blue eye laid level over the sights, his yellow face screwed up in determination. His walk gave a sort of serpentine effect, his head and shoulders carried forward, threatening but coldly genial.

All this time our military education advanced little. Once or twice we had a two-hours' gun drill in the morning. In the afternoon most of us slept through an hour's Morse signalling on benches laid round the schoolroom. Riding school from three to four was the most arduous exercise of the day. Most of us feared the riding-master. Time after time the remounts would refuse, or run off or buck. We revolved in a cloud of powdered tan, sneezing and crusted round the eyes, formed fours, inclined left and right, jumped without reins and stirrups, filed left and right, went in and out of the box-jump, vaulted off and on, changed horses, sat in silence while the riding-master handed out some bitter insult on the point of his whip. Some were injured and went to hospital; some answered back. Those who did got a worse horse next time. The gun drill was displaced by two-hour rides into the country over flinty roads traversing bare moors sprinkled with snow. Arrived at some level space the riding-master put us through our tricks again.

At night we dined in some delicacy, with fragments of presentation plate among the finger bowls. It was impressive to see that even grapes were eaten with knife and fork, and the most aggressively lofty of our company burned off the spirit in his liqueur. It was his nature to be a compendium of etiquette. Slightly intoxicated one night, he saw a Canadian asleep in the ante-room where others were playing cards. One must not sleep in an ante-room. For

8

the honour of the regiment he turned the full blast of a soda-water syphon in the Canadian's ear. Linton got up and dried his face and collar; then slowly pursued the bully to the doors where he was coyly hiding with the syphon at the ready. The fight lasted only a few minutes before the Canadian had thrown the other down the steps. A sort of mêlée followed the exchanges, and Laverick, wildly excited, danced on a card table among the glasses. In feasting and carousing the days were spent, and gunnery seemed as far off as the grave.

It was a time when we were assumed to be taking the part of glorious sacrifice, and people still were kind and had not been long enough disturbed to become anxious. Sir Owen Seaman had addressed the King's Recruit in grave and flattering words – 'Now is your time of trial, now, when overhead the light of – ' — was it glory? – 'dies,' and his clarion call to duty echoed through earnest hearts. My duty was to go from one large building to another through the slums to inspect depots of two or three hundred men. These hundreds intimidated me, but their devotion to duty made them equable and their troubles were nearly always the troubles of small traders who must get home for stocktaking, or small farmers who wanted to get home to plough. 'We're not doing anything here, sir, and we'd come back at once if wanted.' Their food was far better than we had eaten at Doncaster, and they did not complain. From such pay parades and inspections I went into the town to eat lunch. There was a licensed grocer who ate there, a strange dandiacal figure of a man about sixty. He always wore a morning-coat and silk hat, square pointed collar and white slip. It was assumed we were deadly rivals for the hand of Williamina, our waitress, whose soft complaining accent and whose country bloom adorned the table. If I were there first he would stalk to another table and send me a challenge on the back of a menu card, signed J. A. MacWhirter MacCorquadale. Williamina resisted this foolery and begged us to behave.

She came with me in the cold, grey rain to an enormous music hall, whose warmth and colour overshadowed realities with a dream. The chorus rocked across the stage with legs outflung under stiff frocks trimmed with swansdown. The music poured over us genially authoritarian, with trills from the wood wind and heartening percussions from brass and drum, while the stage business wove light and colour in kaleidoscope. It was not long before we were ready to embrace this bright moment, to welcome the illusion for true splendour, to be moved, heartened, converted. In a little it led to its great moment. Softly the motive began in the orchestra, the dim stage was full of marching shadows, a woman's voice far away translated the inescapable beat —'We don't —want; to— lose – you; but – we think – you – ought – to – go.'

'Do you like it here?' Williamina asked wistfully. Yes, I liked it, if liking was the word. The music was full of melancholy warning and I felt rather like the child who is told that the doctor won't hurt. Time seemed to be running too fast, to have joined the White Queen, faster, faster, when all was burning away, French, Germans, Russians, English. You could not ask anyone to wait a bit. 'For – your king – and; your – country; – both – want – you – so.'

'It's a shame,' Williamina sighed, and huddled closer. Unbeknown she poured a small bottle of scent over the collar of my British warm coat. Gunner Savory looked after me like a polite elder brother, and when I woke in the morning I found him, with a smile upon his face, spreading the collar in the sun. There had been difficulty over his leave; his name had been omitted from the list. It was Maundy Thursday when I went to the sergeant major to beg for Savory. He was full of resource. He took out his copy of the Nominal Roll and solemnly drew his pencil through Savory's name. 'Gunner Savory,' he said, 'your name has been struck off the Nominal Roll, but you got to be back here Tuesday at 6 a.m. or I'll post you a deserter.' It seemed an ideal way of walking round a difficulty. 'Now, sir, perhaps you'll do something for me, inspect the married quarters,' the sergeant major said. A corporal led me rapidly round the tall ugly tenements, in and out of windy, whitewashed passages, into kitchens and water-closets, rapping a loud warning of our approach with his whip.

In the afternoon a party of us went for tea to a café in which a fountain played in a marble basin. The walls were covered with sentimentalized pictures, and strings discoursed cafe-concert music. We jingled our spurs on the marble floor, swinging the skirts of our greatcoats, and sneered at the scarlet pipings of the local yeomanry on the ground that their scarlet was an amusing weakness in men not part of the regular army, and that the terrific thongs on their crops were a form of childishness compared with the short cane ending in a loop which the syphonist had made the mode with us.

There was a poster advertising embrocation, which showed two mounted officers, French and English, meeting on a sandy road by a wood. The Frenchman's riding whip hung from his wrist by a thong as he lifted his hand in salute. War looked like that, a genial, earnest business conducted on horseback with no time for idle chatter. The excitement of war deflected one's eyes from the casualty lists. A few days after I was taken to the Literary Club for dinner and there met Captain K— who had already been out and had returned with wounds. His appearance was grey, his manner not cordial. His eyes, wide open, appeared to be staring at something we could not see; perhaps the shock of disaster as it had overtaken his company on a grassy field during the first of the fighting. They had broken cover from a wood to advance on another and met machine-gun fire which melted them away. He was wounded in the stomach but lay firing up the hill all that day before he would crawl back. His story was discouraging. It was a relief to hear the talk turn back to politics and books.

The city was a friendly place. I was taken to Edinburgh for a weekend. We visited the barbed-wire entanglements round the Forth Bridge and looked on the warships at Rosyth, spread out as far as we could see into the haze.

'You're doing the right thing, undoubtedly,' Mr Dougall said, as he put me into the train, his heavy Scottish face lighting with kindness. The train sped on, and the simple sort of heroism which had suddenly come within the reach of ordinary people filled the carriage like the blooming of a flower.

When Sam and I used to sit square upright on the ammunition wagon, the hand-loop held taut between our knees, he would whisper across to me some lines from *Tamburlane:*

Is it not passing brave to be a king
And ride in triumph through Persepolis!

Thus mock-heroic we answered days in which it was easy to be heroic. Nevertheless it was not devotion to an army so much as to a place.

Far below, the quarrel upon Belgium, the German faces brutalised by *Punch,* these were accidents, irrelevancies, unconsidered. We thought the name of the West Riding was as lovely as any song; wide spreading lonely moors, running down to the silvery coppice wherein the bluebells would soon be shining; the dry walls bleached like bones, the fine cropped turf over the limestone, the murmurous valleys whose very sounds spoke of silence, the villages gathering decently about the church and the inn, reticent and self-respectful; the brown old faces steady like sculpture, unchangeable, pre-occupied by private thoughts; these were the articles of our creed, and hate was not among them.

The war was still going on in spite of our fears that it would collapse before we had shared its glories. Large drafts of men left the barracks every ten days or so. They had been brought in from the depots as the rooms fell empty, and on the day of their departure they were in effect prisoners inside the barrack walls. There was still the wet canteen. Towards nightfall some attempt was made to round them up and see that each still possessed the kit made up that morning, and at eight or nine o'clock the first real attempt was made to get them out on the barrack square.

The sergeant major and his NCOs took this in hand, allowing about three-quarters of an hour's scheduled time for the job. The officer on duty arrived in the dark to find a handful of sober men in the square, patiently waiting for their comrades. Every now and then gusts of wild singing and talking burst out of the wet canteen, and a group would come reeling across the darkness shepherded by a vituperative corporal, their equipment hanging in festoons upon their shoulders, their caps – or probably somebody else's caps – askew. At last the major part of a couple of hundred men were in rows with their kit-bags at their sides, and in adjacent heaps lay their companions who could not stand and who would not be supported. The colonel made a short affectionate speech, and the column moved off in broken order. A wagon accompanied it to pick up the incapables. We had not far to go to the goods yard. There they were packed into carriages, vomiting, shouting, singing, perpetually climbing out and climbing in.

Hours seemed to pass under the blue arc lamps before they were settled enough to start, and likely as not a few would turn up staggering on the far side of the line when the trains had moved off.

The weather became mild. In the middle of April I was lucky enough to get sent to the School of Gunnery at Shoeburyness, and when I arrived there it was to find the fruit trees in the barrack town covered with blossom and the beds full of flowers. We walked by the shore and looked over to Sheppey Island while the grey Thames slapped the shingle under the wind. We had little time for such idleness. The sergeant major had told us what we should do, and of our future state. Chewed string was nothing to it. Moreover, Southend was out of bounds – 'Cos why? Why, gentlemen, because some of your predecessors was a-taken in the hact of increasing of the population under the bathing machines.' But still on the Roach, Sunday hours were free, and I avoided Southend by taking a cab through its streets. In a mill-house by the tidal river I saw my last fragment of peaceful England. The brick hearth had never burned anything but wood and, in the window, Chris, on her holiday from school, taught us how to be brave by reading the gory passages from her books. Alas! neither then nor later did I learn that accomplishment. At the barracks time flew past in arduous schooling, decorated by the bright colours of Macaroni's silk 'weekend' pyjamas, which many visitors admired, and by Errol's casual, companionable laughter. In the evening we walked arm in arm under the blossom and over the edge of the cricket ground, circling the great trees which bound it, and heard the voices, clear and musical, running along the earth. Errol had been at Mons. 'It's fine to be in it,' he said, 'but we may never have such a time as this again; let's turn right down to the fort, and then go back by the chapel.' One by one the candles shining through the trees were going out.

One morning as we were leaving the mess we were stopped by an excited group round the noticeboard. It was covered with typewritten announcements each ending in a list of names. It was a few days before Festubert; and within twenty-four hours all our course had gone. A few hours at home remained, and then we turned overseas.

Chapter 2

Numbers 7, 8 and 9

Pont Riqueul – Spring 1915

My very first bottle of wine was almost empty. The topaz liquor trembled in the white glass, and focused golden lights like peacock's eyes upon the silvery grey of the table-cloth. Around the glass lay the implements of dinner; knives shaped like daggers, glazed fragments of crust, the fluted caramel dish, the brown coffeepot still spreading fragrance through the air. Again I drank a little of the wine. It had astonishing smoothness and sharpness, and an astringent flavour which seemed to employ every sensory nerve of the palate, and enticed them to continue. In the mirrors of the restaurant other diners were reflected bending over the little tables, and curls of smoke rising from cigarettes of Scaferlati started off with eager ripples for the gilded ceiling. The silence carried the shuffle of feet from the pavements, and through the tall windows the sky over le Havre was pure indigo unpierced by stars. The leaves of the trees were shot with golden light from the street lamps. My thoughts echoed in my head like bells and I was both pleased and alarmed at this lucidity.

It seemed ages since I had stripped off my foolish equipment at the British office in the Rue de Thiers; revolver, ammunition-pouch, map-case, mess-tin, binoculars, haversack and prismatic compass. Absurd! As if we were to dash off into battle like the White Knight! The typewritten instructions seemed no less absurd. 'Bromo; relatives and friends send out in letters and parcels.' This was too intimate a duty to put on kind aunts and uncles. I felt that Usumcasane and Techelles would have been very much amused by that, and I wished that Sam had been with me to enjoy the evening. We would have enjoyed a little victory over the awkward globe artichokes. There was so much to talk about, and not least the strange people; black-haired, bareheaded women in tight blue blouses and black skirts, neat, elderly men in grey straw hats wearing corded pince-nez and alpaca jackets. They continued to promenade in my mind as I stared at the wine glass, whose liquor trembled a little as a waiter passed.

A boy brought my cap, gloves and crop, and I set foot on the polished hardwood floor. By some accident the crop fell and went spinning across to the cashier's pulpit. 'Mortified' was the word that came into my head. The boy retrieved the crop. I passed under the gilded cupids at the door and laughed, and noticed that my voice seemed too loud.

The train was now starting out of the goods yard; it went in a jingle, jingle, jar, bump, stumbling over the points. Far up it the men were singing and shouting. The train was full, men in third-class carriages and cattle trucks, officers four and six to a compartment. There were only four of us in our carriage and the next was ours too. It was Thomas who had organized our departure. Easing a khaki stock about his neck he was settling in his corner with *La Vie Parisienne, Le Rire, Le Sourire and Fantasio*, unconscious, apparently, of his brilliance as a forager. He had found two old soldiers among the draft and, in return for ten francs, a bottle of wine, and the promise of room to lie down, they had loaded our four valises and other baggage artistically in two compartments and then stood at the doors keeping off any other comer. I believe he told them to say 'Staff'. My part was to provide the food and drink. It lay above me there in the racks, six yards of bread, two bottles of white wine, two of red, a large jar of *pâté de foie gras*, a jar of conserve of cherries, two Camembert cheeses and a quarter-kilogramme of Gruyere, some melting butter, a kilogramme of pale chocolate, some sliced meat, and the cotton bags of army rations, biscuits, bully, cheese, tea and sugar, and jam. It was an old first-class carriage whose outside moulding was designed to make each compartment look like a growler without the driver's seat; inside it was upholstered in dove-grey cord, with neat antimacassars of white lace in which the word 'Nord' was worked. As we rumbled out of le Havre Briscoe was ruffling his red hair and explaining how the night before he had drunk all the evening in the base camp at Harfleur at the expense of a Portuguese Jew, the civilian contractor who messed the depot. Lemuel was incapable of refusing a bet; he would toss double or quits on any drink ordered up to a bottle of good wine, and his luck was seldom in. I answered Briscoe with a story of the indignation of some doddering old general with cotton-wool whiskers growing out of his throat, who had dined there as a guest one night – and after dinner stalked out in his scarlet and gold while Lemuel danced about in front of him with a greasy palm outspread. Lemuel wanted the dinner money. 'Tree franc,' he was saying. He got it too.

Perhaps we should none of us be there again; never hear the silver trumpets of the Horse Artillery reechoing the Last Post up the valley. For we had at last, surely, broken the links which bound us to settled life. 'We're off!' I cried. The train travelled through orchards half hiding the white plastered houses which kept so close to the earth that as often as not grassy mounds were climbing up to tiny windows. About noon the train slowed down, came almost to a halt, jolted on and finally fell into sleep while the sun beat hotly on the roof. A sizzling set in over our heads. Thomas lazily swung out of the carriage to see what it was, and put his head in at the window to tell us the whole train load was on the track. We all descended. Rows of men were squatting on the grass verge relieving themselves and an agitated captain was trying to drive everyone back. There was no need. The running-boards were so low and so served by handrails that we could swing off and on and travel up and down them with ease. Practising gymnastically Briscoe suddenly dropped off with an exclamation. 'That Scottish officer next door, he's got a bird with him!' We remembered seeing her in the half darkness at le Havre, saying good-bye, we thought.

'Mark me, my lad,' Thomas said, 'we'll have some fun through that spy-hole; she's a damn pretty tart too.' There were small windows in the partitions between the compartments. He passed on to a vivid description of her charms. Briscoe laughed. 'No cop,' he said, 'you're done in, Thomas, Scotty's got her.' The engine hooted. There was a rush for the train by men in various stages of dress; some hurrying on tiptoe carried mess-tins of boiling water from the locomotive, some holding up their trousers, others rushing up and down to find their coach. The carriages jolted into action like a snake unfolding, and as we got under way there was a final detachment blowing themselves black in the face a score yards behind the last coach. We were lively now that the train had started again. Only Dunlop sat in his corner reading. The rest of us travelled along the train by the running boards. A battle developed between Briscoe and a subaltern of the Royal Irish Rifles. The Irishman hit Briscoe over the head with a long loaf. So I went round the far end of the carriage while Briscoe played with the man to keep him engaged. Thus I caught him in the rear and disarmed him, and looking up from the buffers was surprised to see Thomas walking along the roof. We went from carriage to carriage until we came to one of those which had a glass cage perched on its end for the accommodation of a brakesman. Thomas ascended the iron ladder and tried to work the brake. A furious French railwayman came running along the tops of the coaches and evicted him.

In the drowsiness of the afternoon we almost forgot the Scottish officer next door. The train had halted and was bubbling away between long platforms whose granite chippings threw back the heat in waves. Dunlop suddenly exclaimed from his corner. 'They've caught the lad with the girl,' he said softly. There he stood on the platform, as neat a little soldier as ever one could see, his tartan riding breeches perfect over black riding boots, his bonnet aslant on curly hair; and she stood with him, a neat brown bird of a girl wearing a small hat covered with feathers. In front of them a middle-aged OC Train was embarrassed by the attempt to explain his views in polite language. In reply Scotty explained that the girl, though French, was a relation and wished to go to Rouen. The OC Train was very troubled in shocking bad French. He could not understand, he kept saying. If – but he could not understand; and on the other hand, doubtfully, if – and here he glanced at the Scot – he could not understand. From behind drawn curtains the adjacent carriages stared, while the train simmered gently between the platforms. It departed without her; she waved to the lieutenant and swung bravely off the platform to hide till our hundreds of eyes were past. The man next door was under arrest with two subalterns at his side.

Thus the afternoon passed. We pulled the curtains over the windows and tried to sleep. We turned back to our books and papers and yawned and stretched in boredom at the country which passed at a slow steady trot, wide open fields, with distant banks of trees, close orchards and tangled ditches deep in lush grass, brown dusty villages, whose only colour was the powder blue of the hoardings. At last we ran into Rouen. There was an hour and a half to wait. We called up the old soldiers to post over our belongings and made off into the town for dinner. We ate in a glassy cavern, the Brasserie de l'Opera. Strawberries and crushed ice floated in a bowl of dull liquor that smelled faintly of aniseed. The washing place, to which I was conducted by a waiter, was a joint office in which a number of wanton girls were laughing and talking, while one, her heel on the edge of the hand-basin, was fastening her laced boot, with her knee uncovered, and threw some remark at me which hastened me down the right passage, amid shrieks of laughter. After dinner Thomas called for a *chasseur* and sent him for a taxi. We rode back to the station and Thomas told the driver to take us up the ramp and along the platform. The cab threaded its way among the staring troops, and we stepped straight out of it into our carriage.

The night soon fell and our candles guttered on the sills, shivering with each jar, blown by every draught. It was not easy to read. At last two of us went to our spare compartment and turned in on the seats. The old soldiers distributed themselves between us sleeping on the floor among the dirt. Somehow the night passed. Sleep fell on me to break as we ground to a standstill. By my ear a signal bell was ringing with nervous titillation, thin, high-pitched, melancholy. I fell asleep again and dreamed I was in England. Hours passed, there was a jar; I woke to hear the bell ringing still, a sound that was to pursue me through every journey in France in every railway station; a symbol of perpetuity.

It was about twenty hours later that we ended our journey of about three hundred kilometres. Where it was I never knew, the army was taking care of us. I climbed down stiffly on to the platform and looked about in the warm dusk. Hundreds of khaki soldiers were forming up outside the railing on the road, and the horse wagons were standing by small platforms being loaded up with kit-bags and valises. Opposite were the lights of a small hotel. I walked across to it. Already my companions of the train had broken up. I could not see them in the dining room and took the first empty place around an enormous oval table filled with officers. The room had a staircase rising from it to a landing which looked down on the company. A couple of officers had been walking upstairs when I entered. The food was served round to us. After a few minutes there was a call from the landing. We all looked up. A girl was leaning over; she was dressed in nothing but silk stockings, camisole and knickers. While I stared another one joined her. I had never seen women dressed like that before exhibiting so freely the warm pearly colour of their chests. Almost at once two officers opposite me dropped their knives and forks, strode over the bench, and stalked upstairs. Not long after they came down again and another two ascended.

Motor lorries were waiting for us outside. It was early morning and bitterly cold when we moved off. The road was unfenced but lined with tall poplars whose feathery tips caught the gold of the rising sun, the grass was covered with a grey web of dew. The earth seemed quite silent. None of the expected sounds of war broke the stillness. Grey faced and red eyed we yawned and stretched on the top of the lorry until the final breaking up sent me off on horseback to my new brigade headquarters.

A few weeks later I was sitting on the bank of the Lawe fishing with bread paste for coarse fish. The roach and tench and bream swam disregardingly among the weeds. Fateh Chand the mess servant with his turban all on one side came up the towpath and grinned. 'Any gottim fish, sahib?' he asked. 'No,' I said. 'Him bad fish,' said Fateh Chand. He passed into M. Bourdon's brewery in which the ammunition column mess was quartered and left me to my reflections. My entry into the regular army had been unfortunate. At the end of my three day journey I had been sent to a battery at rest. The officers were taking tea which tasted strongly of tinned milk and chloride of lime; an opaque sort of tea which one more nearly ate than drank. By dinnertime my valise lay behind me on the stone flagged floor and when the port had passed twice Major Nankivell and Captain Adam carried on a soft and endless exchange of old stories, while MacArthur, a ranker, sighed to himself and said nothing. Sleep was possessing me so that I could scarcely hear, scarcely even observe the patch of summer sky shining into the room. Still the talk went on and on as dusk faded into darkness and candles were lighted by the mess servant. I held on as long as I could and then begged permission to go to sleep wherever I might. They looked at me with polite incredulous stares. I explained fumblingly that I had been two nights on the way and parts of three days. The major laughed shortly and Adam stared even more obtusely. I was too tired to care, I went to bed, undressing miserably before them while the conversation from an immense distance still flowed dully. 'In Lahore, in nineteen-seven . . . jolly fine gal . . .' 'Was that the fellar . . .?' I turned over on the rustling straw. That experience took me into the line and then backwards to the ammunition column. I was not wanted by the regular army.

Fateh Chand came out as I blushed at my recollections. He carried a gauze flytrap and plunged it into a bucket of water. This signified that Captain Stiff, the officer commanding the column, had a visitor and had had a bet with him on the number of flies in the cage. The waiter was arranging the corpses on the hot pavement in rows of five. He got a penny a hundred for counting them. My excursion to the real war had been a humiliating business altogether. They did not want officers like myself: middle-class Nonconformists scarcely out of school; and it was natural that they did not desire to help them. One had to learn by falling. With the completest contempt they left us out of any conversation beyond the official greetings. It was exasperating to them if one joined in their talk. 'I think you had better go to bed if you can't keep quiet,' Adam said. He took my crop and had it burned. It would have been simple to explain. There was nothing in one's green experience to supply a knowledge of appropriate behaviour among this particular sort of aristocracy. In some despair I attempted to fulfil the requirements of the drill book with the battery in action. That seemed to embarrass them more, as well it might, under the trees of the orchard where the guns lay hid in grassy mounds. I went to an observation post to observe the Hun; that was the phrase one used. 'There's nothing to do,' MacArthur said. 'You can't do anything to please them except please them, and God knows how. Keep your mouth shut and keep out of the way. But we've no ammunition – we wouldn't have, in a first class war – so you won't need to observe fire, and the Germans won't do anything, you may be sure. Keep under cover and out of sight and read a book. But watch out for the major, I'll telephone you when he's coming, if I can.'

Thus on a glorious afternoon I went walking by pollarded ditches to the OP, led by a telephonist who carried a sack of bread, sardines, and cheese. The sun beat heavily on the sleeping landscape and threw a dreamy haze over the front, seamed in a disorderly pattern with dun brown trenches rising to Aubers. I ate and watched the full moon rise over the deserted street behind our loft. A volley of machine-gun bullets rattled among the ghostly houses. The solitude became more intense as the night grew, and the movements about the moonstruck village exaggerated it, so that I wished to call out. A pump handle was squeaking down the road. I slept in a rabbit-wire bunk, and the mice rattled on the underside all night. The point was, when I woke, that I hadn't enough to eat; my belly was so hollow that the bread crumbs tickled it. When Nankivell arrived in mid-afternoon I was ravenous.

Sitting by the canal at Pont Riqueul I had to admit to myself that it had been a bad mistake to tell the major that I would rather go back to the battery than watch him shoot. It was the worse because we only had a small allowance of shell; four rounds a gun a day. I was so hungry, but I could have sustained life cheerfully on a few amiable words. So that evening he took me for a walk in the green cornfields and talked about keenness. I wanted to be keen, but how? I asked. I had never been taught this sort of war. I gathered that my question was too big an order. I must just watch others. In the Indian Army an artillery subaltern was not considered competent until he had been in a battery for an enormous number of years – eleven years. Nankivell wished to be kind, but eleven years was too much of a drawback.

We were living in an *estaminet* at the four cross roads known as Croix Barbée. The German gunners put a 5.9 howitzer shell through the roof and wounded several servants. So we moved into an orchard and lived in holes in the ground under corrugated iron and green turves. I smoked my pipe in the largest before the major came in for breakfast. Thus I worked my passage to the Brigade Ammunition Column. My bait was sucked off. I put on some more and reflected that this was easier, if less glorious. A regular battery was too much of a good thing. Surprisingly I caught a fish. Fateh Chand ran out with a pail and put the fish in it. The captain and little O'Connor came out of the mess. The captain said, staring at me with bullish, wondering eyes, 'That'll do for my breakfast! You thought you'd have it, eh?'

'Oh, no, sir!'

'Time you and O'Connor went to the lines.'

We put on our belts. Stiff jerked us back with his head, and winked slyly, opening his hand to show two ten-franc notes. 'Ten for the flies, and ten for the height of the picture. Measured it beforehand.' He let out a single roar of laughter and stamped back into M. Bourdon's salon. That was the sort of man he was, easy to understand. Stiff had been one of the most distinguished sort of warrant officer, in India. O'Connor too, though junior. 'He's a cure,' O'Connor said, chuckling. 'Damned unfair, but amusing to see him do in the nobs.' On the way down the river bank we met Wratt, the fat old regular *padre.* I was humming an Indian soldier's song I had heard accidentally from O'Connor.

It was an indecent song called 'Seven Long Years', but like everything else it sounded innocent enough on O'Connor's lips. Wratt reproved O'Connor and chuckled at the same time. We moved on. 'He'll tell us some hottish stories to-night,' O'Connor said.

The horse lines were tied between ammunition wagons on a field of baked clay on which not one single blade of grass was growing. At regular intervals between the lines curls of blue smoke were rising from braziers in which the horse dung was burning, and the faint breeze brought the strong bitter smell to us. The smoke kept the flies from the animals, and the dung was slowly destroyed. The jemadar sahib salaamed before us. He was a tall handsome man with a curling brown beard, and his belt and buttons shone with a perfect gloss. O'Connor talked a mixed jargon to him, and he replied in English. Then the sergeant major followed. He had been a pork butcher in Yorkshire, and his face had a fat sullen expression. They were always quarrelling, the sergeant major and the jemadar.

Everything in Stiffs lines shone. Most of the horses were Walers, with here and there a small-boned delicate Arab like O'Connor's rig, Jehosophat. The jemadar led us to Challenger, the show piece. He had the horse led out and made as if to throw a lump of sugar. Challenger stretched his neck and opened his mouth. The jemadar threw the sugar neatly into his throat. 'He can catch!' he said in his husky whisper. The drivers laughed, showed shining teeth, and wrinkled up their brown eyes. The native sergeant, Fakir Khan, was with us. His nose was shaped in a sharp curve, and his long grey moustaches dropped downwards and then turned up, increasing his appearance of craft; but when he smiled the harsh lines of his face disappeared in a multitude of wrinkles and made him look kind. He took me to see a horse that had been a man-killer.

'Walk up to it boldly, Sahib,' he said. 'Now, come swiftly, not straight back, but to me, and watch.' As soon as I left the horse's head its ears snapped back and its eyes rolled.

'Ma!' the havildar shouted derisively, 'you are nasty but you are beat; we know you.' Then turning to me he told me the story.

'There was a driver in the column had this horse,' he said, 'and it was a bad horse. Once he was careless in the school, and it threw him on purpose, and savaged him so he died. Now this man had a brother, a gunner, and this so grieved him he drank himself to madness, and begged the captain: "Let me take him to the school, sir, alone, and I will cure him." So the captain agreed; and the gunner borrowed the sergeant major's – no, not this sergeant major – wire riding whip and took the horse to the school. It was wonderful to see. I saw it. I saw the fight, how the horse tried every trick, forcing the rider to the boards to crush his leg, bucking, rearing, kicking, charging the barrier, snapping back to the gunner's knee, tossing his head back, far back, jumping, cat-jumping, rolling, everything . . .' The havildar smoothed down the air with empty palms. 'I saw the gunner, streaming with sweat in his shirt sleeves, his spurs cutting and pricking, the whip cutting the horse's flanks; it was terrible to watch. Then the horse broke down, foam fell from his muzzle like tears. He tried no trick even at the gate. There he is. He is beaten. But he has vice as you see. So nice to the face, so wicked when you go.

Ma! Ma!' the havildar shouted derisively, and spat on the ground. The man-killer snapped back his ears and rolled his eyes.

The lines were as clean as a dinner table and the dung smoke floated about us acrid in the hot sun. Stiff made his inspection and looked in the nosebags. We watered and fed and watched the drivers running off to their little ramshackle shelters made of waterproof sheets and boughs. Stiff stood at the end of a line and made the running men jump over his crop. They laughed and called out remarks to him in their own tongue. He walked over to the detached section to look at a man strapped to a wagon wheel for insolence, and refusal to obey an order, and stood before him with his fleshy jaw outthrust, his hands clasping his whip behind his back. 'Farrier,' he shouted, 'tell the sergeant major to release this man. He's had enough for the present. But mark you,' he added, staring at the prisoner, 'one more word and you get your full measure.' Stiff sucked his teeth and watched the gunner unfastened, and walked off. He laughed at my question. 'Can't hurt a man like that. Damned uncomfortable, though.' He glanced sideways to see if I were trying to be clever, and decided that I was innocent.

We dined upon a dish of stew; and John, the red-haired Canadian, told us stories of his veterinary college. He said that freshmen were offered choice of initiations; either they must step into a tub of horse offal, or they must ride upon a horse's carcass which had been flayed and was now to be hoisted on pulleys to the roof. 'Then the boys sort of jerk it about a bit,' John concluded. The padre laughed till tears came into his eyes, and told us about the gayer dogs in divinity colleges.

Since I could speak some French, Stiff sent me out to buy clover, in the morning. I rode along the clay banks of the river and the canals, by the growing maize and the uncut wheat, as far, almost, as Bethune. The pollard leaves glistened in the sun. A party of soldiers bathed, stark naked, in a lock. O'Connor rode out to meet me on my return. He was on Jehosophat, who leaped about like a violent kitten.

'How do you manage this lingo?' he said.

'I say *"Ou se trouver* when I want a place or a road or anything, with the name of the stuff after it,' I said, 'and *"Combien* for "How much?"'

'I know *combien,* he said, 'but tell me the other.'

We rehearsed this simple *passe-partout* on the way back till we came to the lights of Pont Riqueul and the dusty road to the village. The bascule bridge was down. Old M. Bourdon was lamenting in his falsetto voice that 'They' had taken all his alcohol for explosives. He pushed his sailor's cap to the back of his head and scrabbled in his beard. We gave him what consolation we could in amorphous murmurs meant to be Gallic. 'Combien?' said O'Connor startlingly. The word opened gates to a flood which I had to try clumsily to stem. We drank a glass of beer with him. Two of his sons had been killed, the other prisoner. Madame gave me a rose. 'J'aime les roses,' she said, 'c'est ma seule distraction.'

The nights were warm and velvety. I slept between sheets in the house of an old spinster, Dieudonné Vittu, and her brother. Two bats came into the room and disturbed me. I pursued them with a shoe till I had killed one and driven the other out of the window. The small furry body lay in my hand, the grotesque little face screwed up in death. That seemed strange. In the morning I found Vittu, rubbing his grey moustache while he watched the death agonies of a large rat. He had caught it in a wire cage and had thrust hat pins through its body. He explained that rats were evil beasts and deserved death. It lay transfixed by four or five pins and quivered feebly. 'If you like, you may drown it,' he said, 'but it will die very soon.' We were both red handed that morning. He took me into the garden to give me some fruit. When I got across to the mess I found that Madame Bourdon had taken five pairs of socks from my kit and was mending them. 'It is just what I did for my sons,' she said, 'England is so far, is it not?'

At about six o'clock every Sunday morning the cracked bell in the small church summoned the villagers to Mass. The old men wore black or grey of an antique cut, with enormous top hats so heavily furred and curled they should have been beavers. In the afternoon each cottage turned out its chairs in a row on the street and the families gathered to chat in enormous parties, twelve or fifteen to every door. Near the mess a house door bore a cross of straw with purple vetch and violets in the arms. From here they took a dead mother and her baby. Children walked by the infant coffin and mothers were the pallbearers.

We were ordered to turn out a party for a church parade to be addressed by the Bishop of Nagpur. Stiff and I marched together with our Europeans, all sweating in stiff khaki and polished leather. We marched to a pasture marked by a rectangle of towering trees, not poplars, but full branched like beeches, with grey trunks rising fifteen or twenty feet before the green spread. The congregation sat on the grass and listened to a tiny figure in robes at the end of the avenue or talked quietly between themselves. At the farthest point from his lordship a little group were throwing dice.

Stiff bought a cake from the new Expeditionary Force Canteen, seven pounds of it for 2s 11d (15p) or fifty centimes a pound. It tasted like it but we were very pleased. Near us a party of old French territorials were digging a line of reserve trenches, very pretty, about four feet deep, revetted with thatching reeds. The poppies grew on the breastwork and the dry earth continually fell through the stalks.

One of our batteries had a gun blown up by one of the new defective HE (High Explosive) fuses, and a man was killed. Another gunner was killed by the blast from a gun. He was in front of the gun pit, and the concussion was fatal. Except for such things our front was quiet and my leave was due. It confirmed one's impressions of war to hear of these sad accidents and to see the groups of Indian lancers trotting through the countryside on slim Arab chargers with high bred heads and flowing tails.

Chapter 3

Nuts in May

Rue du Bois – Summer 1915
Wytschaete – Winter 1915

S tiff came up to me one day with his scrutinising stare and told me to be ready to ride out with him in the afternoon. He handed me over to Major Byron. I was to be with the guns again, and I was glad.

I went up to the observation post in the Rue du Bois very often after that and came to know the place. We entered the street by a broken cotton factory south of Windy Corner, and crossed some waste land littered with the wreckage of Neuve Chapelle and Festubert; broken rifles and bayonets and hundreds of tins of bully beef, most of them hacked open and buzzing with flies which crawled about the black meat. The OP was known as the Leicester Lounge and lay on the German side of the road; thousands of telephone wires crawled over the brickwork into the sandbag shelter on the ground floor.

A large hole had been blown through the wall on the first floor, looking toward the front. I lay on a pile of rubble and peered at the German trenches which rose slightly to the row of houses on the Aubers Ridge. I could see southward as far as the double towers of Loos, rising monumentally from the plain. Staring at the landscape dazzled the eyes. I rolled back to look at the street. The house on my left had collapsed into a heap of rubbish. Out of some hole there came a lean cat, which stole quietly among the broken timbers halting every moment in fear. As I leaned over, the cat looked up at me. The remains of my lunch were at hand; I dropped a sardine to him and poured out the oil from the tin, but he turned and fled, his empty belly shaking as he ran.

The village had a stale smell and, at dusk, when the mist crept up over the Orchard, it seemed that figures could be seen to move there, among the trees. In the short communication trench which traversed it the feet of dead men stuck out into our faces as we went to the front line. A boot showed itself as the trench wall crumbled. The next night the marks in the rotten old sandbags showed that the boot and its fellow had been taken away; and then the grey socks were torn off the blackened flesh.

The front line was a poor breastwork of earth crowned with sand-bags, running along to the la Bassée road in front of Port Arthur, the parados an imperfect heap of earth and rubbish. In the line here I saw my first kill. Through a peephole I saw a German soldier enjoying the morning sunshine between Guards' Trench and the trees on the road. The sniper at my shoulder fired, the German leaped into the air and dropped out of sight. An officer and four men arrived carrying a strange contraption which they placed in a gap in the parados. In a few minutes they began to fire the little jam-tin bombs which were all we had in the way of trench mortars. As they fired, the infantry subaltern ran up and begged them to stop and told us to clear out before the Germans retaliated for our futile bombs. When I got back to my perch over the Orchard the German gunners put four salvos of pipsqueak shells into the front of the OP. That was exhilarating.

In the waste space at the back of the OP I discovered a circle of Gurkhas arranged round a dud 5.9 shell set on end which they were trying to detonate by dropping bricks on its fuse. They were throwing the bricks in rotation, and laughed at each other as they threw. After I had chased them away I settled down to study the front again.

The Gurkha officers had a mess in some ruins a couple of hundred yards north. They had sent out patrols night after night to get identification, but no prisoner was brought in. At last the colonel summoned the Gurkha NCO. He was at first crestfallen, and then apologetic, but begged for a few minutes' absence. When he returned he carried a sack which he emptied on the floor of the mess. There fell out four German heads hacked off at the neck, and he explained that the patrol thought that it was sent out to fight people. It had taken its prisoners and despatched them in no man's land with the kukri. The Gurkhas had some lovable characteristics. I came upon them playing with a catapult which had been sent up for experiment. It was about seven feet high, shaped like an easel, and was designed to throw jam-tin bombs. The Gurkhas had set it up and aimed it at the door of the colonel's dugout, and were heaving bricks with it. The colonel rushed out, shouting affectionate abuse at them, and the little men rolled with laughter, holding their stomachs, incapable of speech. They were so small that had it was said they were the only troops whose heads did not show above the parapet of that sector.

At night the street was full of traffic. Long files of chattering men went to the pump, laden with rum jars or petrol tins. The pump squeaked so much we thought it must be the very one illustrated by Bairnsfather in a famous picture. The mice in the sandbags round the door came to me when I whistled and ate out of my hand. Then it rained and I went down two steps into the little cellar, where I lay on the bunk to write home in the light of a candle standing on the flat of a bayonet stuck into the wall. The mice also came inside. The rainwater trickled down the steps and a large frog croaked from the top step and hopped down in the puddles to the cellar floor. A rat raced in, followed by a black and white cat. They made several circuits of the walls and disappeared into the street. The mice still stayed with me searching for cake crumbs. Outside a Scottish voice was singing a sentimental song and opposite to the cellar someone was amusing the Gurkhas with a tune on a tin whistle. One mouse had ventured to take my last piece of cake. The OP was dirty and full of lice. I reflected that I should have to spend some time digging them out of my trouser seams.

I awoke to find the air limpid and refreshed after the rain. It was still dark. I climbed the stairs and stood in the broken room to watch day break. The smell of the plaster mixed with the smells of the earth. The darkness upon the Aubers Ridge dissolved into bars of pink, and the houses began to take shape among the trees. The basin between us was still full of mist and overhead I saw the sky a blue which was not quite grey, and indeed not quite light; it seemed that the sky was something growing into creation, an emptiness stippled with particles vibrating into colour, as though it moved like music upon the land. The houses began to show as smears of white. The sun itself touched the poplars on the road and they shed their envelopment of cloud, rising black in the drifting smoke. Sharp reefs of parapet and the points of wired stakes emerged from pools of mist, which, even as I watched, melted upward into haze and left me standing, staring at the front line. Somewhere a rifle cracked and a bullet rattled among the houses. I went down and looked for breakfast.

A little north of our sector Sam was in action. I had news that he had been wounded just when I was beginning to expect leave. He was in hospital in London at Sussex Lodge when I crossed, and so on my way back I was able to see him. His father was with him too. Together we walked in the Zoo.

Sam was strange. His wound seemed to have altered him. There was a strain between the three of us and we did not know what to talk about. But we became more cheerful over tea, as though food had reduced us to a common denominator. On the platform at Victoria he said that it was awful to be wounded. 'It hurts all the time and drains the energy out of you,' he said. Then he laughed shortly and said that anyway the life of an infantry subaltern was supposed to be six months. It wouldn't last forever. This was very strange in Sam, who was the usually the most cheerful of men, the happiest of companions. But before the train left he had become almost ribald again. The crossing was cold and dark, the sea a deep brown but for the luminous feather at the bows. The journey up to the line was very slow and the carriage was so crowded that it was impossible to stretch out. When we de-trained the sun was rising and the mist lay across the road like swathes of butter-muslin. I was glad, somehow, to be back. O'Connor took me into Estaires to buy a birthday present for his boy. In a dark shop I found a table covered with continental editions of English novels, and among them *Lost Endeavour.* I heard that Bull, a subaltern who had replaced me in Nankivell's battery, had been even more troubled than I by the atmosphere there, and had applied for a transfer to the Engineers rather than endure it.

Byron's battery was in a farmhouse under a large walnut tree, and our defaulters were sent up the tree to gather nuts for the mess. The nuts were soft and green, but sweet to eat. The farmer and his wife were still in the house conducting their business among the gun pits. Nankivell's battery was in Richebourg St Vaast looking up to the church tower, from which some batteries observed fire. Adam had built an underground railway to carry ammunition to the guns. The truck fell off occasionally. 'It's eyewash,' MacArthur said, 'but very pretty and all that. It's for generals to look at.' We joined in the Battle of Loos by sending our spare kit home and waiting to advance on taped tracks laid out in front of the farm. Small bridges were fastened on the ammunition wagons. I scarcely knew what was happening. But our orchard was undisturbed. No one moved.

Rain began to fall, and there were rumours of mutiny among the Indians, who had been promised relief from the Western Front and saw no chance of it. One day near Whisky Corner I saw the Brahmas come out of action, strange faces creased in every likeness to woe, their puttees and trousers sodden and plastered with mud, their arms and fingers hanging inertly from bent shoulders wringing wet. Their large English boots looked too heavy for their lean shins, the felted khaki cloth rubbed on their bow legs. There had been trouble with the Pathans and they were set to dig out ditches near Pont Logy, a disgrace which other regiments were to observe as they marched up and down the la Bassée road.

For the first time I had a real command. I was to put a single gun into a cottage between Whisky Corner and Rue de l'Epinette, to fire in enfilade along the German trenches opposite the Orchard. The day had been chosen specially because the heavy rain obscured the landscape and diffused itself in a warm mist between ourselves and the Aubers Ridge. The cottage was concealed by the trees about the Rue du Bois, but Byron wished to make sure that no sausage balloon or aeroplane would observe us at work. The back of the house had been blown out and the bricks lay in the ditch at the roadside. Now we all laboured, Sergeant Bolland, the gunners, and myself, to make a ramp that would bring the gun into the cottage. In a little time the gun came up the road. We dragged it into the house. Then it had to go left-handed into the parlour, and past the chimney stack, but the axles were too wide. The chimney stack supported the whole house. Brick by brick we ate into it, making a nick for the axle hub. The window in the parlour was not in the right place. We shifted the window and put in mortared lintels; we even fitted moveable transoms like the old ones, and then began to enclose the gun within a sandbag cell. The first wall I built was of headers and stretchers in alternate rows, with a rubble filling to make up the full width. When I leaned against it, it fell over. It was some time before we hit on the system of laying headers and stretchers in each course, and alternating the courses. At every difficulty the sergeant and the men looked at me and waited for instructions. This was exhausting. I knew nothing whatever of engineering, nothing whatever of bricklaying, of thatching, walling or building, whether with sandbags or without. I did not even know how to manhandle a gun properly. Yet somehow all the awkward pauses passed, and I laid out a line of fire by prismatic compass and planted an aiming post to serve till Byron should come.

When it was all done the cottage looked almost exactly as it had done before.

Then came the colonel on his light bay charger, and spoke in a superlatively light clear voice. 'Of course,' he said, 'you'll have to cut down that tall tree there. Give the show away if you don't. An excellent aiming point for the Hun gunners.' For the first time I appreciated the army's methods of evasion. 'Yes, sir,' I said, cordially, 'I'll send for axes and a saw, sir. We haven't any here. Thank you, sir.'

'Ha! Yes! Quite a neat piece of work otherwise.'

Byron took me with him to the OP to see the gun fire. He was a very skilful gunner. Within the first three rounds he had the gun so laid and the atmosphere so nicely judged that the shrapnel burst low over the trench, and the bullets danced along the parapet, fetching up points of dust where they hit. What happened in the trench we could not see.

We had a detached section of guns near Pont Logy by a broken old farm a little behind the sodden straw shelters of the Indian village which supported the front line. I slept in the kitchen of the farm. When there was nothing to do I could wander up and down the la Bassée road. The little cottages were deserted among their rotting crops. Masses of tobacco leaves hung in the roofs, spoiled by the rain, and devotional tracts were littered on the floor. The rain added to the solitude. The road shone with rain in the evening as we stood waiting for the mess cart to bring our letters and our food. Later at night a Frenchman, enlisted with the RAMC, came across from his aid post. In the kitchen, where we sat playing French whist, the winds blew the candle flames about, slammed the extemporised door against the lintel, and filled the air with smoke from the broken stove.

Sam wrote frequently. He sent me some *Times* broadsheets, but I found them difficult to read. The war seemed to have trodden on fine prose, by accident, perhaps, and crushed the life out of it. It was irrelevant, low, it seemed.

My tour ended with duty in the line. The rain had filled the trenches with sandy mud, and on my way past Port Arthur I found a party of infantrymen hauling a soldier out of the slough at the bottom of the trench. His mate had been with him, and had gone under. The other man had his shoulders above the porridge and was supported by ropes. The tips of some long planks showed above the mud, and as he pressed upon them he screwed up his eyes and rocked his shoulders from side to side, while the party above hauled on the ropes from the ground level, in view of the enemy. It was a very English face the man had, broad and mobile, with heavy, well-cut lips. When I left they were lifting him out of the coffee-coloured mud. His body was stiff as though he were paralysed.

When I got back to our new mess in a small cottage, the gramophone was playing 'The Farmyard,' a composition of Jacob's Trocaderians, the stove was glowing and tea was on the table. Taylor, a temporary subaltern like myself, poured out a cup for me and in his cool Canadian speech asked for news. This seemed at last like home. He had pulled our straw beds inwards from the wall of the loft because the rats had bothered him so much running obstacle races round the floor. The major, he said, was going to keep me if he could, and Brand, our temporary captain, had found a horse for me. The mail brought *Land and Water, Punch,* three letters, a copy of *Wine, Women and Song,* and a parcel from Sam of cigarettes and the Oxford book of sonnets.

'I think I rather like the old Boche,' said Taylor. 'So long as he keeps the war like this.'

'He knows a thing or two,' Brand said. 'I bet he's not drowning in the mud. Why should he worry? Let's all have a small little drink of rot-gut.' He poured out vermouth and put 'Watch your step' on the gramophone. 'Have you heard of those fools in the —th Company? They put their dugout door facing the wrong way and got blown up.' Everyone laughed. Taylor said the rain was 'doing his darnedest' to make the war unpleasant, and he put some sentimental songs on the machine. Brand cursed him, complaining that they made him feel gloomy. Taylor declared that the Chopin Funeral March and the Dead March, from 'Saul', 'were the only cure for gloom'. He said they sounded screamingly funny in the front. Brand capitulated and poured out another drink.

As we were sitting at breakfast we heard a big shell coming upon us. In the brief second of its descent I saw ourselves like people seen by a lightning flash, petrified with shock, knives and forks arrested in mid air. The shell burst on the ground at the corner of the cottage, and a servant fell down the loft stairs and ran at once all the way to the wagon line. Then life began again. We went to the shellhole and dug for the fuse. It was made of brass and shaped like a toadstool. I kept it to take home for a souvenir.

A month after we marched by Aire to Renescure and billeted at the chateau rebuilt in red and yellow brick after its burning in the Revolution. The rain fell with solemn monotony and we began to search for waterproof garments. I ordered seamen's leather thigh-boots, and a long waterproof lined with leather. We were resting in the kitchen of the chateau, and dried our clothes by the stove. Taylor produced the gazoos, metal instruments shaped like oysters, through which one hummed, and we sat together trying to harmonise 'Michigan.' The major told me I was to go back to the column, at Stiff's request. 'But I've sent a good report in about you,' he said.

No doubt Stiff wanted someone. All the Indians had gone; we had said goodbye to them and their commander on the way out. Even the division was being split up. The Connaughts – and we were the Connaughts' own battery, wearing their crest on our wagons – had turned out and presented arms to us in farewell as we marched past. Stiff had two or three hundred new men to train. So I joined O'Connor and John again, and we made a thirty-mile march to the Coq-de-Paille farm, below the monastery of the Mont des Cats. We looked up to its ascending walls through the sheeting rain. It overtopped the land like a building seen in a dream, the towers so high and inaccessible it seemed they must have been nailed on. I had a sack of hop leaves to sleep on and could not wake in the morning. Never in my life had I slept so soundly that anyone had needed to throw me on to a tiled floor before I could wake.

We settled into winter quarters on the bleak hill above Westoutre, where the secondary roads were already liquid mud. On the way the blanket wagon overturned into a stream where it stayed half an hour and the bread-cart lost itself. Our working day was seventeen hours long, the last two being devoted to Stiff's command game of bridge. Even O'Connor grumbled. The Belgians about us spoke English and treated us with the professional air of traders; and the grey scoured skies and dark walls were no kinder. The very daylight seemed less within the zone of the Salient.

Eight days before Christmas I had two pieces of good news. I was to go on leave and I was to return to the battery. I went with delight. There was only a paddle steamer to take the leave men across. Upon the quay I met a Jew who had been at the depot in England with me. He was carrying an unexploded German 4.2 shell wrapped in a blanket under his arm. The ship was crowded and the sea rough. The lights were out and the leave men lay about in their sickness on the deck like corpses waiting to be thrown overboard, but still animate enough to retch and moan. There were so many heaps it was nearly impossible to move about, for each fell where he had stood.

The early train north brought me to Leeds at half past six. The Midland Hotel porter refused me a bath and breakfast unless I took a room in the hotel. It was rather a shock in those days of patriotic enthusiasm. But it seemed too good to be true to walk the streets and taste the familiar town smells, to see the shutters taken from the familiar shops. In foolish lightheadedness I had added to telegrams home one to Berenice challenging her to a game of snooker pool. There would be people at home, I should sleep between sheets, walk at ease by the shops under the trees, I should drink coffee in the morning, thick black coffee, with yellow cream, and buy things. Yet it was not the same. Sam was out of my reach; Eustace had been killed, Eustace, who had been ashamed to walk in the street with a naked pair of boots in his arm. Berenice's dignity had been hurt by my invitation to a 'pot-house game'. It was harder to get home than one had expected.

I returned as I had come, by a journey which seemed nine parts night. The leave men crowded in a dusty herd along the platform by the notice board which announced the names of people for whom telegrams were waiting. The physical crowd upon the returning leave train made one feel choked. At railhead I found Stiff's trap waiting for me, and felt flattered.

The battery was in action near Mille Kruis, off the Dickebusch-Bailleul road, in a cunning position sunk below ground behind a hedge, and shooting across a track, so that the blast of the guns did not show. The whole position was hidden under growing grass, and thorn hurdles disguised the mouths of the gun pits. The mess was in a wooden hut covered with tarred felt, and there I found Major Byron, Captain Brand, Taylor, and Puncher, an Australian of about forty-five, who had been too impatient to wait for the Australian contingent. It was still Christmas there, and my parcels were unopened; blessed aunts sending plum puddings, cakes, even fruit pies, crystallised ginger, chocolates and books, socks, cigars, cigarettes. We opened them all out and stowed them away for our last festivities. The gramophone I had ordered arrived with a package of records and Byron fell on them, handling them with his delicate fingers and gazing with romantic blue-grey eyes at the musical comedy numbers he had wanted. There was a girl in one of them, we understood 'Puncher, gramophone duty,' he said. We turned to the mail as the new machine spilled out coon songs, Offenbach and Harry Tate, in indiscriminating stream. 'Puncher, damn you, you've got the taste of a hooligan. The boy is arty, let him perform and soothe my harrowed soul.' Thus ordered I performed till Puncher took me across to sleep in the angles under an enormous inverted pyramid of brick, which we took to be concerned with malt. I tripped over some wire on the way and Puncher chuckled with joy.

'The major calls it "Taylor's patent pulley-hauley long distance bell-pull and looney-trap",' he said. 'What is it?'

'It's a bell wire; when the telephonist pulls it in the battery it rings a cartridge case in the mess. And have you heard about his patent shell deflector? It's a stiff ramp of concrete he's going to make over the slit at the OP so that when shells fall on it they scoot off it clean out of the back window into the road.'

We half undressed, shivering, and rolled ourselves in blankets and British warms. I topped off my bed with the leather-lined waterproof whose riding skirt made it almost eight feet round the hem; and I slept like a log on the brick coping.

The next day Brand went on leave, Taylor to the OP and Puncher to act as liaison officer with the Canadians. The night was still and the rain soaked down steadily. Byron was working with coloured inks on a large-scale map. There was a violent knocking. 'Come in,' Byron said in a bored voice. More knocking. 'Come in,' I shouted. Silence.

'Damn that machine gun,' we said simultaneously.

It was New Year's Eve. The Canadian battery on Dickebusch Lake pooped off twelve rounds in a rafale to welcome 1916. We supposed they made their own ammunition, they threw it about so carelessly. We were still short. 'Our boys are so light-hearted,' they told us, 'when a gun's dirty they just shoot off a round or so on their own.' Such naughtiness horrified us.

An easterly gale blew the sky clear on my first day at the OP. It was in a forge at Vierstraat, looking up to Wytschaete. Snow fell in the night and filtered through the holes in the roof. I was awakened by wet blankets and found myself covered with the snow. It was very uncomfortable.

The road behind the forge led between an avenue of trees to Ypres, not far for a ride on a bicycle but now hours away. From our crossroads the clean washed cobble stones dropped downhill, and over the tree tops we could see the broken towers of the town gleaming like bleached bones in the sun. As I turned to go in a salvo of woolly bears arrived over the trees, big shells whose black bursts unrolled in animal curves after the first cracking detonation had sped the hot metal. Then the storm followed, one after another the heavy 5.9 howitzer shells came howling steadily into Vierstraat all about our ears as we crouched in our sandbag shelter. The small pipsqueaks whipped full up against the front of the forge and salvos of 4.2 howitzers crashed into the field across the road and among the brickwork.

Smoke tinged with pink brick-dust billowed past the door and the fine pulverised earth from the chicory field spouted up in front of our eyes. The whole village was covered in shell bursts and the hot opaque smell of high explosive reeking out of the shell holes sickened us as we sat watching. Suddenly the air about us was shattered by a near explosion and our ears drummed with its roar. A beam fell across the door and a succession of crashes followed on our shelter roof. 'They've got us all right,' the telephonist said, clearing his throat, 'and there's nothing on the roof.' He relit his cigarette. The frenzy of this shoot was new to me. I sat and quivered at the torrent of heavy stuff which poured in. The diarrhoetic explosions of the biggest shells sounded to come from the crossroads fifty yards away, while the 5.9s and the 4.2s were shooting at our block and falling with accuracy short and over and sometimes upon us. We felt the whole house quivering as a big one, off the line, plunged into the garden in front of us, hesitated and burst with a roar which blew half the tiles off the roof and dropped them crashing into the road. A fine powder dropped steadily from the air carrying grit into our mouths and noses with the smell.

The telephone wire had long since gone. A whole bundle which had crossed the road on posts was lying on the ground. A tree crashed on our right and we felt the bat of a howitzer shell in the next house. The wall shook and bulged. A flying figure came through the window seeking refuge. 'My front wall is blown in,' he said, 'God! What a strafe!' We cowered together, numbed by the fury of sound and metal. Then suddenly, after an hour, it was over. We sighed and filled our pipes, waiting a little within safety to make sure it was not a trick. One shell came over and drove us pell-mell to the shelter. But it was the last.

We expected to find Vierstraat razed to the earth, all about our miraculous forge. But the village stood as before, broken walls lower but no more grotesque, the old mill with a bigger heap of brick about it, but still upstanding. A 4.2 had burst in the upper room of our house, close by the slit through which we had observed, but the walls were still sound, though the floor had suffered. Soon we had the wire going, and by the time I had climbed upstairs again our 12-inch howitzers were throwing their terrific shells in retaliation at Wytschaete church, throwing up volcanoes of white stone dust and red brick. We could hear the shells rumbling like trains over our heads. Taylor relieved me and we discussed means to strengthen the interior shelter and to build his 'shell deflector'. For the shelter we decided on additional outer walls supporting steel rails, sandbags, concrete slabs and more sandbags alternately, as far up to the forge rafters as we could get. Then I went along the ingenious path serpentining through the tall chicory back to the guns.

That night the Canadians were conducting a bombing enterprise, a device of their own invention, in front of Petit Bois and we had to stand by in case they wanted help. I picked my way to the guns over and under stray telephone wires, round a deep hole and over a potato pie and dropped into the deep sandbagged trench which ran behind the trails of our 18-pounders. The water dripped incessantly through the roof and Sergeant Charles was manning a hand-pump to drain the water away from his gun. In the middle of the row of guns sprawling each in its own cave, surrounded by gleaming shells ready fused to fire, a glimmer of light came from the top of a dirty canvas curtain. I waded along the submerged duckboards and pushed in. The telephonist was reading an old magazine with the ear-pieces held over his head by a small harness. We sat there smoking and waiting. At every half-hour he tested his lines to brigade and to the OP and the infantry, buzzing their call and listening to their reply while his ration cigarette, damp to start with, gathered long streaks of nicotine as he relit its dirty, diminishing stump.

The drops of water fell with maddening plops into the pool of water in which the duckboards were now floating. One wire gave no answer. The sentry woke the wire patrol and he went out holding the near end in his hand. The sergeant major snored, and the sentry came to warm his hands at the brazier, which kept up a hissing accompaniment with the telephone. Half-past three and nothing doing. Then suddenly our call buzzed out of the receiver. The telephonist leaped into action. 'Infantry request covering fire.' In a moment the firing began, each discharge shuddering in echoes among the hills, the shell hissing on its way like a fiery serpent. 'All quiet now?' we asked. All quiet. We slept while the sentry and the telephonist went on spitting and coughing and wishing their tour were over.

After a rest I went up to live with the infantry, sleeping in their headquarters at the Rossignol estaminet near la Polka. They had one of the new steel helmets which Byron and all the rest of us swore we should never willingly wear. All manner of indecent comments might be made on the thing. But the Canadians were only lukewarm; they thought it would be useful. Their colonel was a card and carried a full dinner service in crockery round with him. Many of his officers were French Canadians and wore the soft-soled shoe-pack, where I wore my heavy sea-boots. They had found a German sniper and were excited at the idea that we could 'wipe him up'. In the morning we took a periscope overland by Vandamme Farm passing the enormous grey-lined shaft leading to the mine under Wytschaete. Our spot was opposite the Petit Bois where we could see the sniper at work, even to the recoil of his rifle. I telephoned to Byron and he laid out a gun on the target. It was less than a hundred yards from our trenches, and the Canadians cleared the trench for fear our rounds fell short. By good fortune the second round hit the sniping post and we saw the sniper rush away, and followed him with another four rounds which screamed over our heads so low that the Canadian captain danced with joy.

'Darned near took our caps off,' he said. 'Guess I'd be satisfied if I'd been where that fellow was.' I reported to Byron that the sniper's position had been 'registered'.

On Kaiser Wilhelm's birthday Byron called us in and said there was to be no firing; the Prince of Wales was in the neighbourhood and was expected to visit the front line. I went up to the infantry at night and saw a small, distinguished group making up the road near the Rossignol. One was a slight figure whom the others addressed as 'Sir'. But it was too dark to see. 'He really shouldn't,' said Byron, 'besides it interferes with the war.' Puncher thought it very sporting and Taylor was deeply concerned about the monarchical position. 'Has he any right, in a limited monarchy?' he asked. The papers were full of talk about conscription. Byron was revolted in an aristocratic fashion at the idea of commanding conscripts. 'But it may be necessary,' he said. Puncher thought there ought to be conscription; Taylor and I hated the idea of fighting side by side with forced soldiers. We were quite opposed to steel helmets and conscripts, and talked like Henry V; 'We happy few!'

We changed about at the battery and the wagon line. As soon as the horses got off their log platform they sank over their fetlocks in mud. It was impossible to keep them clean and many of them got greasy heel. The room we slept in had a slate floor and seemed as cold as ice. Sometimes the old Flemish woman would come in and chat as I sat in a fleece coat and a blanket. Usually she spoke Flemish and some English and was proud of her few words of French. Every morning during the bitter weather she insisted on bringing coffee and biscuits to me. I rode into Bailleul and lingered in its handsome square before I turned to my shopping. Books and cigarettes were scarce, but I found notepaper and cherry brandy and carried it back carefully hugged in my arm. We could buy cardboard boxes of cigarettes at the canteen in Cheapside but the damp was in them and they drew hot and bitter.

We started building new horse lines on the windy summit of Mont Rouge, under the windmill, but before they were done we had orders to move. Meanwhile the road to the gun pits through the farm was over a foot deep in thick mud glutinised by the frost. We pulled our guns out and were away by starlight, but the battery who relieved us were unlucky. Two horses fell in the slough at the gate and before they could be released, had drowned, suffocated by the mud.

Byron had told us in euphemistic English that we should find it futile to think we possessed our souls as soon as we arrived at our destination. But we did not know what was to happen. We marched by night, south-west to Bailleul, and there entered that road through Meteren, Fletre, Caestre and St Sylvestre, which unfolds like a jointed foot-rule on the ground; a grey shining repetitive ribbon of pavé bordered with trees, a slight rise, topped by a spire and, again, at the same distance, a decline, a rise, and a knot of trees, through which a spire points to a grey sky. We climbed Cassel Hill at lunchtime, and by act of grace Byron agreed that we might eat in the inn. We walked across the dining-room and found the plain of northern France at our feet. The ragged clouds rolled over mile upon mile of country, brown fields and green fields and black woods, dissolving to neutral colours under the ragged sky. But the rivers shone coldly like steel.

'Did you notice what there is on the tables?' Taylor said. He came walking to the window holding a torpedo-shaped roll delicately in his fingers. 'White bread! Rolls!' We stared at the brown crust, broken by twin mounting waves. There were cloths on the table and rough glass dishes full of coarse salt.

'And there may be beds tonight,' he said.

'With sheets.'

'I wonder if there's any chance of a bath, and then a change. I'd like to be quite free of lice for a bit.'

When we arrived at last and turned in to the markers Puncher had put down in the field he came up first to one and then the other, smiling all over his face. 'We all have spring beds with sheets on,' he said, 'dinner in an hour. The old woman is making it.'

'God bless you, Puncher.'

Chapter 4

Conrad

Gris Nez – Spring 1916
Notre Dame de Lorette Bully-Grenay
– Summer 1916

W e were standing in a frostbitten field near St Omer. It was very cold and the cold was increased by my nervousness. The sum would not work out right on the Number IV Director. I checked the calculation on the squared pages of the army notebook. But I was again incapable of making the imaginary line of fire coincide with the imaginary target. Captain Conrad stood by with his contemptuous eyes upon me. One hand was in his British warm pocket, the other grasping the handle of a Malacca walking stick. Now and then he stamped on the grey-fringed grass. Taylor had turned away; he also had come out of the examination without much credit, but the sum of the compass had worked all right for him; he had only taken a long time. Conrad's lips curled under his ragged moustache and as again the compass settled and I laid off the line I was aware that it was wrong and that Captain Conrad was an interloper. 'Can't you lay out a simple line of fire?' he said, 'any fool could see that's wrong.' 'I can as a rule, sir,' I said, sullenly. 'I'll give you another chance then,' he said, walking rapidly up to the director. He unscrewed its clamps and shifted the tripod as I paced up and down in frozen dejection. Conrad set the tripod again and bent over the compass. Then suddenly he leaped at me and thrust his hands into my coat pockets. He laughed abruptly and pulled out the enormous door key of the billet. 'Ass,' he said, 'frightful silly ass. Now turn out the rest.' I produced my cutlery and dropped it into his cap. 'I suppose you've got a dead mouse there too,' he said severely. He seemed to be smiling. The compass waved wildly as he swung the handful of metal in front of it. Then

CONRAD

I succeeded. We were in Wulverdinghe near Watten in process of reformation. To our six guns two had been added and the eight were then divided into two fours. Byron had ordered that Taylor and I should belong to the new group. That night as we sat disconsolate in the chenille-draped room of our billet, listening to the rain beat down, there was an imperious knock. A stranger came in and said he was Conrad, the new battery commander. We looked him over in curiosity and he said abruptly, 'Where's Major Byron? Why isn't he here to meet me? Has a room been found for me? I want a man to take my horse.' We obeyed and scowled. I took his horse, a beautiful chestnut, and prepared to take it to the grooms. 'Don't ride that mare, she's tired,' Conrad called, 'and see she's properly rubbed down. I shall come over later.' Taylor sat over the stove and scratched his head. 'That guy seems like a bit short,' he said, as we heard Conrad making free with Taylor's room. 'Seems a bit Tartaric. I've sent for the major.' They quarrelled in a hot and dignified way over the sharing of the old battery. Conrad swore he would lodge an official complaint. Byron became more and more short with Taylor and me. Meanwhile Conrad left nothing undone. We stood for hours in the snow teaming the new horses until the sun's brilliance on the snow nearly blinded us. Conrad's manner made it clear that I was expected to be doing it myself, and was not there for discipline, company or ornament. In less than a week every man had learned to fear Conrad and the new battery was roughed out. Walking back to the mess one evening Taylor and I came to the gun park where the gun park chorus was singing 'Eva' in doleful harmony as the water dripped frostily from the poles. The fat sergeant major with long black moustaches was standing in his fur-lined coat watching them and smacking his whip in his enormous hand. He walked across to us, saluting deferentially.

'I should like a word with you young gentlemen,' he said, 'if you'll pardon an old soldier's frankness.'

'We should be glad to hear anything you want to say,' Taylor answered.

'I'd like to say you've got a grand officer in Captain Conrad; but what I want to say: I go about and I don't want to hear the men saying Mr Taylor's a real kind fellow, and Mr Boyd's a nice kind gentleman. No; I want to hear em say T's a b — and B's a bloody swine and when I hear 'em say that, well, then I'll be satisfied. Mind you, and you must excuse me again, you're shaping to be good officers but what you've 'ad's nothing to what you've got coming.'

Conrad suddenly announced that we were going to the sea to retrain.

Taylor would become acting-captain on the march, and I should go on and billet for the battery with Bryson, the quartermaster sergeant. It was the end of long negotiations with GHQ. My billeting party moved off early in the morning, and Conrad, leaning out of his window, suddenly called me back. 'As usual,' he shouted, 'stirrups far too short!' grinned and slammed the window. 'Heaven knows what to make of the man,' I thought. 'At one moment the south wind, and the next tearing you to bits.'

It was already late when we arrived at the village to find it no more than a four cross roads with two or three farms clustered about it. We had ridden about thirty miles by main road and by-road, through the rides in the great woods and over sandy bridle paths fringed by ash and birch trees. It was March and the wood was beginning to smell sweetly. Every step took us farther from the front and from occupied areas. The biggest of the farms lay at right angles with the road up which my mare trod wearily, forging and letting her head droop to the mud. Bryson was chalking up the billeting marks with his groom. But there was still daylight in the yard, enough to make out in the centre the immense pit of high-piled manure where a young woman stood with a pitchfork in her hands. I saluted her and rode round the cobbled causeway to the house door from which a pale lemon beam of light flowed over the manure. A lame man with very bright eyes came to speak to me. The kitchen had eight or nine people in it, most of them sitting on the long bench with their backs to the window, their elbows on the farm table. The table was partly laid for supper, with blue-and-white-checked napkins and soup bowls. I bowed to the company, rather embarrassed by their number, and explained baldly that I sought hay and corn for four horses, shelter and straw for two soldiers and beds if possible for a quartermaster sergeant and myself. 'But for that,' I said 'a truss or two of straw will do, in your barn.' The bright-eyed man talked rapidly to the woman of the house and nodded to me. Then he asked if we had eaten. 'No,' I said, 'not since lunch.' 'My God!' he cried, 'but what to do?' 'No trouble,' I answered, 'if we could boil water we have biscuits and beef and cheese.' 'Where? Where?' I showed him the linen bag with my rations in it. He untied it and spilled it out on the table for the party to see. They immediately broke into talk and laughter, picking up the biscuits and throwing them down on the bare board. 'No,' the little man said, holding my arm, 'you shall sup with us, you and the sergeant – but still, perhaps it is not right you should eat with a *sous-officier?* ' I told him that strictly he might be right but that there would be no difficulty; but should we not interfere with their supper? Not in the least. Then it was agreed he could find us shelter and forage. Oh yes, certainly.

The two others had not yet arrived. I went to the door to search, but he drew me back and passed out first, holding a tin candle lantern in his hand. 'Marie,' he shouted, 'there is a British *sous-officier* and a soldier looking for their officer; they must come here; go and find them.' She wore a checked apron tied tightly round her middle, a blouse tightly stretched over her bust and a skirt of coarse blue stuff solidly draped over wide hips. I protested. She gave me no answer except a glance from deep grey eyes set in a fat and pallid face. Her dark hair escaped untidily from a bun over her smooth round neck. Rogers had off-saddled the mare in the heavy blue dusk and rubbed her down with straw. We watered the two horses before I heard the jingle of army bits on the road. I heard Rockway saying 'This isn't 'alf a rum go,' and then the procession came in, the girl at their head. The QMS was a young eager man, a regular soldier, prepared always to go one better than circumstance. The girl stood watching with the lantern as Rogers and Blackway unsaddled the roan and Bryson's negro rig. They tied them up in an open shed. The patron came along with a sack of corn and some indifferent hay and watched with much surprise the measure of grain we poured out. I assured him we would pay for it. 'Naturally,' he said, 'I understand that the British Army pays; it is that it is hard to get corn, nowadays.' When we had finished he planted the two men at a side table near the conical stove, whose walls glimmered faintly with a livid heat and whose Cyclopean eye was gleaming with a white incandescence. Marie gave them soup. We were placed with the family at a large table by the patron who was running about whispering into the family's ear. It was plain it was a party. Clumsily I caught him as he was passing. 'Pardon,' I said, 'but we intrude; it is too kind of you to take us in. May we not take a candle and go in the barn; there is a block there we could eat from.'

'Listen, my friends,' he called out laughing, 'they would rather go out than eat with us here.' 'No, no,' I said, still more embarrassed, 'but we fear to inconvenience you.'

'If you fight for us,' said a fat man at the far end of the table, 'you must be also good enough to put up with our manners, is it not?' Everybody laughed, and a thin woman in the usual black whom I took to be his wife leaned over the table and said very slowly, as though she were talking to a child, 'You are too thin. We are going to fatten you. Then you will make a good lover. Like him.' Everybody roared with laughter, including Bryson who asked me what she meant. Marie was frying an omelette on the flat top of the stove and lifted it moist and sweating on to two plates which she carried to the grooms. Then we all began with delicious *croûte au pôt*. The two grooms had undone the necks of their tunics. The patron poured out wine. The QMS lifted his glass, ducked and bowed to the little man and saluted the company. They all rose, clinked glasses with us and wished us good health. Rogers and Rockway had finished. With natural good manners they had tucked their cigarettes behind their ears and were standing about waiting to speak to me. But the patron saw them first and rushed across. '*Estaminet*?' asked Rogers, jerking his head to the outside. But there was no *estaminet*. The patron stood in thought for a moment. He danced out and came back carrying four bottles of home-brewed beer. He looked at me questioningly and I nodded. So he pressed the men back into their seats and left them. Soon they beckoned Marie and she went over and sat with them.

We finished supper with cheese and coffee and handed English cigarettes round. The wine had travelled freely, a red sour wine but strong and pleasing after the open air. The party was shrieking with laughter at jokes we could not catch but very soon everyone began to yawn and fall quieter. We went out to see if the horses were all right. Bryson flashed the lantern. The mare turned her head and her eye gleamed a deep blue aquamarine in the candlelight. She whinnied gently and the roan replied tossing his head.

When we returned to the kitchen we suddenly discovered we could have dropped asleep on the floor. We must have looked it for the patron at once offered us beds. 'Now, come along,' the fat man's wife cried, 'it was I who won the *maréchal des logis* wasn't it?' 'And I who won the lieutenant,' a younger, fatter raman added.

'Why, seeing it's a birthday, they can sleep with whom they like, isn't it?' the patron asked, laughing.

'All the same,' said the thin woman, 'those who've changed beds must have a choice of sleeping partner – my husband may sleep on the manure if I may have the *maréchal?*

'My choice is fixed,' her husband answered, 'I sleep with Marie and also with Thérèse.' The patron led us to the door remarking loudly that we must, being Englishmen, be told where '*Ici*' was. He showed us the door of '*Ici*' with the heart cut in the wood, in case we might have need of it during the night and then took us to rooms with fat beds where we slept in great comfort.

CONRAD

We were wakened at 5.30 by Marie, with coffee, and found the grooms also with bowls on the straw, sleepily preparing to move off. No one else was up. When we were packed we found omelette and coffee and several scraps of very salty bacon, which had perhaps filtered through from army stores. Marie stood over us to watch us eat it, sabreing strips from a cart wheel of bread. The dung heap was smoking, webbed in dewy fungus. Its crude energetic smell mixed agreeably with the smoke of my cigarette. The patron came down, and I asked what I owed. He had figured it out faithfully; in addition to the billeting certificate which I signed, I counted out more, explaining I owed that addition for the trouble I had caused. He took it graciously and said Marie should have it. He called to her to bring cognac and insisted I should take a drop in coffee before I went. We pledged each other and at last clattered out of the yard on our way to the sea. As we walked the horses past the gable end a window rattled open and a woman's voice called out 'My lieutenant —' I looked back – 'Do not forget our night of love, and call here on your way back.' Her face disappeared among bursts of laughter and the fat man took her place. 'She is a wretched creature and you may take her with you,' he bawled. I waved to him and she reappeared and kissed her hand to me. The QMS rolled about his saddle, laughing, and I fear that with only the briefest salute I turned and trotted off into the mist. Soon there was nothing about us but the muddy road, the jingle of the bits and the steady trot of the horses, turned towards Audingham, near Gris Nez, only a mile or so from wonderful sands running sparklingly to Calais.

Taylor looked at me, too gloomy for speech. In the distance Conrad, clipped neatly on to his chestnut, was cantering swiftly away from us by the water's edge. The battery, its horses sweating in the spring air, stood around us in confusion, arrested in the middle of a complicated movement, designed to get the guns in action in a few parallel ridges of rock most awkwardly placed. Conrad's words still reverberated above our heads. Automatically we had swung round to watch him ride off; upon the intervening faces not a smile showed. It was too serious for that. Taylor had been battery commander, and I actually in charge of the guns, signalling to the teams orders intended to bring the guns in action in this particular spot. It was difficult. And then in the middle of it I saw Conrad suddenly bend forward from his position of vantage and gallop straight for us. I was petrified. All the way across the shining sands his grey eyes burned at us under the visor of his cap. He reined up within a yard.

'Do you know what you can do?' he said, 'You can both of you take the battery and drive it into the sea, and I hope I see none of you again, nor such careless inefficiency.'

There they stood about us, the complete outfit, guns, ammunition-wagons and third-line wagons, traces slack, men rigidly attentive, horses tossing their heads and jingling their bits, as nearly turned into stone as live creatures could be. The QMS was turned half left, preparing to take off the third line into an imaginary wagon line. The gunners grasped the handrail preparing to leap off.

'Well,' said Taylor, miserably, 'I suppose we gotta do something.'

'Go home,' I said. 'Tell the QMS to take them back.'

The QMS came up. 'Not lucky this afternoon,' he said. 'What can you expect with drivers like they, real raw they are.' We turned away as he began talking confidentially to the battery. 'Now you've got to use some savvy and *help* the officers; when you see that there director there, and Mr Taylor a-holding up of his arms . . .' What use? We walked on as the battery came filing after us, like a funeral procession. And how were we to face Conrad again? We spent hours in stables practising all the care his scathing tongue had taught us, upon every single horse, every little scratch, every nosebag; pushing our fingers into the crests to search for scurf, opening slavering jaws to look for lampus and rough teeth, examining the chest, the withers, the breast, under the stifle, the hoofs, everything. But at last we found ourselves at the end of all evasions. We had to go. Solemnly we walked through the village to the mess. Silently we entered and took off our belts like a pair of churchwardens with collection plates, in consentaneous gloom. Conrad was sitting there and I saw his face twitching. Suddenly he let out a shocking burst of laughter. 'Never saw such a pair of dumbstruck fellows in my life,' he said. 'Wish I had a photograph of a couple of hangdog damn fool fellows like you two when I left you. The picture of bliss!'

'We were quite a bit upset, Boyd and me.'

'Oh, how I wish I could draw! Upset! Here—'

He poured out cups of tea and joined the QMS in the garden. A moment later we heard them talking quietly. '. . . shaping fairly well, sir, so far as I can see. . . .' Conrad came back humming and with the news that Bryson was now sergeant major. The blood began to run its usual course in my veins. We all went to watch the new sergeant major try to break in a yellow horse with a wedge-shaped head, and drifted back smoking Conrad's cigarettes.

At dinner time we sat down by candlelight to drink our thin gravy soup.

'In North British America, Mr Taylor,' Conrad said, 'you doubtless have some of the amenities common to civilised countries.'

'Well sir, I should say we are just as civ —'

'You're talking sense, Taylor!'

'Well I guess I just had to say —'

'Out, Taylor! Out in the night to let your blood cool.'

Taylor gulped over his soup, disappeared through le door and entered through the window.

'You spoke of my country, sir. It is considered less than the truth to say it is God's own country.'

'I understand the country is highly religious. But I wished to speak of its means of locomotion. Do you, in any of your larger towns, enjoy the aid of street cars?

'We have been so fortunate sir, as to possess the original charabanc used by the Pilgrim Fathers; this has been converted to the use of steam and may be seen regularly every week drawing passengers from the mail packet to the seat of Government. My Nonconformist friend here will be interested in that association with the Godly heroes of his faith.'

'Indeed,' I observed, 'you surprise me, Mr Taylor, with the recountal of the Old Dominions enterprise. Why, in the North of England we still have to rely chiefly on asses — '

'True,' said Conrad gravely. 'And tell me, do you have baths in your new won territory?'

'Not as such, sir, yet the wise government of our populace has taken advantage of nature's bounty and caused to be preserved the various waterholes misnamed puddles, which here and there decorate our streets; for the purpose that when one of the Watch — '

'The what?'

'The Watch,' Taylor continued, 'discovers any person slightly or more deeply soiled, he may forthwith hale him to the nearest and therein immerse him until he be clean.'

'That is found effective, no doubt?' Conrad said.

'Effective indeed, with the proviso, that annually several thousand of the poorer sort are found to have been drowned.'

'You astound me, Mr Taylor,' Conrad said, arching his eyebrows. I laughed.

'That's enough,' Conrad said. 'Outside.

'No sir, I — '

'Outside with him, Taylor.'

Together they carried me down the passage and dropped me into a garden bed.

'We'll make music,' Conrad said, when I returned. 'Out with the cuspidor, Taylor.' Taylor got his clarinet. Conrad and I accompanied on kazoos.

The morning came fine and clear. The sun was warm and after drill we rode the horses into the sea. Some of them rolled in it, with their drivers. Then we took them to the soft sand of the dunes and they all rolled and kicked. On the headland, we three stopped for a moment, and looked west. There clear enough was the low line of white England lifted from the sea. This year, next year, some time, never. Conrad took off his cap.

All the afternoon we watched drivers burnishing the harness links and greasing with dubbin the breast harness and breeching straps. It was to be worked in until the leather was all soft as silk. At tea Conrad told us a man called Meyrick-Hardisty was coming to dinner, and that we must think carefully of him since he might join us. Or not. He had a long dragoon's moustache and sat opposite me listening with solemnity to Taylor's description of the Canadian Imperial Bodyguard. 'It never was up to strength, and so it just has to drill with an invisible rear rank. It would be real cross now if that rear rank ever came true. But they use all the orders.'

'Really!' our guest said, 'really!'

The conversation continued by jerks.

Meyrick-Hardisty was a Yorkshireman from the Plain of York. 'It is a very large county,' he said, looking round solemnly, 'and some important men were born in it. Very important. Priestley, for instance, the discoverer of oxygen.'

'Science is very interesting,' he added after a pause.

Conrad stroked his moustache. Taylor clapped his hands to his pockets as if for a pipe, and went out of the room.

'Do you do much science?' Conrad asked, with a wooden expression.

'Not much, I fear. I am rather more on the literary side, myself.'

'Ah, you read?'

'I always like to have a book, you know. Books are often very interesting. Conrad rose without a word and followed Taylor.

'I read a little,' I said, and as I spoke I noticed from the rustling behind my back that Conrad and Taylor were in the garden, by the open casement, listening to the conversation.

'Ah! What sort of books? Real literature? Not sport, I mean?'

'Oh no, not sport, exactly.'

('Stick into him, Boyd,' said Conrad's voice.)

'I was wondering,' Meyrick-Hardisty said, 'whether your captain was possibly related to Joseph Conrad the novelist.'

A groan came through the window.

'I scarcely think so.'

'Have you read any of Conrad's books?'

I admitted that I had read one or two.

'I always feel that Conrad's books unroll themselves like pictures before one's eyes.'

There was a loud snort from the garden.

'What's that?' Meyrick-Hardisty said, startled.

'I think it is the good woman's goat,' I replied, 'but let us go into the lines where the captain is waiting for us. He would, I know, like your opinion on the teams.' I rose and evacuated the position with dignity.

'We must say goodbye, Meyrick-Hardisty,' said Conrad, as we separated. 'Such pleasant meetings in wartime must be left to chance.'

'Chance! Ah! you also are a reader?'

'No, no!' the captain hastily replied, 'God forbid! Goodbye! Goodbye!' He waved him off the square with a handshake. 'The man is a professional,' Conrad said. 'We cannot have him here.'

Instead we were provided with a small Jew named Kreuz.

Conrad discovered that my twenty-first birthday was to fall that week. We borrowed a lift in a motor ambulance to Calais. Conrad wanted a haircut and I went with him. I was deep in a chapter of a novel, not I fear by the author of *Chance* but by Stewart Edward White, when I observed that the barber had cut a swathe from the back of Conrad's head with a close set machine. I was too horrified to move and nervously fingered the pages. The little man might have ordered it so. But he couldn't! At the moment he looked at my image in the mirror, and saw the truth. Such confusion followed. The assistant barber walked out in the street biting his nails and sweat poured off his brow. The proprietor left a lathery chin to trim the crop as best he could, and his black eyebrows went up and down in terror and dismay. Outside at last and shampooed, and amused at the barber's refusal of money, Conrad took his first whisky and soda since living, as he said, with a gang of temperate hooligans. Taylor turned up with four dozen oysters, three bottles of champagne and a box of cigarettes for me. I bought myself a silk handkerchief. The dinner at Audingham was an anti-climax.

SALUTE OF GUNS

Byron, Brand and Puncher came over but they could not harmonise with our orchestra of gazoos and so we entertained them to 'oriental songs' whose chief peculiarity was that they ended on the wrong note. Then we played bridge. The oysters were off colour; I found I did not care for champagne. A remark of Taylor's came into my mind: 'I guess it's just the ordinary thing when you expect something for it not to happen.'

One afternoon of the next week we marched away. Everything was sleek, everything was glossy, everything was in order, from the whiskers on the nose of A Subsection's rangy black leader to the painted emblem of the elephant on the back of the last wagon. We entrained at Fontinettes siding under glittering arc lamps. The horses were shy of the trucks and, once they were in, kept on breaking into hysterical confusion and were all in a second a melee of hoofs striking over some unfortunate beast on the floor. Even the heavy wagons were easier to handle. However difficult, Conrad knew it all. It was quite suddenly that we found the job done. Two o'clock in the morning and the lights of the refreshment hut were still alight. The English women who ran the place had waited for us. It was built to look like a cottage and the food lay about so that one could take what one wanted and pay by the card. The women were pouring out coffee and tea. We were so full of gratitude to them that we could not say anything.

We slept as the train rumbled on. At times a message would come that a horse had fallen. Along the footboard then to wait for a halt, while someone held down the misfortunate. The candle lamps glimmered high up the wooden walls of the vans, the floors were slippery with stale and at the stations the signal bells whistled through the night.

A few days later we joined a territorial division and were inspected with a few other half-regular batteries by the major general. Conrad came up with the news that the general said we had the best turn out he had ever seen. 'And I'll swear we had, too.' Conrad added. 'We'll go and watch the clouds,' he said. We lay on a blanket in the sun, and stared into the sky.

It was almost May and in Noulette Wood there were rivers of blue running through the grass under the trees, and the smell of lilies of the valley rose from clusters of green. The guns hid in an angle of the wood and the mess and dugouts had been carved by the French out of the face of small limestone quarries hidden under great beeches and sycamores. The very paths to the guns were bordered with flowers and when we examined our quarters we saw for the first time timbered shafts running twenty or thirty feet underground. Far below the stone was carved into graceful compositions. A girl's head faced me from a wreathed medallion; the French arms stood out from a block in the mess. So rich was the soil that a crop of tall disguising oats of our own planting grew round the gun pits within a few weeks. The dugouts we built were fully concealed. There were French units still in the sector and the commander of one of them, a fat middle-aged artillery subaltern, called to pass the time of day with us. He had a sporting gun under his arm and his dog followed at heel. He had been shooting in the wood. His battery of '120 shorts' were not far away. On the plain to our right two batteries of French dummy 75s marked tracks across to the ridge of Notre Dame de Lorette and we climbed up past the sentry on the trench through the splintered trees now budding again, to look on to Vimy and the parallel roads in Lievin.

The war stood so still it was almost terrifying. All day through the misty morning, the hot sun of afternoon and the violet evening, I pored over the landscape with glasses flickering over the front till the rim of houses below did actually seem to lift themselves up and perch, like cardboard models, on the grass in front of our hedge. In the dusk great moths came fluttering about, and I walked above ground on the friable earth whose every inch seemed mortal. The skulls and bones of Frenchmen littered the ground where they had been left. Miles of trenches in the course of dissolution seamed the ridge in an intricate web, like a secret to which the key had long been lost. Here and there wooden rifle embrasures still looked to the east and sometimes a rifle, broken, rusted, burst, lay across the sandbags which were falling to pieces like old tapestry. There were needle bayonets half hidden in trenches drifted up. Broken earth walls disclosed tufted skulls, water bottles, ammunition pouches. The cavernous dugouts exhaled a cold damp air, descending in flights to chambers in which men had prepared for dying. One explored timidly, arrested in silence by echoes of voices long since dead. On the very summit of the ridge stood a pollarded poplar thick with gum about which scores of moths flitted as though they were ghosts coming for orders, and on the forward slope where the ridge dropped to the glimmering spectres of Souchez or Ablain St Nazare I found the stones of the shrine of Our Lady now thrown down and serving to hide another OP.

The moon rose as I made my way through the witching solitude back to my hedge. The telephonists were reading some of my last parcel of books. The moon was so brilliant that it seemed to assert possession of the night, and as I stared at it I had the illusion that it was growing before my eyes;

and with a menacing, devouring look. Just so it had looked down upon the agony of men dying in the battle for Lorette. However we might struggle in the muck it remained a spectator insanely chaste, its silver face bland, blank and cruel. I could have accused it of all war, of being the indiscoverable poison in life, the origin, as it swelled and shone, of the mysterious insanity which possessed us.

The bombardier-telephonist pushed his way under the canvas which curtained the dugout door, his soft cap on the back of his head, a mess-tin steaming in his hand. He was a schoolmaster.

'Some tea, sir.'

'Do you suppose the moon has anything to do with the war?' I asked.

'There's lunacy, and Mr Chesterton's views on the moon, and dogs,' he said, 'and that wicked old moon there might be anything. Won't you come in and eat a bite, sir?'

We went in and ate bread and the remains of bully, whose fine luncheon bouquet had died away quite. It now seemed dry and fibrous. The other telephonist was asleep. We talked of books and slept alternately while one kept watch, and in the early morning I went along the slope again and watched the veils of smoke lifting from the hill where the menfolk of a whole town had been wiped out of life within a few days.

The mist slowly melted from the hill. The sun shot golden arrows into our eyes, lighting the long grasses in front of the hedge with a shimmering web. It was nearly noon before it got high enough to allow us to face the lines of dazzling chalk on the slope. Backwards and forwards I traversed my glasses, and suddenly halted them at the sight of many little specks moving through the air over the trench junction we called J 1. They were rifle grenades rising in flights from the German lines. The bombardier called the orders into the telephone, 'Right section action, J 1, one-o minutes more right. Number one HE Number two shrapnel. Stand by for two rounds gun-fire.' I fixed the spot with my glasses.

'Ready, sir.'

A moment after another flock started through the air.

'Fire!'

I heard the infant plop of the guns, and the whistle as the shells passed over my shoulder. Oh, good! One right in the trench; now the next pair, a shrapnel burst not too bad; that ought to shut him up. Report a direct hit. Stand by. Register as 'Grenade!' There was some movement in the trench. A stretcher's handles tilted up. What marvellous luck, I thought; and then,

'Poor devil!'; and another voice whispered that walking back over the plain someone on the other side might see me and the telephonists, and sing out to his telephone, 'Target: Noulette 3, two – o minutes left, add 100, HE . . . Fire!'

It was no part of my plan to get killed. I saw no reason for it except accident. So when the stretcher handles moved over in J 1 I called 'Stand easy,' instead of 'Repeat.' Someone was wounded, after all. When we had first taken over there from the French there was an *entente* with those others. Newspapers were handed over; an officer lost in the 'grouse butts,' so the story went, had been humorously directed back to his lines by a German subaltern. Even now when they prepared to fire the *minenwerfer*, a whistle blew which could be heard away up on Lorette. But our staff hated that. The offensive spirit must be cultivated. Though our men were only sheltering in holes on the slope up to Vimy, they must provoke and sting and bite, even though they had to dig all night to join up the posts.

Taylor had gone on leave and a new man had joined. He came surrounded with the suggestion that he was too difficult a man for the Territorial Division. Conrad told him he would be junior to me. We walked through the wood. 'Is this fellow Conrad any good?' he asked.

'He is,' I said, 'the best soldier in this part of the war and probably in any part.'

'All right, all right,' C. said, 'I'm all for a quiet life; if a man will tell me what he wants I'm the man to obey; but I can't stand these off and on soldiers. Does he like the staff?'

'He does not. We're having a strafe over the general's mess cart pony. It got lost and he can't find it'.

'Has he looked in your lines?'

'Why?'

'It's there. I saw it today.'

'Yes, he has; but neither he nor his sergeant spotted it. They think another pony is theirs.'

'What has Conrad done?'

'He's sending the other pony back with a note "Error very much regretted" and a word to say it had strayed in.'

'Oh, I say, that's the stuff; they'll never know the difference even if they do wonder why their pony is such a dud.'

I had to go up to spend three days with the infantry. The battalion lived by a junction at the end of a tremendous chalk communication trench running from Bully-Grenay through gentle downs towards Angres. I reported to a colonel of the 60th Rifles.

'Do you know your job, Gunner?' he said.

'I hope so, sir, but if there's anything you want doing I should be glad if you would tell me.'

'Your job for the next three days is to keep the stove going and to pour out my whisky at dinner and at any other moment when you see me wear my thirsty look. I'm wearing it now.'

I glanced at the brilliant blue eyes in his sandy, chubby face and at the fair trimmed moustache and hastily reached for the whisky bottle.

'And now go and play with my orderly officer outside, he's a spirited lad and needs conversation. Help him with his fretwork. Damned good, that "fretwork".'

I found his orderly officer outside in the sunshine, sitting on a step in the trench carving an enormous phallus out of the chalk. There were fragments of others on the parados.

'Isn't it bitter?' he said. 'No sooner do I get well established in my work than the stuff breaks. This one is supposed to belong to a general. The others here are for COs and orderly officers; and that little one there' – pointing with the knife – 'is a gunner's. Shall we walk?' He picked up his tin hat, saying, 'The colonel will be quite disappointed with me if I don't get out of his way and look at the war.'

The condition of the front line was not bad, but the old sandbags were beginning to stink with a sour smell. Insects like dragonflies darted about the top, flashing in the bright sun. The men were sitting on the firestep with their tunics undone. We called on C Company and I met Colefax at the door. He was so pink and flaxen, so clean and pretty, he might have come straight from the staff. Brighton, the orderly officer, talked about J 1. Colefax was not enthusiastic. 'Lots of you gunners want to stir up the war,' he said. 'Damn it, the war's quite bad enough when a man can't rear in peace. Look at our latrine; absolutely pock-marked with grenades. Spoilt a pair of breeches yesterday: one fell into the hole.'

'Now that's serious,' said Brighton. 'Bloody serious when a man's breeches aren't safe. Let us look into this, Colefax.'

We went along the front line and through a hole like a sheep-gap in a dry wall, which led to a tunnelled sap. At the end a sentry stared into a fixed periscope. We were about fifty yards from the German line. It was hard to recognise the front from such a low level. A stalk of seeding sorrel would obliterate a whole junction. In a half whisper Colefax pointed out an irregular chalk mound as J 1. 'The grenades come from left of that now. We'd better get back before their morning hate; come on,' he said. We crawled back along the narrow sap to the hole in the parapet, and straightened up with relief in the tall alley. Before we had gone a dozen yards Colefax halted. 'There!' he said, vexed. I had heard the faint explosion far away. Then the sliding roar became loud. 'Four,' I muttered. We flung ourselves down on the duckboards. They burst about us, 5.9s, crashing into the chalk, and as the bursts dissipated, the fids of hot steel hummed savagely over the landscape. 'There'll be another two salvos,' Colefax said. I lifted my head. The trench seemed full of dead men. Everyone was lying down. The explosions followed each other at short intervals like bowls hurrying to the jack. They had altered nothing, hoping that the natural error of the piece would give a direct hit. All over, that salvo. Fine crumbs of earth fell on us. A lump of shell whizzed at me. I pressed harder into the board. The metal slapped into the sandbags and a trickle of fine powdery earth fell into my neck. The fourth salvo was scattered again. Colefax half sat up. 'Damn it, they're starting again.' We lay there for half an hour listening to the cycle of sounds, relearning the tune of the big hows. One arrived too soon. 'God!' Brighton said, as it screamed down. It burst over our heads, a hot draught eddied about us. It had burst on the lip of the parapet and a fume was rising from the black scorch there. Colefax doubled down the trench waving us on. In front the men crouched running as they cleared the bit of trench. We had a drink in the shelter where Colefax lived. 'Only strong men can drink that ration lime juice and live,' Brighton said, looking at my glass. It was always difficult stuff to drink. 'Why are there no deep dugouts like the French ones?' I asked. 'The ground is dry enough here.'

'The staff, who live so comfortably behind, won't allow us,' Colefax said. 'They say the men would never get out in an attack; though why they should stay in them to get bombed to pieces I'm damned if I can tell you.'

'The troops call them bloody, to use the politer of the popular words,' Brighton murmured.

They ride about in gorgeous cars
And simply sit for hours and hours
Softening the hardships of campaign
With magnums of the best champagne —

I quoted. Brighton added:

... whose ceaseless toiling day and night

Should earn from those who merely fight
Both reverence and respect.
'The "Hun-Hunters",' Brighton explained.

'Sounds a bit stiff,' Colefax remarked, 'but anyway any excuse for a glass. Here's to them. The trouble is mostly,' he said, turning to me, 'this new Toc Emma, the Stokes, that bumps out of the gun by its own power. The fellow's just behind and poops off in absolute joy at all hours. That's what they're after.'

Brighton and I went to have a look at it. The subaltern said he would have liked to 'slosh a few over' but had just had a man wounded and lost a couple the day before. The Boche, he said, knew where it stood, to a T. The ammunition was stored in shelters round the mortar, white metal cylinders in neat piles. 'You see the pin at the bottom of the mortar; drop in the bomb, down the piece, on to that, and out goes she. My troop call it "Ena meena". Come up and see us during the little show.' That happened during my next tour of three days with the infantry.

The rain had fallen heavily and there was nothing to do. Another battalion held the front from another headquarters and I had to invent new duties. I left the battalion front and pushed south in the front line on to the low-lying ground under Lorette. The trenches were waterlogged and low, and had suffered severely. Frequently they had been blown in by 5.9s or the trench wall was pot-bellied, its corset of expanded metal torn into an entanglement of sharp edges. Constantly some sentry would tell me to crawl if I wanted to escape the 'spat' of a sniping bullet. I thought I spotted our hedge on Lorette but could see no sign of the actual OP. The trenches were sinister and half-deserted. On my way back I watched the sappers fixing pipes on to the parapet for the emission of poison gas. There was to be a raid. I saw nothing of it. I stayed with the CO in a new deep dugout and watched him wearily pacing to and fro all night waiting for news, while the candle flames followed him backwards and forwards and the runners came in with confused reports. But we did get a prisoner in the end.

When I returned Conrad tossed over to me a wad of telegrams from the general. 'Please report if Lt P. has yet returned,' one said. Another ran 'Can you recall Lt P. immediately.' Another 'Please report if signpost party is safe,' and so on, up to a final frenzied appeal: 'Please make every effort to bring in Lt P.'

'What's it all about, sir?'

'An idea of the general's to plant signposts in the waste land round Lorette; must be done today. He was so cross when I suggested it would take some time he sent a young and pretty orderly officer here to go round with C. to make certain it was done. The lad could scarcely read a signpost, much less a map. I think C. is doing him proud.' We had dinner. Taylor was ill in England. "Fraid we shan't see him again,' Conrad said. 'He'll be all right. Get a job in England.'

C. came in at last and saluted. He was covered all over with mud, but still smoking his large bulldog pipe.

'What have you done with the ADC?' Conrad asked coldly.

'Oh, he's gone, sir. Wouldn't stay for a whisky, wouldn't wait for a meal, didn't want to see the position. Couldn't do anything with him, silly ass.'

'Gone on foot?'

'Yes sir. I offered him a horse, but no, he wouldn't have it.'

'How did you ask him?'

'I said we had horses in a place twenty minutes away, a nice place but got shelled a bit, and that they were jolly fine stuff, a bit frisky and full of beans.'

Conrad pushed the vermouth across and laughed. 'Tell us all; we can bear it now we know he's safe.'

'Really, sir? Thank you; was the general worried? Oh, I see. I gave him a hell of a time. He started by telling me he knew it all and the country and the people, so I decided I'd just see if he did. But believe me, he knew nothing at all, and less at the end than at the beginning. I led him a real dance, all around the old butts near Souchez and even round under T. Deux; and I kept sticking in his silly labels and saying "Keep low now, keep your head down" or "Dangerous spot, this, very, six men and two officers killed here yesterday," or "They call this corner the Morgue." I could have split with laughing. After we'd passed teatime he got fed up and frightened. I dragged him backwards and forwards on the same bits till he didn't know where he was, and the more he groused the more I said, "We must do the job thoroughly." Then it got to dinnertime and he got worse. I told him they had an evening strafe round there, and I doubted if we could get back; at last he begged me to drop the other two boards in a hole somewhere. I insisted that we must plant them properly. One of them I stuck facing one of the others. He never saw. Then he begged me to give up. I said: "Will you report that we laid all these out by compass bearing and dead reckoning?" and he said "Yes." I brought him back by that boggy bit under the hill and his lovely boots are in a frightful mess.'

We applauded and called for his food. 'Well I call this jolly decent to be back,' C. said. We were still talking when another message came in from the general, delivered by motorcyclist. The ADC was back, it seemed, in a collapsed state; he had seen that the posts, were properly fixed, at great danger to himself, but the route chosen by 'Elephant's' subaltern was highly unsuitable in the general's opinion and deserved censure. We roared with laughter.

'My word, he has had the wind up,' C. said.

Conrad picked up his pen. 'When this sort of thing happens, you young feller-me-lads,' he said, 'write on it "Error regretted," or "Error very much regretted," and send it back. Always remember they can't hit you.'

Conrad ordered me to go walking with him in the wood. I had permission to wear what he called my cycling trousers and to bring with me the dead mouse which he said I kept in my pocket. We went up to the edge of the ragged Bois Neuf in which the flowers were blowing, and back by the wooded knolls upon which the infantry in reserve lounged and lazed, killing the lice in their shirt seams. Conrad stopped and leaned over his walking stick. 'Got a pain,' he said. 'Must see to it on leave if I can.' C. had been up at OP adding to the structure in the hedge bottom. 'I saw the General walking overland in full view to our hedge,' he said, 'and I shouted to him to get into the trench or I'd fire at him. He didn't, so I did. I fired my revolver and he got down. Oh, he was cross! But of course I apologised; hadn't recognised him, and knowing how strict his orders were about concealment, et cetera, et cetera, took what steps I could to see they were observed. "Well, we needn't discuss that anymore," the General said.'

I followed C. at the OP and saw on the extreme right of Angres a porthole open in a house. The black hole quivered violet and I heard the crack of a gun. We put a round through the roof and four or five others all about it, and I saw the gunners run away through the back street.

I went on leave in the fine summer weather. The heather was deep on Beamsley Moor. It grew in a glowing fleece from the breast of the Beacon as far east as we could see, branded by the coarse rushes and the rings of the marsh moss. On the ridge we dropped deep into the springing bushes and watched the white clouds roll eastward over a speckless blue sky. Hour after hour I stared up wordless into the sky, a mirror to the clouds, feeling at last I was a nothing jolted temporarily out of its place. It was pleasant to be nothing, to exist without rules, aims, struggle, to be put here and put there by chance, to enjoy the sight of the clouds like a small boy lost to the world staring through a hole in the circus tent. I had no right to be there, but being there, unnoticeable, the mere fragment of a unit, I took what I could and looked up through the quivering bells of heather to the vast sky bearing its caravans of cloud.

The sun slanted over Addingham Moor End; suddenly I thought of tea with voluptuous joy and we all rose and ran through the tough tangled bushes, my father gaily leading, to a grey stone farm. My civilian clothes seemed ludicrously light and inadequate; it was as though I were naked. I leaped a dry wall and fell into the marshy drain. Everyone laughed.

'I suppose you've been out there,' the farm woman said, 'my son's there.'

The next day I went to the boot shop. 'I suppose you're one that prefers to be safe at home sooner than fighting the enemy,' the woman said. I admitted it. One of her sons had enlisted with me; the other was serving in the shop. He came to speak to me. The woman blushed. The village was like that. Many gave white feathers, but I never had the chance of replying to one of them. There was one who had a different view. After church she rushed at me in her black bonnet and ancient silk cape. 'You are one of our noble defenders!' she said, throwing her arms about me. But she was not quite sane. The church collected our names in a competitive frenzy. Everyone who could be dragged in appeared on the roll, a sort of graduation class from Sunday School.

I returned with eight gramophone records slung in a box on my chest, and a dozen finnan haddocks, a present from my father, balancing them on my back. In my search for the battery I found the colonel. He asked me what I was carrying. I told him. Then he asked rather eagerly if I would stay the night – 'and have breakfast with us, or we with you.' I did not wish to expend my haddocks on brigade headquarters, but reason said I must. The colonel, too, was tactful. I gave him a whole haddock and he lent me a horse. So I got back to the battery with eleven fish. Bryson came in, saluting with incredible smartness and rubbing his hands with joy. He also had smelt the haddocks. He took one. Three went to the telephonists and the remainder we ate ourselves, passing a formal resolution of thanks to my father. During my leave one of the Vimy battles had been fought. C. told me all about it. 'That man Conrad is a real sportsman,' he said. 'There was only Kreuz and me to do OP, liaison and battery control, so Conrad mucked in with us and did the dirty work like a subaltern. I'm damned sure no battery commander's ever done that in this division before.' He told me, too, about the two 9.2 howitzers at Boyeffles Farm. I had seen them coming up. One was blown up by a direct hit with a 5.9, and every gunner killed. The other went on firing until only one man was left, and he wounded.

We were now in a position on the gloomy plain of la Rutoire, firing south to the Double Crassier. The position was painfully in the open, and standing on the ground we could see our own front-line trenches, and theirs. All night long we dug deep trenches from gun to gun, and all day long we slept, allowing no one above ground by day. Conrad went on leave and left me in charge. Every day the colonel to whom we had been lent came to see what we had done, and every day our sentry forced him to scratch his field boots with the raw lumps of stone in our deep narrow trench. We had cut it through the cellars of some miners' cottages. C. or Kreuz answered him in gumboots and a waterproof. When he discovered we were, all three, only second lieutenants he was angry, and began to make trouble. C. and I went walks up to our position in the brickstacks by Puits 7, where a single gun waited for a breakthrough, and sometimes at night fired a shot into Liévin. Near the communication trench which wandered by the mine buildings there was a sentry standing by a sandbagged well. He had half a dozen bombs on the shelf, ready fused. The well was the end of the mine workings and it went through to the German lines. We walked among the gardens and houses of Maroc and climbed into the famous OPs of that place, high in a chimney or in the water tower or concealed in a letter box. Soon we went to Bully-Grenay to live among civilians again. Even the houses we slept in were tenanted and the guns fired from positions only a hundred yards in front of the last rows. Here the trouble began to work. Conrad had been away a month; and no one had observed it. We were jarred by the sudden arrival of a new captain, who came from the yeomanry. Michaels was a Jew. He knew nothing about gunnery, he was no Indian soldier. C. went scouting round. 'They want to strike Conrad off the strength,' he said, 'they always hated him, he's too damned efficient for them; you better write.' I wrote at the end of my letter 'If you want to keep the battery for God's sake come back, sir.' My letter went. We calculated how long it would take. He might be back in four days. We sent his horses to every leave train. There were no messages from him. I turned restlessly in the sheets. It was two in the morning. Distantly on the cobbles I heard the clatter of hoofs; I sat up. Without a doubt it was the trot of the chestnut.

I found Conrad in the morning grey and difficult. 'My wife is very angry with you,' he said. I looked frightened at his cold face. 'What could I do, sir?' His face lightened for a moment. 'If you look at it that way, nothing.'

'C. and I thought it was the only thing to do. We didn't want anybody to mess the show up.'

'All right.'

It was like him to turn Michaels out of his bed on the night when I heard him riding up the road. 'I'm ill and I want this bed,' he said. It was like Michaels to accept a blanket on two hard wood chairs. We all sang to think he was back.

The staff wanted us to be warlike. We went out with a couple of guns into the open, running out Japanese enamelled telephone wire to an OP on Lorette and fired off ten rounds for an exercise. It was J 1 again the general pointed out to me. We scorched it with shrapnel bursts till the white chalk rose in clouds. The general was pacified; and this was our rehearsal for the Somme. Conrad composed a 'howl' on the bagpipes I had brought back for him from leave, in celebration of the day. It was curiously like his oriental songs.

Chapter 5

Fare Ye Well

The Somme – Summer 1916

On 25 July we left our wagon lines near Boyeffles bag and baggage complete, the captain's kitten, Tabitha, nesting among old socks in a basket on the mess cart. At Pernes we stopped three days making final adjustments for the march. This, at last, was no routine business. At 4 a.m. on the 30th, while it was still only the half-light, we marched away from the trees of the orchard, the drag-washers beginning their endless scuddering on the axles, the guns grumbling and roaring on the *pavé,* the burnished steel links jingling among the six-horse teams. The chill mist lay heavy on the ground and the sharp ears of the horses rose above it as though they were swimming. We travelled through St Pol. The sun came up blazing hot. It was pleasant marching country, but as we travelled on to midday the blaze grew hard to bear. Along the road we came up with signs of our divisional infantry, and later we passed an increasing number of stragglers. One of the brigadiers, we heard, had found it necessary to march his men with full kit by day under that sun over distances of eighteen or twenty miles. We saw some of the infantrymen lying in the ditches like the dead, their faces streaked with dust and sweat. Some begged leave to put their kit on our wagons while they walked alongside with our gunners. It was easy for us. Our drivers and gunners could unofficially exchange for a rest, and on the flat the gunners might sometimes ride. The bars of the sun fell between the poplars in a furious glow and the slow walk of the column, scarcely three miles an hour, became wearisome. Conrad had the road clear ahead and arranged his own halts instead of using ten minutes of every hour and thus we could spend twenty minutes in the rare shade, with the poles down and the horses free of their weights. We sponged the dust out of their nostrils and gave them a quick rub down. After the midday halt Mike decided to try the yellow horse with a wedge-shaped head. He took some pride in his ability to manage horses, and this one, he declared, only needed 'gentle-ing'. After about ten minutes he had succeeded in drawing it out of the column into the open fields at the roadside and every head was turned to watch the display and to hear Mike's curious horse-language. 'Wonna-manna-boy, then,' he crooned. The yellow horse shied off from his soothing hand and cat-jumped awkwardly. Then it bolted in zig-zags towards the horizon on the open grassland. Conrad was at my elbow, laughing quietly. 'Would you like a ride? Give Mike my compliments and ask if he is definitely leaving the column – say our rendezvous is Conchy-sur-Canche.' I cantered after Mike. The yellow horse would only respond to company, and Elizabeth's docile clumsiness brought her back after a splendid chase of a mile or two.

We came into Conchy's village street at about 4 p.m., all sweated up and covered in dust which gathered about the horses' eyes and nostrils in a fine silvery filigree. C. took the horses to the pond as soon as they had cooled a little. We marched them into the water, the drivers on their backs, and watched the animals playing in the water. The colonel leaned over the wall laughing as one horse and another knelt down gravely fore and aft and then rolled over with enormous splashings. The heat was so great that the cooks had made an immediate cup of tea for the battery, strong, thick, soldiers' tea. When at last the horses were all tended Conrad came walking into the lines wearing a cricket shirt and flannels, with a towel round his neck. C. and I raced after, shedding clothes on the way, and fell into the stream among the rippling weeds and watercress. I had arranged for dinner; on the long table of the *estaminet* there stood a noble salad-bowl full to the brim with lobster and lettuce, glistening with oil and white vinegar, the tiny specks of coarse salt faintly speckling the leaves. The bottles of French home-brewed beer, fresh from the cellar, sweated with coolness. A large omelette appeared. Conrad choked with pleasure and, halting the meal, gravely tore a paper circle from his message-pad and pinned it on my breast.

At half-past three in the morning I went on with other billeting officers to meet the staff captain in charge of such matters, near Outrebois. We were hot, hungry and thirsty, longing for breakfast. He arrived, an hour and a quarter late, in a large Vauxhall car and stepped out of it into our scowling group remarking, 'No billets, gentlemen, remember that we are at war.' His black curled hair gleamed in the sun, and he worked back the cuticle on his nails as he told us in a high voice which could have been heard in Leicester Square, where we were to go. 'He stinks rather,' one of the subalterns said, 'but I should call him a nice polite kind of staff officer. He did call us gentlemen.'

Conrad chose a stubble field that night. It lay in the crooked elbow of the River Authie looking across to tall glistening trees. Silently we stripped and slipped down the steep bank, feeling the sharp cool grasses between our toes. Mike and Kreuz had some modesty about stripping in public, and Mike devised a neat costume out of large handkerchiefs. He was sent in first because he did not dive, to show whether it was deep enough for a clean plunge. The river flowed on majestically clean and wide. The freckles on Mike's bald head rapidly submerged. He came up blowing and laughing and we shot in over his head down among the silver bubbles. Conrad would have us sleep out. He and the farrier rigged up a hammock on two handspikes tethered to tent pegs. The moon rose in full yellow circle, making the stubble pale gold. We lay about the hammock on the sharp straws, and the tobacco smoke rose in silence. A candle lantern glimmered in the horse lines across the road. I fell asleep. In the middle of the night I was wakened by a startling roar. Conrad's hammock had collapsed. The coolness and moisture of the dawn were falling on the earth.

At Genne-Ivergny the farmer's little girl fell in love with Tabitha, and her sister pleaded with Conrad. 'If you are going to the Somme, sir, that is no place for a little kitten.' Conrad held the kitten in his arms and shook his head. The general decided to hold a field day. It was cruelly hot as we climbed the steep hillside. The grease ran out of the axles and grease-boxes like water; the pieces were too hot to touch, the ground in the sun too hot to sit on. C. was sunstruck and had to be carried back. The coats of the horses were soon black with sweat and we could not keep the sweat out of our eyes. But still it went on. In the late afternoon, when the heat seemed to be striking upwards rather than down, the officers' call sounded from a distant hilltop. We cantered across to the general, who rebuked those who arrived for going faster than a trot in such weather. Conrad's calm had been too good to last. Mike fell into the trouble when he tried to drive the large GS wagon up a steep hill through a wood, to make shelter for the captain. It was in a dry valley covered with prickly grass, and there was no water for nearly two miles. The storm spread to the whole battery. Tabitha was missing. I reported her lost to Conrad. It was during stables; a most dangerous hour. 'Thank you, Boyd.' I was puzzled. 'Do you want me to . . .' I murmured vaguely.

'If I do I daresay I shall be able to give an order,' he said. I saluted stiffly and withdrew to my own lines none too soon. Out of all the 150 odd horses and the thousand or two points of harness fitting he had noticed three misfits on the march in my section. That was my fault entirely. No evasions here; the bridle was brought and fitted. It was certainly too tight and as certainly the small keeper on the poll was missing. Another horse had been forging. 'I didn't know that horse forged,' he said, 'did you know?' No, I hadn't known. A bad break. I had the farrier along. We took the horse out of the lines and watched her gait. The farrier admitted he had shod her hastily. He took her away to be re-shod. I observed that Conrad had found the beginning of a breast gall in C.'s section. A breast gall! The fury descended step by step. If there was one ringworm on a horse Conrad, like God, was sure to see it, to walk straight up and run his fingers over the damned spot. If a buckle was badly stitched on a girth the saddle-flap became transparent. ... A dreadful man, a lovely man. Anyway, in my section I was Robinson Crusoe; monarch of all. There was reciprocal and minutely detailed obligation between us, as there was between myself and Conrad. We were Roman Citizens in that battery, and when we passed a French battery on the road the next day, in spite of polite salutes, soon there was some laughter and secretly derisive fingers pointed to galled animals, cracking leather, rusty links, and traces dropped in the dust, while the Frenchmen shouted back, 'Wait till you can fight.'

After all, Tabitha was not lost. Conrad told me he had sent her back to the farm at Genne-Ivergny with instructions to 'get a receipt from the little girl about six years old'. Boothroyd, his groom, had brought the bit of paper with its laborious scrawl, *'Merci, merci, Thérèse.'*

Seated on top of a London bus with Conrad I was silent now that we were close to the Somme. The morning sun, red-gold and dusty, lit the ruins of Albert with a stagey cheerfulness. Part of it looked like the baron's kitchen in the pantomime, but overhead in the blue sky a few aeroplanes swung, and the roads were full of traffic. On the way to Mametz we saw rows of little holes scooped out of the bank at the roadside. Our infantry had dug them for protection, advancing from the masses of barbed wire close behind. Mametz was a pile of stones carelessly thrown on a low mound and in the centre an iron crucifix inclined drunkenly towards the road. There were thousands of horses on the plain behind.

The reconnoitring parties went to Dead Man's Gulch to learn the position of the batteries they were to relieve. But ours was not known; they told us to go and search for it near Caterpillar Valley. We looked at the road on the map and stepped out in the full blaze of the midday sun. As we entered the road the stench struck us in the face, a sweet, corrupt smell. For some miles in front of us the valley called the Valley of Death lay open to our gaze, with scarcely a blade of grass on its wide course, its higher reach winding among sticks of broken timber. The lips of shell craters overlapped in the dry brown earth, and by the side of the road their crests were powdered with paler dust. Enormous speckled horseflies buzzed and darted about the sweat running off our faces. On the left of the track lay several small shattered woods from which arose a sickening hum, as though all the flies in France were meeting over the bodies whose decay pervaded the battlefield. High above hovered two or three birds and a couple of our planes. The dead lying in the open had been buried, but by the side of the track among the rubbish we saw a foot, an arm, a hand, the flesh black and polished, the finger nails a deep blue.

The hill on the right was broken by a cleft, Caterpillar Valley, according to the map. Its black walls were full of shell-holes and in places regularly grooved by the scraping of the infantry entrenching tool wielded at arm's length as the men lay on their bellies, picking feverishly at the unwilling chalk with a small claw and a blade the size of a child's spade. The smell was no less and hung about us as we climbed Pepperbox Hill. Several batteries lay on the upland in a disorderly camp of shelters. At last we found an officer drinking chlorided water out of an enamelled mug in a low shelter by a half-dug trench. It had one row of sandbags on corrugated iron and would scarcely have stopped a rifle bullet. The guns were no better off. There was no guide to take us to the front line; we studied the maps and returned.

Mike was camped with the battery near Bavelincourt and had pitched our tents under a crescent of ilex trees planted about a crucifix which looked perpetually down into the village. They asked us about the new position. Conrad said, misquoting Harry Tate, 'They've made a nice mess of the garden up there.'

In the morning the mist was heavy and the files of marching men on the Albert road looked as though they wore grey. The column wound slowly by an earthen track within an enormous accumulation of horses and men. Two or three sections of 9.2-inch howitzers still shot over their heads. We halted behind Bécourt Wood and put up our lines. The ground was covered with dung, and flies rose in myriads. As soon as we had rigged a tarpaulin over the pole of the GS wagon the flies entered into possession of the shady side so thickly that not a stitch of canvas could be seen. They descended in buzzing crowds upon the food. In a bad moment we tried to burn them off with flaming newspapers. The fire destroyed their wings and they fell upon the floor and table crawling over everything. A painful nettle rash kept me awake upon my stretcher and I had to suffer that wingless promenade throughout the night, in silence.

The Australians near us were disliked by the English troops in the encampment. Each unit had its allotted times of watering at the canvas tanks, but the Australians galloped their horses down when others were in possession, as it pleased them, breaking down the troughs so that the precious water was wasted, throwing the horses into disorder, kicking and plunging in a stupid fight.

There at Bécourt I had news that within the course of ten days Sam had returned, been blown up and sent to hospital in England.

On 25 August we went into action on Pepperbox Hill, just as the light was breaking. The faint colours of the sky, serene, unstirring, promised another brilliant day. When we started for the front line it was hot again. We walked between Bazentin Wood and Mametz Wood by tracks which followed the firm ground among shell-holes and the refuse of the battle. The reserve battalion of Scottish infantry sat among some low mounds which marked the entrance to Welch Alley, cracking the lice in their clothing and smoking, some of them outspread in the full heat of the sun, others singing. They stared at us incuriously as we entered the trench. Welch Alley was about four feet deep, its walls irregular, collapsed, blown in; falling to the trench bottom here and there in miniature screes glazed like clay where feet had slipped upon them. It was full of telephone wires looping across and under, festooned along the walls like architectural swags, sometimes worn through to the bare core or twisted upon the great corkscrew pickets which here and there overhung the parapets.

There were two OPs. One was in 70th Avenue, the front line on the left of Welch Alley, the other in a forward sap ending in a barricade. The 4.2s had been falling sporadically as we came to these places. Now, as we fixed the telephone on to the wire and sent out the battery call, a big shell roared down into Welch Alley. The sky darkened behind us. We decided it was an 8-inch armour piercing shell. Another two arrived at minute intervals making the earth shake, and throwing fans of black smoke which hung over us like drifting fog. We could feel them strike the ground before the long roar shook in our ears. Conrad put up his periscope and started firing the guns. An hour passed. We made some corrections and sat on the trench bottom. Conrad wiped the sweat from his face and shared a sandwich. The crumbs and bully stuck in the throat. The infantrymen squatted down without talk. A man came flying over the barricade. Instantly everyone leaped on him; but it was an artillery subaltern returning from a private expedition in search of souvenirs. There were many dead lying out in front towards the edge of High Wood, on our right. A regular division had attacked 'that poisonous relic over there', as Conrad called it, a month before, and since then again, I do not know how many times, but increasing the gamble every attack. First a company, then a double-company, then a battalion. . . . The Jocks about us said that division had been ordered to stay in action till they could take the wood, and had thrown themselves upon its machine-gun fire until there were so few left that 'they marched out on paper because there was nothing else left'.

In the bright sunshine we turned our periscopes upon its timbers, like rotting piles rising out of water. At the nearer end the trees were broken higher up the trunk and in one we could see a German observer's platform from which a body hung. The whole front was wasted, a land seized by convulsive disorder. The pits of the shell fire overlay one another in an irregularity so great that looking out of the periscope nothing could be seen but the chopped rings of pulverised earth the colour of *café au lait,* intersecting at all angles, and behind them the battered white silhouette of Martinpuich, mocking on the near horizon; an object in itself as worthless as might be. No human being stood up in that landscape unless he had pressing reasons.

We continued our registration of the front at intervals as the 8-inch guns played continually about 70th Avenue and Welch Alley. There was a pause. Then suddenly the note of the shells altered. Everyone threw themselves down. There was a shocking burst which converted the whole world to one noise. My ears seemed to be hurt; they buzzed with the echo of the detonation. We cowered as the vibration passed over our heads. The shell had fallen immediately behind the barricade which now was levelled. One of the infantrymen lay struggling under the broken sandbags. He was dragged out. The top of the trench walls were blown away and we lay there in our hole as though naked. Conrad picked up his map and protractor observing that there was no point in waiting there to be shot at, now. The telephonist, kneeling, slung his instrument over his shoulder.

'After the next one,' Conrad said.

FARE YE WELL

We were all crouching in the butt-end of the trench in the heavy sunlight which seemed to oppress my breathing. Opposite me one of the infantrymen squatted. His long pale face was cut by the parabola of shadow from his steel helmet and his eyes gleamed feverishly from the darkness. We stared at each other. We all dropped flat at the scream of the shell. It burst outside the trench. 'Now!' Conrad shouted. As I bolted out of the hole I was aware in one glance of the soldier's eyes, resentful that we should go, while he must stay. We ran for Welch Sap, and checked a moment, for it had gone. Conrad led in and out of the scorched craters and we followed, dropping to cover as the shells burst behind; then we ran hard for safety down Welch Alley, elbowing round corners and past the little scoops in the walls where the infantry huddled and waited for the next shell. Upon the rough fire steps the dead were lying. The umbrellas of smoke swept up behind us, but we got out safely.

Our own guns at the battery were sheltered at the sides by walls made of brass 18-pounder cartridge cases filled with earth and laid alternately butt out and in. These costly ramparts supported eight wooden rafters, a roof of corrugated iron, and a row of sandbags filled with chalk. The pits stood nakedly on the hill among half a dozen other such rows of guns. There was no safe dugout for the men. We began to dig behind the pits a trench which would wind in and out from one to the other. When that was started I went up to renew my acquaintance with Welch Alley and 70th Avenue. I was to spend the day there. There was no sign of movement on the front, but all day long the heavy shells kept falling about the newly cut trench. It was so shallow I could look over the top kneeling. The sun beat down hotly upon us. Now and then some infantryman would go past crouching or come and beg a light. All day long the barren plain in front spouted fans of black and white smoke thrown up in rigid bars with a white incandescence at the heart. At times the enemy shell fire concentrated on the trench junction a few yards to the right, and never a moment passed without the sound of near explosions. A pitiless sun beat into the trench all day. I returned after dusk, when the fury of the fire seemed to have become more intense. It was new to be in a place where there was no rest. I shared a corrugated shelter and I slept twelve hours. The battery trench was now over eight feet deep and about two feet wide, cut through lumps of chalk. C. threw down his pick and I shovelled. It seemed to us time we might begin to make a safe place for ourselves and we chose a site and started. Conrad found us at work and ordered us off in anger that seemed almost insane. A salvo of 5.9s arrived in the position just as our ammunition wagons were arriving. The first four were just drawing to a halt when the crashes fell among them, obliterating them in smoke. We ran towards them, but before our eyes the plunging teams disentangled themselves and galloped down the hill. Bryson had heard the shells on the way and had led all the teams round. The shoot passed backwards and forwards over the area smashing in gun pits and exploding ammunition. We were firing a slow barrage, every gun a round in four minutes. We stood in the trench and as each shot was due a gunner would jump into the pit, fire, and sight the gun again. The ammunition came up again, two wagons at a time. Everyone helped at the unloading, passing the shells in a chain to the pits. Liaison duty for three days with the infantry battalion was peaceful in comparison. The deep German dugout faced the wrong way and its doorway was protected by a bridge of timber and sandbags thrown across the top of the trench. Here I could sit and write letters in the sun. But hearing a gun one moment I looked up and beheld a black speck in the sky. As I dropped into the shaft below I heard the final scream of the shell. It burst on the edge of the bridge and I rolled to the bottom of the staircase. No man could have better luck than that.

I was still with the Scottish infantry when a runner came from the battery. 'The captain's gone,' he said, and handed me a note. I read it and re-read it. Conrad said he had been ordered to England for an immediate operation. 'I expect you're damned glad,' he wrote in his bold hand, 'but I'll give you hell when I get back.' But I had a doubt that he would not come back, and with that doubt the war changed its complexion. A new landscape like the landscape of Welch Sap presented itself. There was C. left to talk to. Kreuz disliked or despised us all, even the gentle Michaels, but when I returned I found C. and Kreuz agreed that Mike could not properly command the battery. C. thought his lack of efficiency was a public danger. Kreuz also revolted against Mike's arrangements for messing. At any moment a dozen tins of asparagus would arrive, or a large jar of *pâté de foie gras,* with tins of curried prawns, a baked ham enveloped in a skin of shellac or other such coating, tinned chicken, bottles of mulligatawny and *hors d'oeuvre.* None but Mike could reasonably afford such things, and when we protested he always wanted to pay for them himself. That was equally impossible. Thus the small profits from our pay melted.

One morning C. and I went to see Sergeant Sankey, our pink and white pay sergeant, canteen sergeant and general accountant and writer. He was counting out English pennies into a bag. Twelve English pennies were worth more than twelve French ones, though nobody cared about the difference but Sankey. He, industriously enough, paid for everything with the French pennies he had to take, but saved the English ones, pocketing the margin. The ammunition statement was lying on the board which served as a desk. C. put his finger on it and called me over. We were firing about 2,000 rounds a day, but the return showed us with scarcely any in hand. We called Bryson. It was true. There was enough left for only about three-quarters of an hour. 'I've reported it to Captain Michaels, sir,' he said, 'but he's sent no order yet.' We sent off a bicycle orderly at once. 'I wish to God Conrad was here,' C. said.

The barrage continued night and day. At times a storm of 4.2 and 5.9 howitzer shells swept over the area, but did not stop the firing. Walking across to the shelter which served for mess, one night, I heard a strange whistle, a fluty sighing sound which expressed both dejection and weariness. There was a faint plop some yards away. I went to find C. who came and listened. More were falling and the faintest smell was rising with the grey shadows from the earth. It was a sweet smell which burned the back of the nose a little, and rather like the smell of cold mutton fat. We agreed it must be gas if it were anything at all. The quiet whistling increased about us. It was certain; we ran to the shelters to give the gas alarm. I had an experimental box respirator with a nose clip and mouth piece. C. pulled over his head the grey flannel bag which was the regulation gas mask. At that moment the ammunition began to arrive. Everyone turned out to unload, throwing the rounds from hand to hand with the highest speed. The gas shells increased in number, fluttering down among us. When the last wagon had gone three of the loaders were found collapsed on the lip of the trench, and went at once to the dressing station below. There they told us it was phosgene gas. The night air was as calm as in a tomb. The guns still fired, the explosions shattering the darkness with brilliant flashes and echoing over the hill, but the gas in the pits grew steadily heavier. We sat in our shelter between tours of inspection. Mike, C. and Kreuz in their grotesque smoke-helmets breathed out through a metal pipe ending in a rubber flap like a child's squeaker, and breathed in through the flannel. The eyepieces fell forward, distorting the face still further. My respirator left the eyes uncovered, and I could see better than they. C. went over to the guns.

We sat about the candle in our narrow cell. A bench ran along each wall and a table filled the rest of the room. It was scarcely five feet wide. Minutes passed. Mike suddenly became agitated and told Kreuz to take a torch and look for C. Kreuz said it was useless to go; C. would be all right and could look after himself. 'He can look after himself damned well,' he said.

Mike said: 'Please go at once.'

Kreuz said: 'Not on your life. Why should I?'

Mike said: 'I order you to go, as your superior officer.'

Kreuz argued. It was pointless, he said. He had bad sight, and certainly could not see. 'Anyway, I refuse to go,' Kreuz said.

Mike said with forlorn dignity: 'You will consider yourself under arrest.' This exhibition was painful. There was little danger from the shells. They did not so much burst as fall open like rotten fruit. I went to find C. and told him what had happened. Then I found Bryson huddled at the back of a gun pit. He was laughing at these pussy shells, as he called them. We sat together for a while. Then we saw a flashlight, moving about on the ground. Some voice was calling, muffled and hoarse. 'It's Captain Michaels, sir.' We went to him. He was calling 'Boyd, where are you, Boyd?' Bryson smartly reported progress. We were a little behind the total of rounds we ought to have fired. Mike and I went back to the mess. The time passed with hopeless slowness. It was three hours since nightfall, three hours since the gas bombardment had begun. Mike sat sideways on the bench, jammed between the sandbag wall and the table. Constantly he fell half asleep and his smoke-helmet would inflate with each respiration and contract in folds over his mouth when he drew in breath. The spittle dribbled from the rubber lips of the valve. We kept on stirring him and putting the mouthpiece back between his lips. His heavy snore was almost frightening. At last he sighed and rose, saying he would go to the battery again. Nobody said anything. The gas was falling heavily outside and the desire for sleep almost overwhelming. C. put his knees under the table and edged himself along the bench to the corner, where he sat, jammed in his place. Kreuz occupied the other. We none of us said anything. I went out. There was no sign of a breath of wind, nor of the dawn. I went in again. Nothing had changed. The two sat there with grey flannel bags over their heads obscenely pierced by goggle eyes of glass, as though they were some primitive form of fish, and the air seemed also aqueous, as though the gas were a grey tide of fog rising about us. Kreuz suddenly leaped over the table and threw himself upon C. He was making noises like an animal. He locked his thumbs in C.'s windpipe and hammered his head on the sandbags, one knee on the table, the other on the bench. I dragged him off and pushed him in the corner. 'Better luck next time,' C.

said calmly, 'unless you'd like to fight?' Kreuz swore passionately at C. The action was over in a moment, so quickly that, like action in a nightmare, it seemed unbelievable. But there lying on its side the candle still flamed, and C. eased the collar round his throat. Kreuz leaned his head on his hands. Mike came in with news that at least one pit had been struck. We replaced the candle and sat silently in the shelter. Time scarcely moved at all and under our eyes the shadowed pattern of the sandbags played strange tricks, becoming at one moment like stonework, at another a net. The night was still and dark as pitch, as though day had finally fled, the earth stopped in its rotation and everything a dream but this. We could scarcely keep Mike awake. Propped against the wall he would breathe for a moment, slide and fall. This was a time for miracles, I thought, in despair of the night. If they could keep this up and the air stayed still then we should be caught in a springe truly. There was nothing to be done. We walked out again. Five hours had passed and still the shells fluttered down, soft and easy about the position. Still in the cold darkness a gun or two guns of ours would burst into momentary flame and throw their shells whistling across the line. The wire spring of the mask held my nostrils so tightly my head was near to bursting and my mouth felt as foul and hot as concrete in the sun. In the shelter the rats and mice which usually sounded so noisy were silent, probably dead. Occasionally a trickle of earth fell out of a broken sandbag, with an alarming sound. In the solitary candle's light the place seemed to become a filmy grey, and time hesitated between centuries past and centuries to come. I went out again, it seemed still black night, and stumbled across to the gun pits where the gunners tried to lay their pieces through the steamed glasses of their goggles. There was some shouting in front. I discovered Kreuz hauling Mike out of danger. He had wandered in front of the battery. Kreuz took him back, arm in arm. After a while I followed and leaned in the doorway staring witlessly at the sandbag wall. It seemed to change colour. I turned to the candle and looked at that, and then back again. Yes, there was a change in colour. I lounged out and looking up saw a stream of golden rain ascend from the hill about Bazentin. The tracer bullets seemed almost like an omen of good. Beyond them the sky was a tone less dark. The east was lightening. I called the others and we came out into the raw air, waiting for the light that would stir the currents on the earth.

Watching so eagerly, the dawn came quickly, dissolving the black into a smoky grey, and then etching that out into dark bars of wool. The shelling had stopped, and the gunners on duty came from their pits and holes crouched with cold and fatigue, like men at the turn of a debauch. They were wrapped up in khaki wool mufflers, and had their arms over their breasts, moving about in the half light like figures in a play. We began to assess the damage. Two gun pits were blown in, one so badly that the gun could not be fired. Two or three dugouts had been hit but not penetrated. But we had fired nearly two hundred rounds less than our share for the night. That seemed serious. We called the numbers one, the sergeants, and they turned back to the pits. C. checked the barrage lines again, Kreuz and I checked the guns. In two or three minutes our three were firing again, waking the morning with a salute of gunfire to make good the deficit of the night. We all carried shells. A band of light broke in the sky behind us; the siege candles on the aiming posts glimmered more feebly and the shuddering of the echoes came back to us like the only sound in the world. Bryson lifted his gas-helmet and I removed the clip from my nose and sniffed the air. It was better already. In half an hour the gunners had halved the balance and turned out for tea. But some of the twelve could not drink; and five went down to the dressing station and were sent off to the hospital. Bryson roused the day team and C. and I went round the shelters. Sergeant Sankey was lying amid his treasures asleep, a smile on his face. I shook him. But he was dead.

We had been in action a fortnight now, and C. and I congratulated ourselves that our dugout was nearly finished. In the hole, ten feet deep, cut through the chalk lumps there stood two sections of 'elephant' cupola, horseshoe shape, of heavy gauge iron with a rib about eight inches wide. We threw back the spoil on to the iron roof until it made a high mound over the top, and contrived an archway of wood for an entrance, by which we slid down the loose slope of chalk to the level of the floor. There we felt safe, and spread our blankets on stretchers. Between them, upon a box we put an enamelled washbasin and a candle. The shelling began again with a salvo of 5.9s which shook the earth about us. Another put the candle out and filled the air with chalk dust.

We found the crater afterwards upon the summit of our mound; a direct hit, and we reverently filled in the hole and added a few more lumps for luck.

C. and I went down to the wagon lines for two days. We had twenty-four hours' leave for Amiens. We talked about Mike. 'Let's ask the Colonel whether Conrad's coming back, and whether Mike is to take charge,' I said. C. thought it couldn't be done. But about four in the morning we mounted our horses and rode up to Dead Man's Gulch. We roused the colonel's orderly and asked leave to see him. I went in to his cell through a gallery in the quarry face and he leaned upon an elbow and asked about Mike. At length he said, surprisingly, 'You want a new captain?'

'Yes sir.'

'I've been thinking about that.'

'If you could find us a regular, sir —'

'We'll see.'

'Thank you sir.'

C. was waiting by the horses. 'I thought he was strafing you good and proper,' he said. An unpleasant business.

We rode into Albert with our grooms, and a mile or so beyond. It was easier to catch lorries on the road, beyond sight of the Motor Transport Officers. So we stood at a bend of the great Amiens road linking mile after mile with tall trees and waited for a likely lorry. A few passed and then one answered our hail by slowing down. We leaped at the tail board and from above the mixed company of officers and soldiers hauled us up. The lorry driver glanced back through his window and accelerated. The exhaust bubbled underneath and the solid rubber tyres jarred and bumped on the *pavé*. The sun was up and already the dust was beginning to scoop back on to us. There were ten or eleven lorry hoppers in our company. Everyone was wildly pleased to be out of the line for a while. The next lift we got was in a car going to bring officers back from some railhead. That took us about ten miles. Another lorry carried us to the end of the Amiens pavement, and there we dismounted, settled our belts and stalked towards the town. The sun played in the trees and as we crossed the bridge the cathedral suddenly lifted itself above the roofs. The road was full of slow civilian carts and wagons, driven by old men wearing blue blouses and smoking big pipes. 'This is the life,' C. said. The first hotel we came to was the Belfort. C. wandered round the lavatory with his hands on his hips staring at its miniature magnificence, its polished white metal taps and plate-glass shelves. The water was hot, too. Lunch was the most delicious meal we had ever tasted. C. drank champagne and abused my abstinence. The more he drank the more he cursed the staff in his high-pitched, reasonable voice. He described the campaign and explained its defects with the restrained ferocity of a criminal lawyer. But the staff sitting about us were too courteous to listen. We walked out smoking the largest cigars and felt that life held nothing better than this; to be free, and spending money in Amiens. The gramophone shops had half-a-dozen records played by Backhaus; the bookshop some English novels. Then suddenly finding ourselves under the very door of the cathedral, we entered. The sunlight carried blue and purple through the east window, and we stood in its seraphic calm till C. reminded me that we wanted a bath. There was a queue thirty or forty long in the moss-grown courtyard; another shrine this; no less lovely to feel the hot water eddy about every sensory nerve of the skin, to make a smooth bodily lather with the square of fibrous soap, to feel the scrubbed body smart as it re-entered the water. Then to dry with a large cotton sheet and to feel clean everywhere. Early evening brought us to a café for short drinks. People walked under the trees laughing and talking, girls so neat and gay it seemed no war could hurt them. The women were unbelievably lovely. Out of the Hotel du Rhin came a party of British staff officers pluperfect in every inch; looking as if they had come not from a bandbox but from some museum for precious things. We sauntered along the Rue de Noyon, until we came to a semi-circle of French infantrymen on a bench; their blue soiled, their hands and faces covered with hair. The hairy ones! They sat there like apes, arguing vehemently among themselves, making disgusting noises of contempt. They were strange and admirable.

In the street we met one of the brigade subalterns. He had found a girl. She waited for him in the shadow of the by-street, small, dark, with large sad eyes which flamed out boldly as we looked at her. Richards turned his back carefully upon her and handed over to us his spare money and his cheque book. He told us that one of the subalterns in his battery had escaped from a knife in some low place; 'God! but I don't believe it of that girl! Do you?' he said, 'She's lovely, I've been drinking with her all evening, and I've bought her things, you know. Cheerio!'

'Good luck,' we called.

Early in the morning he called at the hotel for his valuables. He looked like a man who has seen an angel. 'I'm coming back here if I can sneak another day; and we'll spend it together, her and me. She's bloody fine.' It was still early when we breakfasted. The sun was throwing red hot pokers between the trees on the Albert road as we waited for a lorry. The river flowed crisply under the bridge. In a couple of hours we were back again in the stench, and Amiens lay behind us as though it had never been.

Our fragment of the war had changed again. The guns went forward a few hundred yards. A new captain joined us, to be OC. His name was Lennards; he was a rowing blue, and a man of enormous proportions. Even his face had run to fat. Mike left us, and we toasted him our farewell with real regrets.

Lennards introduced himself with a dozen of whisky and asked us all to drink. C. and I took no spirits, but Kreuz leaped at the opportunity to explain with bitterness that we meanly refused to pay a share of the whisky bill. C. argued and Kreuz spat. At length Lennards' face grew apoplectic and he let loose a torrent of bad language and abuse which silenced the argument. The physical fury of the dispute was almost painful. It seemed that C. and I had won, though Lennards abused impartially. C. went up to observe from Bazentin le Grand. He came back dead beat after touring the line. But Lennards sent him back again for the next day's duty because he and the telephonist had forgotten to bring back the rifle which we were supposed to carry. Back again he came after nightfall and found the colonel in the mess. The colonel wanted a map drawn.

'You must know the front, C.,' he said. 'Captain Lennards will send you up in the morning.'

'I've been up the last two days, sir,' C. protested.

'All the more reason, then,' the colonel said.

'It's really our turn,' Kreuz said, slowly.

'C. will go and draw the map,' the colonel said.

C. went out to swear quietly on the top.

'Must keep discipline,' the colonel remarked to us. Our faces were blank. Bazentin was horrid.

It was a few days later that we all happened to be at dinner together. The brigade orderly arrived with a message. Lennards read it out – Please detail a senior subaltern to attend at Brigade HQ 19 hours, 13/9/16.'

There was a pause.

Then C. said, 'I'll go.'

'What is it?' I asked. 'What do they want?'

"Spose they want someone to go over with the infantry in an attack.'

We felt ashamed then. We had half guessed that.

The attack was delivered on 15 September. Our barrage had changed its line to the right of High Wood. On the night of the 14th a servant rushed into the mess to say that some amazing things called tanks were on the road below. We were incredulous. He persisted. We all went down to look. But he was right. Among the stream of traffic they lumbered along, the strangest things we had seen. Early in the morning we rose. C. was to go with the first wave of infantry and to observe from the far side of the crest, Kreuz to follow with the third wave and get as far as he could. I was to watch from the hill above Bazentin, observing the capture of the wood. As C. and I stretched in the dawn and loaded ourselves with map, compass, water-bottle, rations, gas-helmet, binoculars and revolver we saw on the skyline above us the silhouettes of cavalry, their lances aligned against the grey sky. 'Poor fools, poor bloody fools,' C. said; 'they're going to be killed in the first half-hour.' It was horrible to think of the horsemen picking their way through the miles of broken wire and broken earth. They could not hope to live. We walked up the German road and separated with a salute. The barrage had begun. In broken ranks upon the hillside the guns and howitzers were firing in primrose flashes upon the half-light. The pitch of the bombardment increased to a steady drumfire which drowned every other sound except the scream of an aeroplane skimming up over the front line. The angle of my trench was built like an earthwork in the bastion of the hill; but it was still so grey that I could see nothing beyond the immediate foreground, and that still smoking with the wreaths of mist. Looking round at the ruins of Bazentin I found it plumed with monstrous pillars of grey smoke. One after another they shot up with terrific velocity and faded away in a grey rain. These were explosions of heavy shells, 8-inch or more; yet not one explosion could be heard, so loud, so various was the bombardment. I turned again to the front. By my side the men of the third wave were waiting for the signal to advance. They looked sleepy and turned in on themselves. By now the first wave was over, the second preparing to follow and the German road below was already going up in smoke. The enemy were trying to strangle the attack here; and later their fire would be worse. Some shrapnel burst over us, but high as usual, too high to be of any use. The infantry prepared to descend into the smoke below, now varied with individual shellbursts. As they went the mist seemed to clear up before them. They deployed on the right of High Wood and moved forward slowly in line up the gentle slope of the crest. As I watched reserves came up to the position and took their place. A moment later a stray captain attached to our howitzer battery came into the angle. He was observing too. He smelled very strongly of spirits and his face was quite grey. I saw he carried two water bottles, a quart each.

'What have you got there, Rattray?'

He lifted them to my lips. One was full of neat whisky, the other of neat rum. He went away from me. Up against High Wood a black lump showed itself, a disabled tank. A handful of our infantry were working up behind it to fire from its shelter into the tangle. Little balls of white smoke and black smoke showed that they were being bombed. The barrage was slackening and lengthening. The fighting went on invisibly in the wood and over the crest. The sun came out; it was late morning and I saw files of German soldiers marching out of the wood, their arms up in the air. I counted a hundred or so and sent off a message. Up on the ridge now someone was trying to semaphore with flags in the smoke of the shellfire there. It might be C, I thought. We gave an answer but before the message could come through the signaller was obliterated by a big burst and we saw no more of him. No wire could hold in the barrage. High Wood was captured, or the main part of it, that was clear. I repeated the message. There was nothing more to be done at Bazentin. We ate some bread and cheese and cake and drank some of the bitter lime-juice. Then I signalled that we were going forward except for one signaller, who would relay messages if necessary.

Men of the German garrison were still coming out of the wood. Our men were loading them with stretchers. Sometimes the Germans threw an arm round our wounded to help them down. Everyone on the slope was walking above ground, a most unnatural sight. Sometimes the shelling was lucky; a little party disappeared before our eyes as we walked towards it. The enemy fire was now heavy on the forward slope where our infantry lay, and behind. There we could see it throwing its columns in the air. In front an angry cloud lay over the horizon, in which sometimes a 12-inch explosion rent all other sounds with its own enormity. Now the men up there were scratching holes in front of the Starfish and others were struggling to reach them with ammunition, others calling for reserves, arranging to continue the attack, some clearing the wood with bombs, blowing in dugouts, hunting out the machine guns that still fired from the hidden concrete emplacements upon our troops. Yet on the ground the movements of the feverish fighting were lost. Nobody knew where the front might be now or in half an hour. At dusk we were upon the ridge, searching for some sign of C. I came upon him smoking his pipe in a shell hole. One signaller had been wounded in the arm, the other he had sent back with a message from the front line.

'When was that?'

'Dunno. This morning, I suppose. When we came back after the first show.'

'What was it like? Pretty bad?'

'Bloody awful. Thousands of dead, our chaps. The wood was absolutely blazing lead all morning, in our backs. A Godforsaken staff. They will have the tanks in the wood instead of outside. An imbecile would know better. Two tanks for High Wood! I say, you know it's really rather rich! I don't think they've seen High Wood. I say, they've read about it in the papers. Mr Hilarious Belloc's articles. That would be good!'

'Come on.'

We walked down in the growing darkness under the crimson sky. 'Those infanteers – I d'no. How they exist; how they manage to keep going. It beats me,' C. said. The shelling wandered about the slope and overtook us. We dropped into a shallow trench. By accident we found Kreuz there, drinking an infantryman's tea. There was a quarrel; and we moved on, back to the battery. Already some of the neighbouring brigade were coming into action near the wood, under a desultory but damaging fire. At the battery Bryson met us with his hands full of telegrams. He was preparing the battery to move forward.

'Captain Lennards is not back yet, sir,' he said.

'Not back?'

Bryson grinned. 'No sir. He went up, he said, to see the battle and have some sport, and left me in charge. Orders to move forward tomorrow.'

Lennards rolled down the steps into the shelter a few minutes later. He had a German helmet hung on his arm and his pockets were crammed with stuff he had taken from the clothes of dead Germans, notebooks, postcards and letters, posted and unposted. C. read some for him. They were much like ours. 'Dear Mother, I am just going into action and we expect an attack, but I shall be all right dear mother, so don't worry. Anyway, you know about giving Eric my watch if anything happens.' The letter was stained darkly. 'That's the beggar that was making all the noise, howling his bloody guts out, by God he was,' Lennards said. 'They were half out already. I finished him off. He was crying out to me. He sounded as though he damned well wanted it, anyway so I risked it.'

'What did you do?'

'I blew his brains out.'

Lennards mopped up a few whiskies. He had already had some with our howitzer officers. Rattray, it seemed, had been picked up senseless by the ditch of the German road, unscratched but swearing he had been knocked unconscious and lain there all day. His canteens were empty and he had been removed in a dreadful state, swearing and shivering and slavering at the lips.

We laid out lines of fire by map and direction from our new position on the high land and went up to watch the guns fire, waiting till the front was quiet enough to spot our own shells. In the waste of torn earth where the front lines lay invisible there was no recognisable landmark between the Butte de Warlencourt, a chalk mound which stared over the fold of land from the left front, and the ruins of Flers in which some of the tanks had made their last appearance. We did our best to recognise the bit of front and corrected the fire as we could.

The front had an exhausted air. A few shells sighed overhead, and the snipers lying in their shell holes fired occasional rounds. On our left High Wood lay in its corruption, its timber scarcely rising more than two or three feet over the immense crater field. Upon that deeply marked skin of earth it looked like the outbreak of a disease; it was revolting and fascinating. Within it were men dying but not dead, with others whose wounds had become maggoty while they lived, men living and whole, but fatally wounded in mind, cut off from the living, terrified to move. There were dugouts full of men, dead, dismembered, disabled, who would lie there forever. The war had passed over it and left it a discarded instrument which had cost ten thousand lives and now was worthless, a broken copse not a half mile long.

When I called at the howitzer battery on my way back Major Lucas was talking with agitation to 'Spadger' Dickinson. Spadger was a merry lad, but now he sat with his head in his hands and said nothing. 'He's been blown about a bit,' the major said. Spadger had been doing the ordinary dirty work for a long time. 'Here Spadger, have a drink, old son,' Lucas said. He lifted his dazed and vacant face and drank from a shaking hand. 'Now go and have a sleep.' Spadger went out with old uncertain movements, peering into the darkness from the door. After a few minutes he came back and tried to smile and broke down. 'I daren't stay away alone sir, I can't, I can't.' The tears ran down his face. A big shell suddenly swept down on us. Spadger leaped screaming into the air and cowered under the table. Lucas went white. The candle was blown out by the blast and the earth fell about our ears. We relit the candle and sat wondering whether others were coming; whether it was better to stay or to go. We looked at each other across the table wordless while Spadger sobbed and moaned upon the floor. They saw him to hospital that night very late when for a little the road was quiet.

Then the rain came and turned the roads into mud. The German road ended in a slough under Bazentin and all day the wagons and men struggled through it. Night and morning the crowd of travellers increased. The heavy shells plunged persistently into the broth, throwing up dismembered horses to heaven, adding constantly to the graveyard, and to the wreckage by the side of the track. You could sometimes hear them coming all the way, while the wagon wheels sucked at the mud, axle deep, and the muscles of the horses quivered in their flanks. You could hear the faint report, and then the distant 'Whee' broadened into a terrific scream as it fell upon you, 'Crash!' and then the bits sang among you; and the wheelers, that had plunged and trembled at the explosion, gave another heave and drew the wagon a few yards farther. If they and you still lived.

The coming of the rain gave a darkness to the landscape as definite as the brilliance of the heat. The rain drained the light out of the shattered soil. Instead of powder-bright earth one walked through the half solid mud which steadily increased its depth. Under the grey sky the ragged files of men passed up and down to the line, bowed under their burden, their leg wrapped in ragged, sodden sandbags which flapped about their feet, their haggard faces half- hidden under the ungainly helmets tilted forward for comfort, rifles over the shoulder, gas-helmets, ammunition, bandoliers, sacks of food. They struggled on slowly, dragging one foot out of the mud to immerse it again up to the calf, plunging in and out of the invisible shell holes in the slough, falling flat and rising again with the wet mud smearing face, breast and hands, flinging it off with weary patient gestures and scarcely smiling. It was a joke that had been worn too thin. The crater field accompanied them wherever they went. Not a thing stood up, not a tree, not a house, not a blade of grass. Even the signpost lay on the ground. The deep brown track spread indefinitely into the shell holes at each hand, and by night, as the 5.9s pursued each other to destruction, it was a journey of the damned that the infantry made with their steaming kettles, their overburdening ammunition boxes; a journey which gave in two miles the labour of twenty, and torment enough for a lifetime.

One evening Kreuz came down the steps of the new mess in a good mood. He had been at the wagon-line for a couple of days. His boots were nicely polished and his nails trimmed. He had been shaved in Albert by some regimental barber and had added a haircut and a perfumed shampoo. He was very natty and he sang in a high, corkscrew voice —

We're so glad to see you're back, dear lady,
We're so glad to see you're back!
Where have you been?
What have you seen?
Tell us all about it, you delightful little queen!

Lennards sat in arrested attention for a moment and then bellowed. His laughter rolled round and about the position, peal after peal succeeding. The sweat ran off his quivering cheeks and his face grew a deep leaden colour. The breath whistled in his throat and he rocked backwards and forwards on his couple of ammunition boxes, slapping hands like hams upon the table. Kreuz smirked for a little and then grew cross.

'By God!' Lennards roared, 'You've got a voice like a strangled hen, you little – . By God! You singing! I'll teach you to sing!'

Kreuz made dignified protests. After a while Lennards subsided into a good humour. He told C. and me to spend a night in the new wagon line and we turned out by starlight to walk down the spit of land towards Mametz. When we came to our lines in the great multitude of horses we found New Zealanders camped all about us. They were going up at dawn and had begged and stolen great numbers of wooden ammunition boxes to make fires. The blaze rose to the open sky with dancing flames and they sat about, fine clean brown men in tidy uniforms, laughing and singing. The light silhouetted the rows of standing horses. They tossed their heads and stamped on the wet ground, looking curiously to the flames. 'They're asking to be bombed,' C. said, 'and we shall get a packet, too.' We found Raven in the mess censoring letters, and helped him through the pile. Some New Zealand officers came in for a drink and played cards. Then they went off to extinguish the fires. Raven played the gramophone. He sat with his head in his hands thinking of his new wife, and listened to the record: 'I know of two bright eyes, waiting for me.' He was inexpressibly sad and oppressed. Then we heard the planes coming along. They dropped their bombs between us and the Montauban road. A horse screamed for long minutes, and in our lines the teams moved a little and then slept again with their heads dropped as though in thought.

C. went up to our new observation post a few days later. It was on the forward slope by the south-eastern point of High Wood. He came in long after nightfall dead-beat and covered with mud. He would not eat, he said he was so tired. He lay down on his plank bed in our little shelter and said, 'I'm done. Absolutely whacked. Blow out the candle.' He woke about fourteen hours after, and said, 'Did I tell you I was going?'

'Going?'

'Concluding a separate peace. Can't be helped. I hate to, but I simply must.'

C. was prepared to be firm with Lennards but there was no need. 'I think I ought to tell you, sir, I'm going sick, and I don't suppose I shall come back. I'm very sorry. I've been out eighteen months and I can't stand it any longer.

I shall go off my rocker if I stay.' 'Do what you — well like, C.,' Lennards said, 'I've nothing to say.' We shook hands by the control pit. 'I say, you know, I really am frightfully sorry. It's frightfully low to leave you,' C. said. 'Oh no.'

'I'm a stinking correspondent, but I will write.'

'Yes.'

He walked away and I stood staring at him. Suddenly he stopped and turned and came back.

'Forgot to tell you, the way to this OP; the landmark is a dead Scottie near the crest whose kilt has uncovered his buttocks, he's lying on his side facing south in a big shell hole; leave him on your right and go straight over the crest, about a hundred yards, then in a blown-in trench, twenty yards right is the place. And for God's sake take care of yourself. It's the most bloody place I ever saw.'

I nodded and smiled and watched him walk off along the hillside and then down to the German road. Absently I felt in my pocket for my pipe, and stared at its lovely straight grain, loading it carefully with dark Virginia. It was good, perhaps the greatest good, to have tobacco for a companion. But C. had gone, and I was as much alone as I had been sixteen months ago. I wondered how much more there was to come.

In the half darkness of the morning the telephonist and I walked up the road to the end of Elgin Avenue, a trench which now was a track broken in a hundred places. We slid and climbed in and out of holes by the side of High Wood where the dead of half a dozen countries lay rotting, and at last as the wood tailed off into something and nothing I saw C.'s dead Scot on the right. One could not miss him. He had been a fine handsome man, with stiff fair hair, but now his distended skin was the colour of old lead and had a gloss upon it like the skin of an unripe potato. We left him on our right and did not delay crossing the crest. Beyond lay the track of an old road blown to pieces, and now no more than an earthen gully looking towards the German lines. At the corner there was an old German dugout which went down about twenty steps, and tied to its lintel was our telephone wire. The opening was about four feet high and three feet wide. The steps descended abruptly, and all but the top two were occupied. The men clung together on the stairs and leaned against each other in silence, and from the short passage at the bottom there rose the moans of the wounded. With them came a draught of hot air smelling of dirt and animals. The mud had gathered in a pool at the threshold and now had begun to travel over the wood and down the steps in a thick slimy cake. We occupied the second step and tested the wire. Fortunately it held. The morning was grey again, and with daylight the routine shelling began. From a large shell hole across the gully we could see the front, inactive and secret. When the shelling became worse I took shelter under the foot or two of earth over the dugout door, and the mud crawled down and round me and on to the next man. After a while stretcher bearers came for the wounded. The dugout had to be cleared. The little movement attracted fire and in a moment or two the first 8-inch arrived and burst in a great balloon of smoke which seemed to hover in meditation over the scene as if it wanted to see us dispatched. Then its companion arrived. They were shooting a few yards over. I sat in the big shell hole with my back to the bursts leaning into the earth. Two machine gunners crouched with me on the bank. The younger one was sobbing and crying and could not stop his teeth from chattering. The elder held him in his arm. We sat like little grey monkeys huddled together for company. The big shells pounded away all about us, filling the air with acrid smoke and flying metal. The warmth in my middle receded until there seemed nothing there but a cold emptiness. My fingers were clammy, like tallow candles. At the back of my throat was an obstruction which prevented me from swallowing and I was aware that my face was quite grey. As the bursts shattered the world around us and obliterated the face of the day I had an odd realization that the bombardment would look very fine from somewhere else. Immense fountains of soil and smoke with trunks of trees and pieces of men crashing upward from the earth, moment after moment, scarcely varying by thirty yards. All the blood in my body seemed to have gone to animate my nerves, and every one of them ridiculously dispatched messages of caution to consciousness. I spoke to the machine gunner and my voice was a hoarse croak. It was difficult to force my hand and body to move and to take a large aluminium cigarette case from my pocket. The older gunner shook his head and stared when I offered him one, but he could not speak. In about an hour the stretcher bearers had roughly dressed the wounded and had got the stretchers to ground level. They picked their way devotedly over the top. The garrison poured back into the dugout.

At nightfall the telephonist and I climbed out of our holes and began our journey to the battery. The crest was roaring under the shellfire. We moved like very old men, too exhausted to run, not speaking a word.

It was cold and solitary now in my shelter. Foul, dirty, verminous, I took off my boots, collar, tie, and tunic, unfastening my breeches at the knee and pushed into my sleeping bag and there I lay asleep for twelve hours.

We moved the guns forward to High Wood and prepared for the attacks of 1 October and the 7th. The weather brightened, but the ground was too wet to recover. All ammunition for the battery went up by pack mule. The canvas packs were made to carry sixteen rounds, but we loaded eight or twelve on each animal. One after another, head to tail, they picked their way fastidiously among the crumbling craters and old wreckage. The mess was under a few sheets of corrugated iron thrown across a ruined trench, the ends stopped with tarpaulin. The guns were in the open. The slope was dreary beyond description. The infantry were to attack the Butte de Warlencourt across a thousand yards of country under view through its whole length. The Butte was full of emplaced machine guns. No one, except possibly the staff, expected they could do it; no one of them believed he would return alive. Early in the morning I stood by the guns as the grotesque mules filed away in the darkness, and I saw the infantry coming up rank upon rank. Colefax passed me within a yard, wearing soldier's khaki instead of officer's uniform. His blue eyes were fixed upon the horizon, like a man in a dream. The attack was in broad daylight, just before two o'clock. The infantry moved forward in perfect order and were mown down piecemeal as they advanced, and Colefax lies out there somewhere on the way to the Butte. Again the guns moved forward, to the crest, and were laid direct on the enemy lines to support another futile attack on the Butte. On the night of the 13th we pulled out the guns and brought them slowly down the crater field. It was dawn when we got to Albert, and the rain was falling.

Chapter 6

Winter Rain

Hill 60 – Winter 1916

A N enormous feeling of relief possessed me as we passed under the arch of Albert railway bridge. I tasted it to the full as I looked up at the dark and ugly tunnel, dripping water and stained with lime, and I thought I could never feel like that again.

Soon we left the main road for the north, and came to a hazel brake which almost made the road appear an English road, with hedgerows at each hand. We halted. At the head of my section a small *estaminet* had just opened its door. It seemed that one might celebrate by ordering coffee for the fifty men. In twos and threes they entered the house and stood about the glowing stove, returning with every appearance of pleasure. Sergeant Trevor came to bring their thanks, and brought a glassful for me, and as I lifted it I smelled something that was not coffee. The wise woman had laced every glass with cognac, tactfully breaking military law on my behalf. Then Bryson came up, that fine soldier, and accepted a glass, having no doubt caught the odour half a mile away. He rubbed his hands and told me how disappointed he was not to have had 'a smack at them in the open'.

We hoped to have rest for a week or two. The battery had been in action for six months, and two of those were spent on the Somme. But we marched with all speed to the north. The cold October weather drove the rain flying before the wind. The last day reveille was at 2.15 a.m. By four we were moving off and we marched all morning and all afternoon. Darkness found us at Boeschepe and the rain still falling. We stopped at a dirty farm near the Mont des Cats at the end of thirty miles. Next morning the little endives in the garden were sprinkled with frost. I marched away early with my two guns and brought them into action by the Kemmelbeck, two miles south of the Lille Gate of Ypres immediately in front of Woodcote House. We were in the southern half of the saucer looking up to Hill 60 and the German crest. The weather was set foul and there was no sun. At twelve inches below ground level there was standing water and all our living places must therefore stand up naked. The gun pits stood up as clearly as haystacks in the row of pollards fringing the beck. The control pit looked like a corrugated-iron cowshed in an empty field. The water flushed up round our boots as we walked about and we had to lay duckboard tracks to get about the position. Forward a little copse lifted black branches to the grey sky. In its cover two shelters of curved corrugated iron had been built for the officers. They huddled close together in an old sandbag skin, put on for warmth as much as safety. In one end was the door, at the other a celluloid window looking to the ruins of Ypres. An iron stove with sliding doors stood halfway along the hut. The battery map was stretched on a triangular drawing-board under the window. The quadrant was rayed out by degrees, and cut longitudinally in arcs at every hundred yards. A pin was stuck into the position of the guns and to this a piece of thread was fastened, so that the officer on duty could quickly find the angle and range between the guns and any target. The leather thigh boots and the leather-lined waterproof came back to duty. An air of apathy enveloped the Salient, and yet it was not quiet. Sudden short storms of shelling burst over the area, and the smoke drifted up from Ypres with a pink haze of brickdust about it.

Fenton, our new subaltern, spent the day with me putting up what we called 'panelling' on the upright part of the walls. The wood was old floorboards so well covered with mud that we had to scrub and scrape them. I rehearsed Fenton in a Chinese Labour Battalion song so that we should get the right spirit into the work. Lennards had just finished breakfast and was beginning his morning ritual. He lit a cigar, grunted, stretched and belched, and stamped about to ease his joints. We raised our Chinese song and beat on the corrugated iron. Lennards cursed us roundly and announced he was now going to the latrine and that we had better keep out of the way, or he would tear the bloody tripes out of us. He splashed past us to the old gun pit, planting his enormous stick like a lance in the doorway, as a signal of occupation. From time to time a burst of indecent song came from the gun pit. It was always the same song. Lennards enjoyed that daily half-hour more than any other and grudged us no details.

By nightfall the hut was tidy and as comfortable as might be. Kreuz was riddling about with a small box like a doll's house. He looked up at

Lennards' question, his wide lips pursed forward, his spectacles reflecting the candle flame. He looked a queer sort of small animal under the immense bulk of Lennards.

'It's a prophylactic medicine chest, sir.'

'Can't you use — English?' Lennards shouted.

'It contains various means collected by myself for the prevention of venereal disease.'

'Do you take them with you when you go whoring?'

'Yes, sir, as a rule.'

Lennards was very shocked, and described his own views quite shortly. There was an argument over the chest, whether whoring was worth the risk at all and whether, if one did go whoring, it wasn't rather worse to take the chest. Lennards dozed and we played the gramophone. We still had from Conrad's days the 'Casse Noisette' suite, parts of the 'Twilight of the Gods,' 'Thais,' 'Les Erinnyes' and 'Paillasse,' several of the Chopin studies, some Chaminade pieces, the first 'Arabesque' of Debussy as well as a great quantity of lighter music. Any of these we might play. But Lennards, reading and re-reading the *Pink 'Un,* would leap up with strong objections to an Andante in G Minor by Debussy. He recognised that disc even if we played the Tchaikovsky Andante Cantabile on the back; either of them fetched him from his chair. We sat on ammunition boxes with hands between our knees and stared at the hot stove while the music travelled on and on, into countries that it seemed we could never know, now. The soft glow of the candles wrapped the dying sounds in a regretful pause, and Kreuz shook his head and put on the 'Bing Boys'.

One morning Lennards found an old stray dog, fleabitten, lean and misshapen. It had been white, but now was nearly all mud. It looked up at him and barked and wagged its tail. Lennards was delighted to organize a rat-hunt. The dog played its part well, starting a rat in the neighbourhood of the mess. It dodged from one shell hole to another, running on the narrow pathway above the water line under the beard of sour grass which overhung the lips of the craters. We followed with pick helves beating at the ripple of the grass, till Kreuz landed fairly and squashed the rat flat. For variation we turned out with revolvers, but that was less amusing. The dog soon deserted us, to Lennards' chagrin. Instead of ratting we stood on the banks of the swollen beck and shot at the bottles and tin cans floating rapidly into Ypres. At night we manned an OP in a farm by Zillebeke Lake, staring out at the black crest in which the Very lights shot up greenish-white. The road behind was busy and at odd intervals salvos of pipsqueak shrapnel came tearing across to harass our transport. We watched till dawn and then returned in the raw air by the dyke of the lake. A deep trench had been cut in it, now fringed at its lip with long melancholy grasses. The exits were well marked by shelling.

We went up to the line by Blauwe Poort farm and the railway cutting. There the water had seeped into the trough and now lay stagnant and foul between the raw earth walls. The duckboard track up to Larch Wood sank continually into the mud and the shellfire drove the hurrying traffic of men to the sides, where they pressed against the mud. The wet earth filled the skin with grit, till it never would come out. At Larch Wood the track entered a trench leading straight to Hill 60. They had a minenwerfer aligned on it and shot with accuracy. We hurried up the hill or halted, pressed into the walls, to allow a stretcher party to come past, and overhead about the stumps of the larches a few sprigs of green still hung. On the right we used the trench happily known as 4711, for its smell. The whole trench system there was mined, and might go up at any moment. There was scarcely any garrison in this quarter-mile and the trenches had fallen in. One stride after another we laboured along 4711, each viscous whirlpool of mud releasing a foul smell of sour earth and corruption. On the crest we crouched to escape observation and squatted in the mud, looking through a periscope at the flattened perspective of the Caterpillar and Hill 60. Their wire seemed enormously thick. Across the cutting to the left our trench was fully manned, and elaborated into many alleys from which men mined towards the German front. We observed from the fire step, searching for the emplacement of the minenwerfer. A sniper followed the periscope head as we dodged from place to place. After the fifth or sixth the minnie took a hand. 'Plut,' we heard the soft explosion, and then saw it in the air, like a flying trunk. We ran round the traverse. It fell with a shattering discharge in the next bay, the earth trembled. 'Look out!' the sentry shouted, pointing. They lodged half a dozen in the line. The trench was blown out and three men killed, two others blown to pieces. The little sentry was one of them; nowhere to be found, but in a mess plastered to the trench wall.

When darkness fell I found my sleeping place was a low corrugated shelter built into the wall of the communication trench, its back to the cutting. I wrapped my coat about me from head to feet and tried to read by the light of a candle stump. The minenwerfer ranged up and down the trench, advancing and retreating with a fury more violent than any other projectile, its hideous crashes penetrating every cranny of the night. The cold was very great and the light of the dip did not travel even into the near corners of the place. In the other half a man was asleep on a stretcher. I rose and lit a cigarette and bent over him. He had no head. I thought it a little impolite of the infantry to put me in the regimental morgue; at very least, a few minutes early. I reflected in my sleeplessness that it was likely that one would grow responsive to nothing but shellfire, every nerve so alert for that, that it would appreciate nothing else.

Fenton succeeded me at the OP in front of 4711. While he was there Lennards developed a desire to shoot over its summit on the German line. Fenton protested weakly that our shells could not clear the crest at so short a range. Lennards became abusive and ordered the guns to fire. They came belting into the parados of the trench, at 2,700 yards range, and covered the party with earth. Fenton reported, and Lennards called him a liar. He said he would go up himself and see. An hour later he arrived. Fenton and the telephonist lay in the trench bottom while Lennards ordered a couple of rounds. The earthen clods knocked Lennards' helmet off. 'My bleeding Christ!' he shouted. Then he fetched me to the telephone and told me the guns were laid wrongly. He was still obstinate and reluctant to believe that such a bit of theoretical mummery as the angle of sight, and a hilltop, had anything to do with it. Fenton helped in peaceful persuasion.

The colonel came to see us and went back to the Ramparts by the road. At Shrapnel Corner he was caught in a sudden burst of fire and wounded in the lung. His orderly ran for help but the ambulance was so long coming that he died in hospital from loss of blood. The infantry on our right asked for help. The line of fire was over the wood. Lennards would have us fire. I objected. A look up the gun showed plainly that we could not clear the treetops. Lennards refused to believe. We fired and watched the branches toppling in clouds of smoke about the cookhouse and the mess. The cook came running to the battery under the impression that an attack had started. The staff developed a slight fever and required every unit to make bakehouses and ovens and to limewash them in a clean and orderly fashion. The cook was Irish. His oven was a beautiful sight. But it had no flue. 'It has no flue at all, sir,' he said, 'I thought you would be wanting it for nothing but to show the general.' It was necessary to order a flue. The staff also wished to encourage the offensive spirit. A gun was to go up by night on the Verbrandenmolen road among the limbers carrying hot food to the infantry. It was to fire thirty rounds, but without any preliminary registration. It seemed even odds that gun, gunners, limbers, drivers, and food would be blown up within the first five minutes. At best the shooting would be uncertain.

'You'll do this, Kreuz,' Lennards said.

Kreuz looked on the floor and said it was my turn, not his. Lennards' temper drove Kreuz out of the mess, trembling with passion.

He went up.

He fired twenty rounds as fast as the gun could get rid of them, and buried the rest in a shell hole, to square the daily ammunition statement. He was bitter against me and Lennards. Fortunately a new subaltern came to ease the duties.

Day by day the water increased. Every hour or so the gun pits were pumped out into the beck whose swift stream was lipping higher than their floor. At length a day came when we could not get the water below the breech level of the guns. We waded about slowly so that we should not splash over the tops of our thigh-length gumboots. Brigade was angry that we reported the battery out of action. Divisional CRA was shocked, and sent an engineer officer and two sappers to drain the position. The officer stood with his hands in his pockets by our melancholy pollards as we waited for him to say something. 'How they expect me to drain the lowest spot in the Salient with two sappers I'm damned if I know,' he said. He made a long speech about the staff in the most furious language. 'Let them clean up the bloody canal with walking sticks first,' he concluded, 'and then I'll promise them to drain it.' He went away a little softened by whisky.

In Poperinghe the shops were open. Riding in, one passed the miserable huts of refugees, made of old biscuit tins and laths, decorated with paint in the most pathetic attempt at pleasantry. Tin stovepipes stuck out of roofs laboriously tiled with bits of old bully tins, and the wind tore the smoke off into the grey sky. The huts were labelled Villa Lucerne, Villa Pompeiae, or Villa Paris, according to fancy, and in the windows stood a sewing machine, a shoemaker's last, or a few lumps of chocolate with the notice 'Café, tee, chocolat' or 'Fried fishachips.' In the notepaper shop we spent a long time buying records and worshipping the businesslike girls who served there, satisfying our taste for minor luxuries, English and American fountain pens, fine soaps and books. We had tea in the long room of La Poupée, once a millinery shop but now Anglicised into an officers' tearoom. Brooks told me our veterinary officer was there, recovering from a blind. He had been given his leave warrant but he drank so much in celebration that he slept in Pop all night. The next night the Railway Transport Officer would not let him on the train. It seemed too dreadful to be true. To console himself he drank more. Now he had finished his precious leave, and here he was recovering.

As we spoke he came down, hanging on the banisters, his ruddy face blotched and sullen. Our table laughed loudly and waved. He leaned over the banisters to peer at us and screamed out: 'All the odds and sods, all the old odds and sods.' He was still far gone in drink and would eat nothing. Then we all went diagonally over the stony square to a bar which he recommended. Dusk had fallen and hid the mean streets. The bar was half full of officers roaring with laughter at a girl behind the counter. 'I taught those girls English,' Dobson said, pushing his way through, 'and bloody good English they speak.' They spoke perfect English, but every other word was foul. No man ever spoke so horribly. We took a few glasses of *vin blanc cassis* for the good of the house and pushed on without Dobson to Skindles. The smoke was already thick in the room and the ancient waiter shuffled at a run with huge piles of plates. Knots of subalterns fringed the narrow room waiting for tables. The smell of the food was exciting, a robust smell, full of suggestive flavours. Very soon we sat down before real dishes and glanced lovingly at the golden stars spangled over the green tinfoil of the Ayala bottles. The room was jovial, full of laughter and the explosions of bottles. Men moved from table to table to drink with old companions. Here were half a dozen of our infantry subalterns, known by their old hospitality in the line, whom we sought to entertain. But at last we came to coffee, dessert and a bottle of port, lit cigars, and knew regretfully that we must make room for others. As we rose a short man with long hair went across to the piano and began to play the Chopin Fantasia in F minor. We edged nearer to the piano to listen. The noble and grievous music seemed like an elegy upon the company. He finished. Some cried out for ragtime. 'More,' we said. The shadow of a smile came into his face. He shook his head and shut the piano. We walked out into the rain and sought our grooms in the dark square. My man had a parcel of fresh fish in his wallet, and for breakfast the mess cook served whiting.

Up in front the minenwerfers fell with continual fury. One landed down in Larch Wood. It blew in five feet of earth over battalion headquarters and killed the orderly officer. The communication trench kept falling in as the ground grew more sodden, and the minnies blew great holes in it. It was clear that from the enemy lines one could see every movement in the batteries. Kreuz came back from OP. As usual they had come out with minnies crashing at their backs. 'Faster, sir,' the bombardier called, with an eye on the overtaking bombs. 'Can't,' Kreuz shouted, stretching his short legs to the uttermost.

'If you were Mr Boyd you'd have been at the battery by now, sir.'

I maintained that I held the record for the stretch from the front line over the broken duckboards past Larch Wood and out.

The rain persisted and the mail was held up for three days. Three nights we went down furtively to wait for the ration cart coming past the Trois Rois *estaminet*; three nights we were bitterly disappointed. In that we were united. Then news came to me that Sam had been out again. The train in which he travelled was bombed heavily at railhead. At last they got on the road and began to march. After two or three miles he collapsed on the roadside and the doctor sent him home again. There was something wrong with his heart. 'It doesn't really matter,' he said. Nothing really mattered, I thought, staring at the stove. The war went on by itself like a perpetual-motion machine; something enormous and overpowering which dragged people in without any reason except its own existence. It had a mystical existence apart from men, although men were necessary. We had become the moving parts of the machine; some to move, some for the machine to hit against. A certain number had to be killed to keep things going, but it didn't much matter which. After the Somme our artillery general explained that he would recommend no officer for decoration because there hadn't been enough officers killed; an annoying point of view, but no doubt reasonable.

> The aim for which each general strives
> Is losing other people's lives,
> And no exception to this rule
> Was General Augustus Moore O'Toole . . .
> When they had no more men to spare
> They sent him back to St Omer.

It was true enough for satire. Therefore I thought that in ordinary circumstances there was no necessity to stand up when a safe shell hole lay at one's feet. My friends were all scattered. I had been out two or three times as long as any of the others in the battery, and I felt old and solitary.

WINTER RAIN

It was now the middle of November. The rain had been followed by six degrees of frost and a biting south-east wind. One of our subalterns in 4711 shot two wild geese with a service rifle as they were crossing the line, but the birds fell behind the German front. At night we made a treacle posset with strong ration rum and tinned milk to cure colds. Thereafter we tried to waltz to the 'Blue Danube' in our clumsy boots until Lennards found himself in danger. I was building a double roof over the control shelter, putting a skin of bricks and concrete over the cupola and roofing that again with steel. The concrete was not thick. The Germans might build their solid square concrete pillboxes all over the front, but we had none; and we had to beg for every pound of cement used to protect that flimsy shelter. One determined shoot would have knocked the whole battery out. *Punch's Almanack* arrived with a picture in it of piano removers, 'From me, to you.' We were very pleased with that.

Then I was lent to another of the brigade's batteries, quartered at the Doll's House on the canal bank. It was a Territorial battery and different in its ways. Its officers were charming but strange. Up at OP and liaison I had time to hear how time stopped dead while the war sought us all out. One could hear the minutes ticking away, but knew that for a mere illusion. Time ended things, but not the war. It was outside laws. As time added up enormous sums of minutes, so the war malevolently grew worse, the mud thicker, the rain more penetrating; peace and peacemakers as remote as the bottom of the sea. There was none to be seen anywhere. The war threw one back to past time and past places, and showed how much it had learned while we stood still. The crumbling parapet creaked with the rain, and the water gradually lifted the floating duckboard up and up. The minnies were dropping in the cutting and the slope of Hill 60 squatted over us like a toad. It was the top of the world, a barren slope of mud; as though man had tried to make the world and had not succeeded very well. At the Doll's House the wood smoke blew in gusts about our tiny cellar, and in the celluloid window were framed the heads of horses taking our letters home to England. The rain ran down their cheeks, their ears sagged with dejection. Every day our letters went home, full of inflated cheerfulness; 'We shall have a few swimming matches here soon,' or, 'If the frost holds we shall need skates ... we are in a quite quiet part of the line now, and my job's as safe as houses.' That was a religion. I looked at my letter. 'In nineteen months I have never felt so very tired mentally, so stale and so useless.' I read it again, surprised. The corporal came in, his mackintosh cape and tin hat streaming with water.

'Letters, sir?'

It didn't really matter. I sealed it up and gave it to him.

Harrods' Christmas catalogue arrived. We ordered presents for the people at home. The mail stopped for four days. The leave list halted again. There seemed no chance of a rest anyhow. My next two days in the front line were spent dodging the minnies and sniping rifles while the mud leeched further into us. Feet were like leaden lumps, uniform sodden and stiff. At night I retired to sleep in the flimsy shelter by the cutting. Liaison duty in front of Hill 60 was a sort of solitary confinement for forty-eight hours. Lying awake in the shelter, staring at the low black roof and listening for the drop, drop, dropping of the water which survived and overrode the occasional bursts of fire, I decided quite suddenly to follow C. I did not care what people might say, and so it was not difficult to start.

About ten days before Christmas I found myself resting, with others, in the Trappist monastery of Mont des Cats. I thought that it was no rest to be under that grey sky so near the gunfire. We killed days as we could, talking sometimes with the lay brother, and one day two monks under the vow of silence pulled my arm and pointed to the sky. Two planes there fought an engagement. They followed the combat with the most expressive of grimaces. We gesticulated to each other, the three of us, our surprise, concern, bewilderment and excitement. They jerked their bodies up and down like clowns on the stage. They gave me a look of intense gratification. I saw then that the German was in full retreat, a plume of growing smoke following his course. Two or three of us begged leave to attend the Trappist service. They allowed us to watch from a high gallery their downcast entrance into the chapel, their disappearance into stalls from which each other was invisible. The voice of the abbot, commanding and remote, broke into Latin. We stole out and saw them file away. Beneath the robes of two there showed the horizon blue of the French uniform. They were monks on leave to their monastery.

An infantry subaltern called Barclay, a thin agile man with red hair, got leave for four of us to go into Hazebrouck by ambulance. We went to the magazine shop beyond the square. A girl was serving there, ill favoured, but sharp and bold. She called us to an inner room where there were many indecent pictures which she made worse by putting false titles to them. Several other subalterns came in. She pushed against one of them, and touched him, throwing up her chin and looking at him from drooping lids. Then she showed a three-quarter length nude by Raphael Kirchner. 'Twenty franc,' she said, while her hand caressed the boy. He quivered under her hand, starting back against the table. Her body followed his, pressing upon him. 'Lovely lovings,' she said, holding the picture before him.

He stammered.

'You would like to touch . . . here,' she said, taking his hand.   ,

Barclay and I moved forward at the same moment. Barclay swore at her. She drew off and laughed and picked up a pack of postcards, disclosing their charms fanwise before our eyes. 'Three franc,' she said.

'She has the reputation,' said Barclay later, 'of being the nastiest woman in Belgium, and she never lets a man have her.'

A few days later we both went to hospital at Hazebrouck. Barclay swore to rape the woman. Two or three subalterns followed him into the front shop. She went inside with Barclay, her face dropping into heavy sensual excitement, but cold. She found fresh pictures to show him and stretched her body catlike against him, then swayed away and began slowly lifting her skirt against a silken knee. Barclay glared at her with his green eyes, and manoeuvred slowly, holding the pictures in his hand, until her back was to the table. Then he threw her down amongst the drawings. She screamed 'Frederic! Frederic!' The others rushed in. The table was upset, the indecencies littering the floor. Barclay was laughing in long yelps and the woman was adding up the amount of the damage. Frederic meanwhile tried to push in from the back. Barclay laughed at her and threw some money in her face. 'You filthy bitch,' he said. They all went away telling Frederic they would break up the shop if there was any fuss. That was on Christmas Eve.

I woke in the small ward next morning and found there on my table a Christmas parcel. How it could have come there I could not guess; but there it was, brown paper and string, my name upon the label. 'A happy Christmas!' It was too wonderful to open. I lay there looking at the skylight holding the parcel in my fingers. But I should have guessed. Here there were nurses, English women; and they had forgotten no one. We all had a present. How wonderful of them to think of that, here! A toothbrush and a packet of Gold Flake, I had. There was nurse, just come in the ward. 'And did you sleep well?'

'Yes, nurse, but – ' We could only smile foolishly. 'This Christmas present – '

'Oh that's nothing – a joke.'

'Oh no – so surprising! So topping of you!'

'We aren't ogres here!'

'No! I mean . . . Oh, thank you awfully.'

'Thank you.'

'It is topping.'

In the middle of Christmas dinner we were told to pack at once. An ambulance train was due. We travelled all the afternoon and by night, in the bitter cold, to a canvas hospital by the sea. One of the wounded screamed all the way. The tents were coloured rose and softly lighted. The nurses moved about and one watched them. Then the doctor came.

'What's the matter with you?'

'Nothing, except that I can't stand it any more, just at present.'

He took my temperature and listened to my heart. It seemed to be beating very hard.

'How long have you been out?'

'Nineteen months.' He wrote two initials on the chart at my head. After a while the sister came near.

'Sister! sister!'

'Yes, laddie?'

'What do the letters mean, sister?'

She laughed. 'Back to the line at once, laddie.' That demolished one's hopes like burned paper. I turned over. This seemed to be the finish. I would as soon die where I lay. Presently she returned and glanced my way.

'Is it true, Sister?'

'Is what true, laddie?'

'That this means back to the line?'

'Why no, ye puir madman; it means walking case to England; ye shouldna ask questions, then folks'll tell ye nae lee.'

On the way back there was an hour to spend in Boulogne. The lounge of the Hotel du Louvre was full of officers sitting under the cold blue skylight. It was a depressing place. I saw an empty chair and went to it. An infantry subaltern with a grey exhausted face stared at me. 'Where are you from?' he asked.

'Ypres.'

He continued staring.

'Not looking for anybody?'

'No, only for a drink.'

'Thank God! I thought they'd sent you after me; they're always sending people after me. They think I'm dotty —just because – Do you know a place called the Switch in front of Martinpuich?'

'Yes.'

'I was there with the remains of my company, right in front of the front line. No communication. Three days and no rations, four days, not a word. Well, then I sent a man back. No answer. Perhaps he was killed. Next night I sent two. They copped it, I suppose, or perhaps lost—' He suddenly shouted. 'We hadn't had any sleep or food! Perhaps they went the wrong way – savvy? – Oh God! Then the sergeant. I saw him coming back. He was killed before he got to us. Then there were ten left. That night I took them out. We crawled about for an hour. Then they fired on us. I shouted 'Friend, friend!' but two were hit. Then we got to the front line. They weren't our lot. Our lot had GONE! Gone and left us three days before. Yes, but that's not all. My colonel had reported us all dead. They never came to see, never came to see. So when we did get in, they arrested us all, and still he says we're dead. I'm alive, so I'm mad, instead. I must be dead or mad. See? He keeps on saying we're all dead. But they've sent for him. I'm waiting, and when he comes I'll spit in the face of the stinking bloody swine. I've got documents and orders!'

He pulled out a handful of message forms. Just then a military policeman stopped at the door and stared in. He began to make his way towards us through the chattering crowd.

'There's an MP,' I said.

The infantryman picked up his papers and ran off. It was time for me to go and embark. We drank while France sank behind us.

The hospital ship slowly entered the harbour and the gulls came wheeling about it, gleaming in the winter sun. The siren blew and made me jump in the air. The grey lucent land shone before us. And all about were the happy voices of those who could stand and stare. Only the wounded lay listless in their beds.

Chapter 7

Third Ypres

Menin Road – Summer 1917 The Ravine

That winter we shivered in Manchester. The heart of the frost was in the wind and the water turned into polished black ice where it trickled down the wall. The men newly returned from France told us certainly that able-bodied men going up the line had been frozen to death in the goods wagons, where they lay with their mates huddling under the great coats. Meanwhile a company was playing 'Romance' at the Gaiety, José Collins was 'The Maid of the Mountains' at the Opera House. Harry Weldon sang about 'a dark green camisola' in the Palace pantomime, and the fairy queen came to amuse the wounded officers. In the enormous sick ward the company lay in various degrees of illness and recuperation. One of them was a boy of eighteen, remarkable for his long, smooth, chestnut hair and his long, sharp nose. He might have been the Pied Piper's son. When he saw my brilliant forage cap he ran across the ward and said, 'You're mad, too; come and join me.' We made up a farcical band and went about the hospital wheeling our fiddler in a chair. His legs were paralysed by shellshock. One of us had a piccolo, another a gazoo. Nobody could tell whether Crashaw were really mad or not. 'I'm going to be a poet when I grow up,' he said, fantastically, 'we shall have enormous jests and sit up late drinking punch and feel no worse in the morning. I shall adopt you as an uncle and all the day we shall ride and walk. We shall go over Edgon Heath and by your place with the funny name, Beckermonds, and my places in Wales, walking and talking and singing, till we've been on every hilltop and worn out six pairs of boots. We'll have a cottage in Craven and one in the place you can't pronounce and perhaps afterwards one in Porthgwarra and one in Wessex. I love Cornwall. The war will be over then, and a grateful country will provide.'

He went out again to his battalion before I left, and I suppose he was killed.

In the spring I went to the artillery depot at Newcastle for light duty. A great many of the people there had never been out at all and the young officers were fresh from school. It was lonely, being there. I even went twice to a Congregational church, but the churchgoers were afraid of subalterns and nobody spoke. That was a great relief. Three of us one night dined in town and were stopped on Grainger Street by three girls selling flags for some charity. Someone suggested we should all go to a picture theatre. Thus I met Edward. She was tall and slim and had a large mouth. Edward had met one of the subalterns from the barracks and spent an afternoon with him at Whitley Bay. He was too crude and she pushed him over a low grassy cliff. His face was badly scarred in the fall. She was as simple as a child and liked fairy stories. Almost every night we had dinner together. Sometimes when I went to inspect the depots in the town she came the round with me, waiting out of sight till the guard had turned in. She told me that all the girls watched the casualty lists and always loved the regiment that was getting it worst. Just now the names of gunners filled the columns. But that, she said, was not the only reason. . . . We were in love but never thought of marriage. We never met except in a street or a restaurant or a theatre.

Just then about a dozen officers from hospital came into the mess, all with long service. The colonel was kind enough to let us alone in our duties. He was charming. He said to the young officers, when we went to take our gun drills, 'I shall work out a nasty little sum, perhaps two nasty little sums, and I shall come to you and tell you to work them out on parade; I shall know the answers, but you will not; if you don't get the answers out quickly, then I fear I shall have to punish you.' Yet things were going wrong in the depot. The QMS of my battery was defrauding people in wholesale and detail. He persuaded young officers to pay him two pounds above the proper price for field glasses, on the ground that they were made by Zeiss. The glasses were stamped 'Zeiss, London, 1916'. He withheld goods ordered till officers were spending their last few days at home and then wired for more money than they had cost, holding the goods till the money came. Afterwards I learned that he had an arrangement with a civilian laundry agent who gave him every week a bill for the washing of army sheets and underwear that had never been washed, a hundred or two at a time. The drafts got dirty linen instead of clean and the two confederates pocketed the money. It was another habit to debit the men on draft with clothing which they never got and to sell the clothing they should have received. There was a chance a man would be killed before he had time to find out how his account showed such a debit. In any case it would be difficult to prove trickery at that distance. Some of the permanent staff ought to have known of these abuses. Perhaps they did.

We played snooker in the evening after dinner. Once several of us went to the padre's billet for cocoa. One of the young officers, Whitfall, was there. He was a divinity student.

'You don't seem very enthusiastic about the war,' he said to me.

'No, I'm not.'

'That seems shameful.'

'Why? Everybody thinks the same, whatever they say.'

'That must be a lie.'

'Oh, nonsense! Ask padre.'

'Isn't it, padre?'

''Fraid not; it's quite true.'

'I know you're wrong, both of you.' He jumped up, very angry, and spilled his cocoa.

'Hold hard,' the padre said.

'I'll not hold hard. I think it's damned shameful to talk like that about gallant fellows; I think the war's a damned fine show. The sooner I kick in the faces – '

'Wipe up the cocoa on your breeches.'

' – the sooner I kick in the faces of those Boche swine the sooner I shall be pleased.'

'They're not swine.'

'Of course they're swine.'

The padre shook his head, but made no answer. He was grieved at this outcome of his party. We all said goodnight.

The presence of the long-service subalterns increased my unease at being there while my friends were in action. In ones and twos they slipped away. When the news of the Messines battle came through it seemed clear I must return. They had at last blown up Wytschaete with the mine we visited in 1915. I went to my medical board with this determination and walked back into the city under the dusty trees, relieved that it was done. Then I told Edward. We walked round the little square making inarticulate remarks. The square was empty in the dusk. We sat on the coping of the garden and the yellow laburnum dropped in her lap. After half an hour of stillness we walked slowly to the red pillar box at the corner.

'We shan't kiss goodbye, shall we?' she said, 'it isn't regimental.'

'I can't say anything,' she said. 'Keep your heart up and your head down.' Then she suddenly kissed me. The tears were running down her cheeks. 'Goodbye.'

I went down the hill to the station.

It was the last day of July 1917 and I was following the road that would lead me to the old position of Christmas 1915. It had been raining and the earth was covered with a mist. I put my kit into a tent whose floor had been lowered as a protection against bomb splinters, and had tea in the horse lines of the Divisional Ammunition Column. The place was full of horse lines and heavy-gun positions, crowded together as far as one could see. As I stood by the muddy track a passing wagon caught my eye. It had an elephant painted on the back. I followed it to its wagon line. Bryson gave me news of the battery, but it was all bad news. Conrad, I knew, had never come back. Even Fenton had gone. He himself was not Conrad's Bryson. The spring was out of the man. The battery was no longer with the division and we might never meet again. We shook hands and parted. I walked along the level ground to the old position from which that battery had sprung. No guns were there now. The farm was in ruins, the malthouse obliterated under its thatch, which it wore askew, like a drunken woman with an old hat. The hut still stood under the tree, wearing innumerable patches of tarred felt. I remembered Taylor and Pincher had put one of them there. The branches of the tree had scraped patterns all over the roof. It was deserted now except for ghostly memories which I fled. Up front the guns were making a low continuous rumble as I walked back to the wagon line mess. The rain dropped on to both ends of the table and between its pools two of us ate dinner. The other man was gloomy and kept remarking on the gunfire. 'I've looked at it all over and round about,' he said, 'but I can't believe it's worth it, all this.' He repudiated the whole war. He took me out with him to hunt up some people for a game of bridge. Later the whole of the night barrage started on the crest, lighting it up with a high surf of flame. In the misty rain the bursts were less clear than usual and their colour was gold edged with pink. The thunderous rumble stirred and steadied itself, throwing into high relief the irregular explosions of the big shells which sounded at that distance like the loose clattering of a train over a succession of points. The

Very lights sailed up into the black night like haloed stars, molten white. I could not get to sleep. I tried to think of black night, sheer blackness, but the exhausting thoughts incidental to fear revolved endlessly in my mind until a 12-inch gun close by fired one round. Its violent report made the confusion worse, and as I was cursing it an orderly brought a message written in indelible pencil on paper sodden with the rain. It was for this I had returned, this order to report in the morning at a point near to the Spoil Bank. But the message would not be assimilated; and the barrage in front, in a fantastic way, tossed it continually uppermost in my mind. I argued furiously with myself, turning about in the harsh army blankets, but the adversary had the better of it, so maddeningly loud that I felt he occupied me to the complete exclusion of every communal tie or human relationship. I felt completely isolated by this preoccupation. Meantime the barrage continued unabated; that was no fantasy. Its volume pursued my feverish mind as though the genius of war, the thing apart from its instruments, was in pursuit. In the pitch darkness my imagination portrayed the filmy grey after-smoke of the bursts, shredding itself upwards like the pause that should follow a crime, and I felt the shells animate, crouching and teasing as they burst now here, now there. I got up, to read, but by this time was too ragged to follow the printed lines. The only other sure thing in my mind was that I could not turn back. There were three witnesses who made that impossible; the infantry in the line and the artillery behind, my family and friends. It was not permitted to laugh on the wrong side of the face. I made an attempt to meditate on the quality of courage, with my fingers stuffed in my ears, and in so doing fell asleep.

A little after eight in the morning my guide brought me through Voormezeele and I saw on the wide landscape, among the hedges, scores of little trucks on miniature railways, moving up and down. We entered a corduroy road made of sawn timber secured by tie-beams at the side. There were many dead horses lying where they had been thrown off the road. In front the whole of the land was full of activities. Half a mile on the guide halted and pointed out the battery position, on the left of two 60-pounders. He hinted that he would like to take the horses back. I walked on. As I drew near I saw a few men chasing another from shell hole to shell hole. This strange sight held me till I got to the guns. They had now caught him. He was mad. They told me how it had happened. Two nights before the dugout which he shared with his mate was blown in, and the mate was killed. Ever since he had been looking for him, and he would not stand up, but crawled from one hole to another scrabbling in the earth. Several times they tried to catch him but he screamed so that they gave it up, till one man observed that the only other thing he would do was to read magazines. They threw magazines to him till they could come close enough; then they caught him and sent him to hospital.

I reported to Major Stansfield. He had a high narrow forehead, a sharp nose and a prim mouth which moved nervously into expressions of amusement often accompanied by a high pitched laugh. He spoke sharply and hurriedly, brushing things aside as though too difficult to explain. With him was a man whom he introduced as Captain Rawley. Captain Rawley spoke in the most surprising drawl I had ever heard. At first I assumed it was a joke, this affectation of style. Rawley had brownish, animal eyes which he used to express sentimental longings equally with a romantic, full-blooded contempt. He said 'Yaas, Major!' and curled his upper lip, upon which a few hairs had been induced to grow. Outside I found, to my joy, MacVeagh, whom I knew, fat, endearing and cheerful. He said in a soft, husky voice, 'Oh, I say, look who's here, oh what joy. Let us dance and sing, shall us?'

The battery commanders in this Territorial brigade had no system of government in Conrad's sense. They exercised a benevolent despotism which allowed no one to control a job himself. At any moment a major might come rushing in and interfere, nag, storm or bully, even superseding the officer or NCO on the spot. The effect upon discipline can be imagined. Nothing ran itself; it depended on the major. NCOs sometimes would go straight to him and find him attentive. At other times he would tell them they ought to know better than to trouble him. The effect of this was that the section commanders like MacVeagh and myself, were not section commanders at all but merely junior officers useful to man the OP and to spend days living with the infantry in the line. It discouraged us from proper care of the sections by removing us from our proper responsibilities. Conrad would have made us work twice as hard and we should have become integral parts of the battery. It would have moved as one thing. Now we were fragments, loosely attached. The whole unit was extraordinarily slipshod and held together by a constant succession of makeshift orders catching up their predecessors. Nobody was taught by routine to report anything to the right person. Every officer, the major included, had to spend his time asking questions. Thus, actually, one had to work harder, and in the end achieve only a modest degree of efficiency.

SALUTE OF GUNS

The rain fell solidly every day and walking over the slimy mud was hard. Everything in the mess was caked with it and the roof was so low one could not even sit upright. On our right the 60-pounders lay veiled in their camouflage netting, rabbit wire in which knots of coloured canvas were tied. As soon as they prepared to fire, the word was passed round and everyone became wary. The Germans always replied, and not so accurately that we escaped. The heavy gunners got off ten or a dozen rounds and then retreated a few hundred yards to the flank of the line of German fire. 'Whee-whang' the 5.9s came, crashing about the long snouts. There was lots to look at. On our left front the butt-end of the Spoil Bank stood up, a lump of shiny mud with dark little entrances below. The corduroy road ran past it carrying its labouring traffic. Flights of pipsqueak shrapnel and 4.2s smashed into it, obliterating the scene in rapid clouds of smoke and leaving a struggling team, half up, half down, broken-backed on the road, a sight tragically ridiculous, like a pantomime donkey squatting on its hind legs. To get to our OP in the old German support line by the site of Battle Wood we crossed the cutting by Lock 7 and turned east up the track which led through the shattered timber of the Ravine. The OP was like a Punch and Judy stand in a shattered trench. Immediately at its right hand there was a concrete German pillbox. The front dipped slowly from the ridge in a dreary waste of mud. An enormous communication trench slid down among some viscid crater pools on the right. In the evening they were almost green in colour, and the smooth humps of earth which marked the communication trench looked brownish purple. Signal lights in bright colours rose from the German lines but the noise of the shooting was too great to hear what effect they meant. The pillbox was awash and half full of men sitting on ammunition boxes with their shins under water. Perhaps there were dead men in the water, for as night became colder a stream of hot air rose from the door of the pillbox carrying with it so poisonous a smell that I vomited over the front of my Punch and Judy show. It was necessary to rig up a screen of old sacking. The shelling which had flickered about behind us settled on the ridge, and I went into the pillbox. The smell did not seem so bad inside. There were some duckboards floating about among our legs and one man who had raised a duckboard on boxes so that he could lie down to sleep was now lying with his back in the water. It was rising continually, draining the perpetual rain from the surface. We pumped it down about six inches and sat on boxes nodding in the darkness. Some big shells were falling upon the place and the concussion inside the concrete walls was very painful to the ears. One of the sleeping men fell off his box with a loud splash. The quiet running of the rain persisted and we pumped again for three-quarters of an hour. At daybreak the telephonists got the pocket Primus going and made some tea. We had cheese and bread to eat. Then we had about a cupful extra each for cleaning purposes. First I brushed my teeth, then washed my face, and last shaved. I knocked out my old black pipe on the concrete and it cracked open, showing the wood all charred. This regretful accident reminded me how long that pipe had been a good companion; since Nankivell's time. Luckily there was another pipe in my pocket, and its presence endeared it to me remarkably. The day was warm and grey. On the right, below the grim dark embankment of the Dammstrasse the land tilted evenly to the valley, with Hollebeke chateau a sinister ruin in the plain. In front it was less even; the land was like a dirty sponge, but the whole of the front might have been a cemetery for all the movement of men it contained. Two men moving on the grey crust were extraordinarily fascinating, like maggots discovered in food.

It was about six o'clock when we were relieved and an area shoot was falling between us and our road. The telephonists were anxious to wait, and I to push on. We got through without accident. There were letters waiting for me containing the bare news that Sam had been wounded, gassed and shellshocked. 'Dear Sam,' I wrote, 'I hear you have been startled by a shell again. My feelings are mixed; I'm sorry, but at the same time I rejoice to hear you're in England again. Perhaps this time you'll be content to stay in England a bit instead of rushing off to this part of the war. Personally I'm in the pink, hoping for the very best and very much of a hero between rounds. Write me if you can, old thing, and give me all the news of yourself.'

MacVeagh and I began to build a new mess with the help of four gunners and a corporal; two men built while the rest filled sandbags. The ground was so wet that the spits of earth stuck to the spades and when we hammered the sods down with the flat of the spade the water splashed out. The mess had to be above ground, but we designed it low, with its butt end to the front, and as the rectangle of sandbags grew, we built with it an independent wall at the dangerous end, to act as a burster. The roof was carried on steel rails. It had alternate rows of sandbags and concrete slabs over a corrugated iron platform. The first night we were in it there was a direct hit on the buttress and one of the gun pits was blown in, wounding two men slightly. The weather became brilliant again and the whole front was signposted with sausage balloons staring at each other's secrets. We were taking tours alternately at the battery and at the wagon line. There, under soft blue skies swept by streamers of cloud, we could ride out after the day's work, even into Bailleul.

The whole brigade marched out before the end of August, and our lines were pitched in a remote valley near Godewaersvelde, so warm and bright that we could sleep out. Everything had to be polished for inspection by General Plumer. It was spit and polish all day and visiting rounds twice at night, up at 5 a.m. every morning. At last the general arrived, the legendary soldier, the soldier's soldier, and rode round the battery in about ten minutes. He was short, fat, unimpressive in figure, but we still felt it was an honour.

As soon as the inspection was over we went into action again. The rain was back and our first wagon lines on the Ouderdom–Vlamertinghe road were upon a liquescent field. Night and day the flood continued. It was necessary to send for my sea-boots and heavy clothing. We all had colds, and occasionally high temperatures. The German gunners shelled about the road with 6-inch high explosives and some of the horses became nervous, but it was not very near and the softness of the ground blanketed the bursts. At night the enemy planes came over searching for the horse lines with bombs, but the sky was raggedly obscured and their releases not very accurate. We moved the lines up to firmer ground near Halifax Camp. The whole of the roadside was occupied by horses, camps and ammunition dumps. Daily at the noon hour the 6-inch gun turned on us. He shot straight up the road from some railway well behind the line. The ground had dried up and the bursts were excellent. Every day we sat at lunch waiting for those rounds. The shell had such velocity that no time passed between the faint explosion of the gun and the arrival of the shell in a hideous scream the fraction of a second long. We called it 'John Cotter,' it was so fast a bowler. The gunner put down one, then one short and one over. Every lunchtime we sat at table suspended by the arrival of the first, waiting for the second and third. One day the saddler's hut was blown out of its place and thrown fifty yards, and he untouched. The next day the first fell in my horse lines. The stableman was dying with his chest blown in and the lovely chestnuts lay screaming on the ground, mangled and bleeding. Nine of the best of the sub-section horses were shot that day, the very pride of the battery, so beautifully matched for size and colour. The lines were messed with blood. We dug all night a hole big enough to bury them, and the big bombing Gothas came over in the moonlight, their engines warning us with their 'RRR – RRR – RRR.' They hung about dropping their bombs till nearly daylight. John Cotter missed us next day. He hit a dump of tin cans and threw them gleaming in the air. He also hit Halifax Camp and killed half a dozen infantrymen resting in their hut.

After midnight the ammunition was to go to the guns. I stepped into the darkness from my hut and heard the restless jingle of the bits. A few yards farther the masses of the teams, sharp ears pricking the night, stood waiting. We mounted and moved over the soft earth to the *pavé* road, eight wagons with a hundred rounds, with six-horse teams. The night was as dark as pitch, and everybody heavy with sleep. The wagons jarred and clattered on the granite and the drag-washers lifted and fell back, scuddering on the axles; the drivers bent forward over the horses, pyramidal in waterproof capes. There was some frost in the air, and thousands of small stars appeared in the black sky. In front the shellfire pulsed in bright lime-white bursts, and occasionally one of his big ones rushed overhead like an express train, burst behind and clattered away in echoes among the hills. The journey would take between two and three hours at the foot pace of artillery, and I sat my horse at the head of the column watching the almost invisible road and checking the landmarks carefully. It was not a comfortable charge, for any one shell might lay out a couple of teams and jam the road; then the other horses might panic and get off the track into the hopeless mud. Or if we got the wrong road we might never get the ammunition up till daylight; that would be too late, fatal.

Now it was approaching two o'clock and a terrible desire for sleep was overtaking me in spite of the nervous cold. Somewhere among the traffic a man was singing.

I wonder how Canada is getting on;
Much as I left her, still going strong.

The tune, slow and wistful, seemed to embody the immense melancholy of the war. The notes ascended in a minor inflexion as though without hope.

I'm living in dreams to-night,
Hope they may all come right,

He sang in a sudden revival which flickered out all too soon.

Never again to roam
When I get back to home.

The foreboding strain followed me down the road.

My eyelids kept on dropping half shut, and when I shook myself to wakefulness the images in my mind appeared with the raw truthfulness of early morning. The game seemed stale and stupid. We had eight hundred rounds on board to fire into Germans; and they no doubt had their eight hundred, too, to fire into us. There was no reason, I thought, why this should continue. There was scarcely a man on our side hated them; nor could there be any on their side hated us. We all knew too much. The only excuse that could possibly excuse this was that we hated each other. There were quite a lot at home who were successful haters; then, I said, let them come and fight. In the pitch-black night, leading the angry wagons, I resented the orders of the civilians that we should stop loving things. They wanted to denature us. They also wanted the composite mechanism called the soul to be destroyed by some virulent inoculation, so we should go on fighting and killing and being killed. Why should we have to suffer for the sake of King Albert's soul? War was possible to people who hated very much. But when I said 'I like the Germans' in England they pretended to be horrified. Perhaps they were. And when I said that the war was quite stupid and went on destroying good spirits in men, they said: 'Oh, we do appreciate the heroism of you men;' then you replied, 'If so, why keep it up? Why not stop the war?' Then they thought it was a joke or a crime. No, here on the black road with the eight wagons, driven by men as silent as stones, we had no warlike ebullition left, and only resentful, wayward thoughts stumbling about in the darkness among the bodies of dead friends, among the ruins of things which had once been considered splendid. I decided that the difference between ourselves and those at home was that we had acquired a skill in detecting ruins; we knew they had been something once; they were still at least landmarks. But at home they had in effect agreed to accept shams and frauds as the edifices of honesty, reasonableness, respect. Actual war soon taught one to discover those pigeon houses for what they were; but it left one to solitude in the bare ruins. Well; both sides of fighting men had got to the stage of numbness and would go on till everyone was maimed, mutilated or dead. What fine conclusions! One: it was impossible to maintain any degree of hate. Two: we were forbidden by Church and State to love our enemies, and in any case any one of my eight hundred rounds was out for the slaughter of a dozen Cupids. Three: there was no hope of survival. The thought of Edward intruded like a heartbreaking comment on the whole thing. Wherever there was a spot of love left, there it was most likely to be made to suffer. Love was *verboten* now, in England. The war conscience was equally shocked by war babies and war marriages, and if it did allow a marriage the hymn it sang was not, naturally, 'The voice which breathed o'er Eden,' but 'Gather ye rosebuds while ye may'. All those German chaps and their girls loved as we did; all the drivers behind, they had girls or womenfolk whom they left to come into this column, now approaching Shrapnel Corner. Why should Edward and those others, German, English, French, have to cry? Their voices seemed loud in the early morning and above them all there was Edward's voice and in the darkness I seemed to see her face, looking up with her wide set eyes and sobbing as though everything were lost. She was right, on the facts. Loving was too painful a business and forbidden by DORA (the Defence of the Realm Act). Of course a man must have his pleasures. Whoring was encouraged as an alternative. Every officer and man going out of the camp at le Havre had a pass with the addresses of the brothels printed on the back, and instructions for reaching them so that no officer would be embarrassed by meeting his servant on the doorstep, and no soldier would lower military dignity by observing his officer in search of a woman.

The dawn was still some time off, but an infusion of grey occupied the blackness. We entered the corduroy road, south of the Ramparts, which led directly to Birr Cross roads, leaving Hell Fire Corner a hundred yards on the left. We were now within the chord of the Salient itself, and it lay before us muttering and moving uneasily in the darkness. Suddenly a salvo of heavy shell streamed down and blasted the night with a flame, leaving it darker than ever. A horse began to scream; someone in front had got it. The traffic checked, halted, and moved on slowly towards the front. We listened for the next salvo, aware that there was nothing to be done. I wondered what those silent drivers were thinking, whether they prayed, and whether they also were strung up waiting for the next shell. The traffic in front of me was circling the dark tangle on the road. A man came up and hung on my stirrup leather. 'Oh, sir,' he said, 'have you a revolver with you? Will you shoot my horse? He was a very good horse, sir!' I dismounted. 'Here's his head, sir. Have you got it?' He patted the animal and talked to it. 'Pore old Brownie, never mind, Brownie, it's all over now.' I found the spot and fired. The horse kicked and relaxed.

The corporal went ahead to tell the battery of our arrival. The stink of the unseen carcases about us and the blacker line of the Menin road were signs that we were near at hand. The wagons crossed in pairs at the trot and charged the slimy hill. A man was running from one team to the next, taking the bridle of the near lead and drawing it round to the guns. A voice in the darkness was issuing a stream of orders. 'Now sergeant, get your men out, hurry up there. Where's Corporal Bloxham?' It was the major. The first empty wagon came rattling down the slope. I gave my horse to the lead driver to take back.

'Darley – you wait a quarter of a mile beyond Shrapnel Corner.'

'Yes, corporal.'

'Well, get out of it.'

'Yes, corporal.'

I found the major. 'We'll have no more wagons up here,' he said, 'only pack mules. I must see the NCO.'

'Corporal Hall,' I bellowed.

'Here, sir,' he said, from my elbow.

'The major has decided he won't have any more wagons up here, only pack mules. When you get back, you must tell the sergeant major at once.'

'Yes, sir.'

Someone called from the guns.

'Corporal, what sort of ammo? I want some HE. We're full up of shrapnel.'

'Who?'

'Number three.'

'Coming.'

The last steel lid clattered up and the jingling of the harness faded in the distance. The major led me to the mess.

Some weeks ago in Hazebrouck station I had seen an ambulance train sliding through. All the badges I saw were artillery badges. They told me then that there were hundreds coming from the Menin road. This was it. The major led me along a battered trench piled high with dugouts and shelters on the northern side, and looking on to Birr Crossroads a couple of hundred yards south. He ducked down at a small hole and led me into the mess. It was the smallest sort of corrugated shelter. 'We're all right now,' he said, 'the Hun will begin again at daybreak. Mac's on duty, so you can sleep.' MacVeagh woke me at eight for breakfast. It was quiet, and he led me out to show me the position. The guns squatted in front of the trench, a little below the crest. Other guns lay all about. The ground was full of new shell holes. All morning they shelled us with 5.9 HE. In the afternoon the

Somme 1916. Every round had to be unloaded by hand on the battery positions.

Infantry officers with a gramophone in their billet; Boyd describes similar scenes in his battery.

'Under the grey sky the ragged files of men passed up and down to the line, bowed under their burden . . . their haggard faces half-hidden under the ungainly helmets tilted forward for comfort, rifles over the shoulder, gas-helmets, ammunition, bandoliers, sacks of food.' (Page 82)

'Beyond lay the track of an old road blown to pieces, and now no more than an earthen gully looking towards the German lines.' (Page 84)

'We slid and climbed in and out of holes . . . where the dead of half a dozen countries lay rotting.' (Page 84)

An 18-pounder battery moves into a new position during the Third Battle of Ypres.

An 18-pounder battery in a temporary position during the Great Retreat of March 1918, with horse teams coming to withdraw the guns. Donald Boyd was awarded the Military Cross for leading teams to recover two guns abandoned after such a withdrawal.

SOS sounded on the mess buzzer. SOS – SOS – SOS – SOS – SOS – SOS
– SOS – SOS it went, unappeasable. We climbed over the bank of earth and
ran to the guns. They fired at a prescribed rate. MacVeagh checked the
times. When the rate was fulfilled the guns stopped. A storm of shrapnel
burst over the position. It was the first time I had seen German shrapnel
burst low enough to be effective. One of the gunners got a ball through the
palm of the hand. He was trembling and excited. 'That's a blighty all right,
isn't it, sir?' We bandaged him and sent him off to the dressing station.

The hours repeated themselves throughout the days. With nightfall came
an endless procession of large shells, falling about the position at regular
twenty-second intervals. In our little mess MacVeagh held a party. There
were six of us; Rawley, dear 'Daddy' Johnson, captain of A Battery, who
was almost completely bald, and the mild redheaded Anson, captain of C
battery, a short wiry man with a Military Cross and Bar. We raised a little
song and drank. The solitary howitzer was joined by a battery of 4.2-inch
howitzers. MacVeagh silently put on his helmet and slipped two shell
dressings into his pocket and went out.

'I think I must go.'

'And I'll step along.' The two captains went away. Mac came back. We
sat for half an hour. Then some of the bursts came very near. It was my turn.
I stumbled along the trench. At the far end a candle threw a slit of light upon
the mud in the trench; the mud was inlaid with large splashes of blood which
stood out from it, like enamel. The candle threw a thin light into the arched
recesses of an elephant cupola and in the foreground I saw Gerald, of D
Battery, leaning over a stretcher.

'Come in,' he said, 'one of your people.'

'What's done that?'

'Dud, through his thigh, I think. One did fall. I heard it fall.'

The man's right leg was mashed to a pulp.

'Nothing to be done.'

'Nothing.'

The man murmured. 'My puttee strap,' he kept saying, 'my puttee strap's
tight. Hell! My puttee strap!'

We cut the puttee strap on the other leg and loosened his tunic collar. I
looked at his leg.

'Oh God!' I said.

'Yes,' Gerald said, 'pray if you can. You need to, here. Have a drink.'

'I've never drunk whisky.'

'You need whisky too. Thank God for whisky.' He poured out two glasses. It tasted of earth, fiery, crawling like slow fire all over my stomach.

'We can't shift him to the dressing station now.'

'No. Listen to them.'

We went to the telephone dugout. There were some other wounded there. We broke iodine ampoules over the wounds. The liquid stung the raw flesh and made one sick. Then we bandaged them roughly. One of the men fainted. At dawn in the quiet half hour we took the wounded down to Birr Cross Roads. The dressing station was full below and stretchers lay in rows on the ground. We hurried back to the battery. A Ford ambulance came along the grey road and halted. The orderlies filled it up; it started back to Ypres, and as it went the shelling began again on the road, overwhelming the little car, but still it continued towards the town, and we watched it past the school till it had jolted out of sight to the Menin Gate.

We were shooting on to the Westhoek Ridge. The crater field had a sort of slime upon it as though the earth, mutilated, disembowelled, had suffered decomposition in the rain. Upon this skin the duckboard tracks gave foothold and served for direction through the artificial nightmare of the front. One OP was in a mine crater, five or six feet deep in water. Higher up, the walls had been tunnelled in galleries, and dead Germans lay in the entrances like rats escaping from their holes. In front, like a ship in a sea of mud, stood a German pillbox canted over on one side; it was packed inside with German dead too rotten to remove. The other OP was a hole near the remnant marked as Red Lodge, a little shell hole where the mud all day ate through cloth and leather to the bone, where we crouched into the mud under the shellfire. The rain soaked down and crawled up our sleeves taking the colour out of the skin, as though it were staining it white. The rain crawled up inside my old waterproof and filled the fabric. It was stiff with water and cold. It dripped from the skirts of our coats and the uniform sucked it in till every shred of stuff was damp, and our boots were as soft as cloth. The front was inanimate. The infantry lay caked in the slime like some wild outcast tribe. A little distance in front there was a glimmer of water. The earth was liquefied by the rain, and the beck was dismembered by the shells. Here also night and day upon the lips of the water the infantry lay holding the line, clinging to the mud while the shells sought them out, and daily the character and quality of life diminished.

At the guns we had warmth and shelter, and yet, as the days passed, the roll of casualties increased in progression. MacVeagh said that the Boche was going without breakfast. That morning one of the howitzers of D Battery had been thrown upside down, and two gunners blown to pieces. We sent their captain, Truscott, a note asking for information about 'the new type of howitzer which apparently fires underground'. Our cookhouse was blown up. There was no breakfast. We ate cold. Then the regular morning bombardment began. Mac lifted his nose like a connoisseur and said it was the mid-morning hate. In the middle of it the buzzer started again. SOS - SOS – SOS – SOS – SOS – SOS – SOS. All about us the guns took up the battle. There was shellfire of some kind all the day long, and only one silent hour in the early morning.

The mules came up just before dawn and one day as they stood to be unloaded the roar of an aeroplane dropped upon us. It was flying very low. When it sailed down out of the grey light we saw that it had black crosses on the wings. 'Christ!' MacVeagh said. The pilot opened fire with his machine gun and circled to sweep us again. He was so close above us we could have seen his features. The anti-aircraft machine gun in the trench got to work but still he came on. The mules were moving off now. We offered the machine gunners two hundred francs for a kill. But they did not fetch him down. Day after day he came upon us at dawn, machine gunning the population of Birr Cross Roads. And so there was no calm interval now.

The weather was warmer but the rain made a hot mist about the battle front. We had a circular message from the Army Commander. It had come to his notice, he said, that officers and men on the front were going sick in increasing numbers with neurasthenia and shellshock. All ranks were warned that those who so reported themselves would make themselves liable to court martial.

Mac and I sang the news.

For 'tis tidings of comfort and joy
— comfort and joy.
For 'tis tidings of comfort and joy.

We made up a new verse:

God bless ye Army Commandant
Let nothing him dismay,
The boys upon the Birr Cross Roads
Can't live to run away.

SALUTE OF GUNS

They think a soldier's life is foul
And neurasthenia fair
But 'tis tidings of comfort and joy —

Daddy Johnson pleaded for the Army Commander. 'He's doing his best for the army, after all,' he said.

'Well then, why the hell doesn't he use some counter-batteries to shut up those bloody guns— '

'— and a few aeroplanes to knock out the early morning bird bastard?'

My servant Backhouse packed my rucksack. We were going to the wagon line for a day. Backhouse had won the DCM for conduct in the Messines Battle. He won it, Mac said, because he never could keep any shoulder-title or cap badge. Mac said Backhouse was on his way to join him near 4711 when the Germans counter-attacked. A subaltern mistook Backhouse for an infantryman, put him under arrest, thrust a rifle in his hands and said, 'Fire that, all you know.' Backhouse said nothing but climbed on the firestep and got to work. He saw nobody, not a solitary German, but he kept on firing uphill. After an hour the subaltern came back. He was so surprised to find Backhouse still there and firing that he recommended him for the DCM, and it was so rare that infantry ever found artillery worthy of recommendation that the award was made.

It was well enough to have a day off; but just at the moment great 8-inch high explosive shells were bursting with a time fuse about thirty feet above the Menin road, and we could see the pieces ricochet along the *pavé*. The shells tore apart in enormous black bursts. At the first lull we got on to the road. It was quite empty and we trotted gently towards Hell Fire Corner, to be clear of it before the next series began, and succeeded; but just past the crossing a platoon of infantry appeared, solemnly marching forward, and Backhouse grinned as we fell into a walk.

Walking over the bridge in Poperinghe after a bath I met Nankivell. 'I have two guns, one subaltern and five men left,' he said, 'or else I'd ask you to come and dine on the Menin road.'

'I do,' I said, 'I live there too.'

'I expect we watch each other being shelled. It's the only amusement left.'

A few days after a subaltern arrived to prepare for our relief. We thrust all the papers at him, ammunition states, trench stores, barrage schemes, registration tables, calibration records, SOS rockets, charts, plans, notes, aeroplane photographs. His gunners came up before dawn in two small parties. The Numbers One took the detachments into the pits and shelters, handed over the guns, and left the newcomers in charge. It took about fifteen minutes. We moved off, a small party on foot. Although the position had been manned by no more than a handful of men we had lost twice their number in ten days, either dead or wounded. Mac kept saying as we walked back to the horses, 'But it was jolly, wasn't it, really? So full of surprises !'

We went back to the hills north of Bailleul and set out our horse lines under a windmill. It was 10 September. On the 13th, Daddy took the guns to a new position. It was the old sector of the Bluff, but now we were forward, on the high ground above the Ravine, about three hundred yards in front of the broken wood. The Bluff Tunnels lay a quarter of a mile away in the depression on our right. The position was in the crater field. Shallow open pits had been dug for the guns, and each one contained fifty rounds prepared for fire. On the roadside there stood a large dump of boxed ammunition. This preparation was a novelty; but we were in the Second Army, Plumer's Army. Everybody believed that meant a great deal. Daddy manoeuvred the six-horse teams skilfully among the shell holes and wire until the guns were as near as they could be drawn. Then Daddy and the teams trotted away in the fading light. It was a beautiful evening, the horizon a pale lemon deepening by invisible verges into a mauve which illuminated the cap of the sky. As we manhandled the guns about the bare earth I noticed a tuft growing at my feet, a tuft so familiar I could not recognize it. It was heather.

Before dark I laid out lines of fire and prepared an SOS line. Then we began to look for cover and on the right flank found a concrete pillbox half full of water; its top had been blown in. I made that headquarters. Orders came for bursts of harassing fire in the night. Our atheistic sergeant, Peace, masked a torch over my notebook and map as I worked out the orders. We sent the men who were not needed down to the Tunnels. Then we settled in for the night. It was very unquiet there. The enemy was also engaged in harassing fire on the ridge and the road. Several times we feared he would hit the ammunition. Peace was highly critical as we walked behind the guns in the starlight taking cover at intervals when their bursts came too near. War, he gave me to understand, should be conducted like religion, by reason and not faith. 'Couldn't they see,' he said indignantly, 'that this dump should have been spread behind the guns away from the road, which is a fixed point on the map and therefore easy to hit?' I promised we should shift them tomorrow. We should dig small ammunition stores for the boxes. At once his contempt for disorder turned another way.

'I doubt, sir, if you will find the detachments strong enough. We should have the whole battery strength for that and the ordinary work.'

'Still it's better only to have small detachments here, don't you think?'

'In one way, yes. But in another, no.'

I admired him very much. He was an excellent soldier of great courage, but he always argued, either before or after. Mac said Peace would argue with his own coffin bearers if they tilted his head the wrong way. Peace must have been twice my age. We continued the ridiculous conversation for some hours of the night. On the evening of the next day the rest of the battery arrived. Daddy found a cupola dugout beyond the pillbox and made that the mess. We had just got settled when a familiar voice sounded at the door.

'Anybody here from B Battery?'

It was C.

He was attached to another battery not far from us. I persuaded him to share the remains of my pillbox with me. After dinner we pumped out the water and lay down on duckboards to talk.

'I've had the hell of a time with these sods,' he said, 'they're a frightful ragtime crowd. The captain lives in the Tunnels with a favourite subaltern all the time, and leaves me at the battery to do the dirty work. We got badly strafed – oh, by the way, Anson's in for another MC. He's in the next battery. They got two shelters blown in the other day and he went and dug them out while they were shelling like hell with 5.9s. The best of it was, the colonel was watching from an OP in the Tunnels. – But our lot; well, after the strafe we started tidying up, me and the NCOs. A general suddenly appeared on the scene – not one of ours. I saluted in a smart and soldier like way and he said "Well, and what do you think of the position?" I said "Not much, sir." He looked a bit shirty, and said, "Do you know who selected it?" I said I didn't; then he explained he had. Nothing for it. I plunged right in then, and told him it was too far from the road for ammunition supply and too far from the Tunnels for safety. Oh, my God, you should have seen him! He was cross! Then he inspected the position. It was in a mess. I admit it. He said he would hold me responsible for its state. I told him he couldn't because I was an attached officer and therefore junior. So he asked where my officer commanding was. I told him. That made him worse. He said he would make an official complaint about my inefficiency and talked about having me put under arrest. I said "Very good, sir," and we parted. I don't suppose anything will happen.'

I was glad to see C. again. We talked for a long time, and we compared experiences of England.

'Do you know Becker?' he asked. 'We finished up in grand style at home. The adjutant had been swinish and so had the colonel, with all the overseas men. They refused us leave on the last night and so Becker organized a party to shoot up the camp at 1.30 a.m. I had the colonel, Becker the adjutant. There were several others in the hue and cry. We looted the ammunition box and chased them all round the camp, and in and out of the mess firing our revolvers; it was a scream. They were both in pyjamas. We halloa'ed and shot and whooped and shot. They thought we were dotty and ran for their lives. Do you know both those chaps have been there all the war and joined up after the rest of us did? Both perfectly fit, too. They deserved every moment of it for trying to stop leave.'

'How on earth did you start the row?'

'Oh, that was great. We lined up and fired volleys, one over the colonel's hut and one over the adjutant's, then I rushed into the colonel's hut and lashed at the walls shouting "orderly officer visiting rounds," at the top of my voice. I fired a couple of rounds through the roof and by that time he was up and out; then we all screamed after. It was pitch dark and raining, he couldn't recognize us. Then all the overseas men went into town by cars and the following night we met in the Empire bar and had a binge. An APM was offensive. He objected to my pipe, and Becker offered to fight him, very politely. Nothing doing, though. I say, the swine got in some of his military policemen to chuck us out, and I tackled the official chucker-out. He was a good 'un. We had a great time and landed up on the pavement. The APM said, "Your names and addresses, please, gentlemen" and Becker said "My name is Becker and my address is BEF. You can come and fetch me if you like." So then we went to Victoria and stayed at Folkestone the night.'

'You go about asking for trouble and getting it.'

'Well, I say, what's it matter? Might as well get some fun out of this mucky business. Besides, I can't stand these people with cushy jobs at home when they butt into some PB subalterns gratuitously. The ones who've been out and got wounded never behave like that ... I say, water's up again.'

We pumped out the water and rolled ourselves in blankets.

In the middle of the night Peace came to waken me. They were shelling a bit round the guns, especially near the road. We arranged the harassing fire to be done by the two guns on the right flank. The night was dark and starless, but dark with an edge to it, not blurred by fog. The front winked restlessly about us. There was a battle brewing. Night by night the dump of boxes by the roadside was replenished and a new dump was made on the right. The enemy began area shoots, concentrating guns of all sizes on one square of territory, so that nothing could move in or out of it. They fell with incredible fury on our patch, driving us to ground in our shelters, and behind we could hear our heavies start their roaring counter-battery fire. 'Bless them, oh, God bless them,' Mac said, crouching with me in a shell hole. He had come back from night OP at the edge of Battle Wood and was on his way to sleep in the Tunnels.

A battery of 6-inch howitzers came into action on the forward fringe of Ravine Wood and we watched the black timber fall about them when the Germans opened fire. Then another section came and squatted down in the T of the road in front of us. The area strafes caught the rags on the camouflage wire over the dump. In a moment they began to blaze. We baled with our steel helmets out of the nearest shell holes and got the fire out before the wood had caught or the smoke attracted further attention. No sooner was that out than the other dump was fired by a shrapnel shell. We had to run to that, then, among the bursts.

The adjutant called on us with his barrage map and unfolded it on the table. It was a perfect barrage map. There was a pink chalk line, north-east and south-west, marked 'zero,' then a green chalk line marked 'zero 3,' and after that a blue chalk line, a yellow line and finally a red chalk line. These were the steps of the barrage, creeping forward from the German front line to his retreat. Between them were coloured rings of chalk marking machine-gun posts, strongpoints or other obstacles for special attention. Across the map ran parallel lines illustrating the zone of each battery. The infantry were to attack Polygon Wood and Gheluvelt.

'This is you,' he said. 'You will fire for forty minutes. Zero hour is to be announced tonight. Send an officer at eight and he can take the time. The rate is three rounds a gun a minute for the first ten minutes, then two rounds for fifteen minutes and one for fifteen minutes. They will cop it bloody hot.'

It was very sunny. Daddy spent the afternoon working out written orders for each gun on neat pages of his notebook. We gathered for tea. In the dusk the water-cart and the mess cart came up with rations and mail, unloaded and departed rapidly. The Ravine was feverish. Pairs of 8-inch and salvoes of 5.9 fell on the corduroy road. There was a scrawl from Sam to me. He was blind from gas but expected to recover. My Uncle Norman wrote from a Canadian division in the line. Also there was a copy of *Vogue,* a fantastical sight in that place. It was sent for contrast. Daddy poured out whisky and remonstrated gently with my lime-juice. 'It's very lowering,' he said. 'You ought to drink whisky. Lime-juice encourages you to get depressed.' The night muttered on in the usual way, till an hour before dawn. Then it fell silent, and we stretched and yawned behind the guns while the fuse-setters made little metallic knocks on the shells and the tin cups protecting the fuses gathered in piles about their feet. The sergeants went about with electric torches preparing for the barrage. In front thousands of men were waiting till we should have put down the curtain over the enemy lines. A few Very lights sailed up, flamed out white, hanging in the air and died away. Daddy went back to the mess with Mac to check the lines and ranges for the third time, and we examined each of the six guns again. Mac was very cheerful because there was some tinned ham for breakfast. 'That is lovely, my sweet, is not it?' The air was cold and raw and the voices sounded harsh. The guns were spread far apart in among the shell holes, one section lying across the road. We walked up and down, talking and waiting.

'Two minutes to go,' Daddy said at my elbow. 'Go to Number Four and give the orders.'

'One minute to go,' I shouted, with my eyes on the watch dial. The sudden end of small sounds seemed to make the whole front crouch in silence.

'Stand by – fifteen seconds to go.'

'Fire!'

The barrage leaped into flame. The horizon danced and swayed in fiery points as far as we could see. The noise swelled about us with a large excitement, fragmentary sounds seizing upon the ear, the harsh whistle of 60-pounders, the majestic swish of the 12-inch sliding through the air, the woolly reports of the howitzers, the sudden crack of our own guns. As the barrage ground slowly forward, searching and sweeping each step of the front, the guns grew hot and the buffers began to tire. The gunners had to push the pieces up by hand. Number Five went out of action altogether with a broken piston and Number Six doubled its rate of fire.

Day had broken and the noise was dulled into a *diminuendo* in which the enemy shells could be heard. A smell of mustard gas rose from the Ravine itself and the first of the walking wounded began to come by. 'Gone all right,' they said, 'but lots of dead.' About the position were unmistakably new shell holes. We had not noticed their arrival. The barrage was over, and the heavies were putting in their counter-battery work. Soon we should be called to fire on the enemy reserves coming up. Already his tracks and roads were being well pasted. The howitzers kept on. We had breakfast. A party of unfortunate Labour Battalion men arrived to carry ammunition. They did not know there was a battle in progress. They were oldish men, some of them bent and grey. They worked a little under their corporal and then the enemy's fire fell upon us again. At once the Labour men broke and ran. Daddy watched them.

'Damn them,' he said, 'they've gone into the Ravine. They'll all get killed or gassed.' He ran and gathered them, comforting them as well as he could. The corporal he sent back to their bus, behind the Bluff Spoil Bank, and the men he sent through the Tunnels. They passed behind the guns, utterly weary, dispirited old men. A subaltern named Marsh called at lunchtime. He was going up to night OP Marsh was about forty, a gently mannered man who lived on an estate in the country. He never seemed to understand the war at all. We begged him to stay but he would not. It would take him another hour, or perhaps two, to get up to the old trench, and he wanted to be sure. He had a rifle and four new SOS parachute rockets with him in a sack. So he passed forward under the bare poles on the ridge, where the camouflage screens had stood. Some of the wounded stopped for water. They had fought all morning. Our water-cart had just arrived but we dared not spare much. It was not easy to get supplies up there. We fired a great deal, and with the evening there came a lull. The guns were washed out and laid on the SOS lines. Darkness fell on the front and we sat on the earth pulling at cigarettes. Suddenly in the heaven there flowered Marsh's SOS light like a jewelled bouquet. It hung against the black night, red-green-red, in a pause which seemed dead silence for a second, as though everyone stopped and stared. Then the whole of the guns crashed into fire upon the second, a confused storm of sound swaying and shuddering over miles of land, faces lit up with the yellow lime flashes. The acrid smell of the burnt cordite billowed into the air. The whole note of the tumult swelled and quivered and every continuing second burst itself with a multitude of packed voices battering across the front. Daddy cupped his hand round my ear and shouted: 'What do you think of that!' 'Nothing like it in this world or the next,' I answered.

'God bless the sailors on a night like this,' Mac said piously.

I don't know where Marsh spent the next day. He must have gone back to the position for a long sleep. The next we heard was on the evening of the third day of the battle. It had been a nasty disordered day. After dark we heard somebody stumbling about just in front of the guns. One of the sergeants of my section, Wilson, warned the control not to fire and went out to see what it was. He brought back Marsh's telephonist, who was bleeding from the shoulder and had lost his way. At first the only thing that he could say was that Marsh was dead. Then we learnt that a shell had burst at their feet near a pillbox in the afternoon. The telephone wire had gone and he had been trying to get back ever since. We gave him food and drink and telephoned to his battery. Then he said, 'The officer on duty the day before, he was killed, too.'

Mac said 'It sounds very careless to me, don't it? What was Mr. Marsh doing outside?'

'You couldn't help it, sir, so nasty, hopping in or hopping out, they're sure to get you. It's in full view. They snipe with 5.9s sir,' the telephonist said with the ghost of a smile.

'My God! Sniping with 5.9s!'

All this was uncomfortable hearing for me. I was due there next day.

Backhouse stowed stuff in my rucksack. Bombardier Eldred and another new telephonist were waiting for me in the morning. The new man, Hurst, was only about eighteen. We made our way towards Hill 60. At the corner a dead infantryman was lying, a boy with a neat black hole in his head. The flies were walking in and out of it. 'Death with a little pin.' We passed Hill 60 and walked up the railway cutting towards the Caterpillar. It was strange to see into those places. The remnants of the bridge hung over the ravaged chasm, its brick piers eaten away by shellfire. The banks of the cutting were bare and shapeless, as though they were returning to the original slime; and it was as though the molten earth and the lagoons in the bottom of the cutting were the second or third stage of that corruption, no longer responsive to organized life. A few men hurried up and down the shelf on the side of the bank. The enemy fire was hitting the top, and sometimes a shell plunged fairly into the bottom and threw up great webs of mud and water. We crossed to the north bank by a haphazard bridge of duckboards, and laboured in the crusted mud up to the track on the other slope. An infantry guide was to meet us. He took us up to the top of the cutting and pointed out the curtain of shellbursts across the track in front. We sat down in the nick at the top of the cutting and waited a moment. I looked at Hurst and then at Eldred. He had his hands in his pockets; his helmet slanted down and his cigarette up, and his good London face, flexible, inquisitive, humorous and keen, was also turned towards Hurst.

'Do we need Hurst?' I asked.

'Not if you don't sir.'

'Do you want to come on, kid?' Eldred said.

'Well, just as you like.'

We sent him back and started along the track. It was called the Red Track and led between tapes pinned on the ground. It was high, open and under observation. After a couple of hundred yards the infantryman stopped and pointed to a pillbox in a group of broken trees. 'That's the place, sir.'

'All right, come on.'

'Could I go back sir?'

'No, I don't think so; we must get on.'

'It's a dreadful place this, sir. I haven't had any sleep for days.'

'But we must get to the right spot, and I don't know it.'

'Oh yes sir, but that's easy, sir, it's right at the end of the track, there where you can see it.'

The pillbox was about six hundred yards ahead

The man began astonishingly to whimper.

'Do you swear that's the place?'

'I swear it on the Sacred Cross, sir.'

'Very well.'

Eldred and I stepped forward briskly. We came safely to the pillbox and I went in. There was a candle burning in the darkness. A voice said, startled, 'Who's that with a German pack?'

'Artillery observation officer looking for J. 31 c 3.7.'

'Why don't you know it — or why can't you find your way by the landmarks?' he asked suspiciously.

'There aren't any so far as I know, sir.'

I explained myself further to the colonel. Then he was satisfied. It was the wrong place. He told me how to go. We walked forward to a depression in which were a group of concrete pillboxes, all German and facing the wrong way. We slipped in with a chorus of 5.9s at our heels. They told us to take the half-dug trench leading forward. We walked on a step. A trench lay across our path, packed full of men looking up at us with strange twists of the neck. I was about to speak when I saw that they were dead, every man of them.

'Cripes!' Eldred said, 'they fairly gave me a turn, too.'

Our trench lay at their side. It was only three feet deep, hastily dug. We pressed on smartly and uneasy. Suddenly an infantry runner came past, actually running and bent double. He shouted out, 'Bad place, run!' as he passed. Then another followed him, breathing heavily. He turned his head and stared as he passed. It seemed absurd to run when there was no shelling. But when infantry runners behaved like that there was no need for artillery to pretend indifference. 'When in Rome —' said Eldred. We went forward at a jog-trot till we came to a large concrete pillbox with a stumpy tower rising a foot or two above the roof level. It stood far up the ridge, shining in the sunlight, a conspicuous mark for their gunners. Eldred and I peered into the blackness from the doorway. 'Is this J.31 c 3.7?' There was silence for a moment. Then a voice said wearily, 'I should come in if I were you. We've had two gunners killed in that doorway in the last two days, and though I hate to say it we don't want the bother of cleaning your mess up as well.'

We went inside. There were nine or ten officers and men lying on the floor. One of them was trying to make a pillow out of cotton bandoliers full of rifle ammunition. My small pillow was in my rucksack. He took that and went to sleep. The company commander gave me permission to use the tower. It had slits in each wall, so that we could see the sector on which the battery was shooting. The sun was bright, and over the front in parallel rows lay small clouds suspended in the blue sky. The crust of the earth had dried and the front lay an undulation of pale brown earth broken open by innumerable craters. The slope declined as far as the Basseville Beck, which stood in dismembered fragments about a row of broken pollards. On the left the remains of Basseville Wood, black standing timber bare like masts, concealed the opening of the valley. From here it was feared the Germans might counter-attack. But the front lay apparently in the indolence of exhaustion. At intervals a storm of big shells fell upon the shallow trench behind, tossing the earth sky high in cones of black smoke. There was no cover there at all and the fire took the solid squares of earth and left no yard unturned. About noon we took the air for a few minutes, never far from the pillbox, and met some men of our neighbouring brigade mending telephone wires. It was as quiet as the grave, and they were moving about crouched on the ground. Our wire was through to a group headquarters in the tunnels of Hill 60. We could only communicate by means of an elaborate and difficult code which depended on a codeword and then was translated by means of numbers. In the afternoon smoke rose from the valley behind Basseville Wood and we reported that. A small storm of artillery fire developed on the front. The light faded and left the landscape cold and bare, the black stumps gathering darkness against the pale brown earth. Before dark we got an order to come in. We gathered what information we could from the infantry and I drew my pillow from under the subaltern's head. He was still fast asleep. Then we hurried back to Hill 60. The slope was full of odd parties of men moving about among the bursts of shellfire. We went over the top to look into the enormous crater, as big as a quarry, which our mine had torn out of the hill. A few yards further, upon the unrecognizable earth, we found a deep shaft, its hind wall built perpendicularly of sandbags, its forward slope at an angle of about seventy degrees, so that it was shaped roughly like a canted funnel. It was about twenty-five feet deep to the bottom. Then we realized it was the emplacement of the minenwerfer which had so often plagued the old front line. 'They knew a thing or two,' Eldred said, spitting with accuracy down the shaft. The mortar at the bottom was made of wood.

When I arrived at the Bluff Tunnels I found Rawley squatting in our alley. They had been shelling outside and he was trying to evacuate into one of our 3-inch cartridge cases, while one of the mess servants kept guard on the entrance to the street. He was a funny sight.

Mac poured me a stiff whisky and said he must kiss me for coming back alive. Backhouse brought in an enamelled plateful of thin soup and a hunk of bread. There was beef, baked in fat on the Primus stove, spotty potatoes and cake out of Mac's last parcel from Fortnum and Mason. Mac lit his meerschaum pipe, carved in the shape of a parrot's head, and discussed the way up to OP. The chamber, like all the rest of the Tunnels, was floored, walled and roofed with wood. A wooden framework supported bunks of wire netting, shiny with use. I rolled in my blanket and slept, while Mac went down to the wagon lines. Two or three days later he relieved me at the guns. My horses were waiting at the bottom end of the Tunnels. On the dressing station at Voormezeele there was a huge poster published by the Scripture Text Association. 'Underneath are the everlasting arms,' it said. I trotted along wondering if it were true. I went down the dark road I had used in the winter of 1915, past the forge at Vierstraat, and saw there Taylor's shell deflector still intact; then straight down to Kemmel, and by Kim's Road to la Clytte. The freshness of the grassy hills about Scherpenberg was astonishing. I finished my twelve-mile journey as the moon was rising, to fall on the bare hop-poles, crossed like gigantic fencing sticks, in the field below the windmill. A track on bright sand made a short cut to the horse lines. A bath of cold water was poured out for me and stood in the moonlight in an alley between the small fabric huts. I stripped and scrubbed and changed my lousy clothes for fresh ones. My hut was in the middle of a cabbage patch which seemed to stink abominably. But it was half-past eight when my servant woke me. 'How's this?' I said. 'I've missed parade!'

'Major's orders to me last night, sir, not to wake you till breakfast time.'

'God bless the major.'

'A cup of tea sir, and hot water.'

'And God bless you.'

Two days later the major called to me.

'Boyd, we're fetching the guns out tomorrow. We shall have a harness parade this afternoon.

'Very good, sir.'

Everyone was very pleased.

Later in the day he called me again.

'Boyd, there's some confusion about OP duties. You'll have to go up and do OP tomorrow.'

This was bad hearing.

'Damned bad luck. You may not be wanted but you'll have to go and see.'

'The usual place, sir?'

'Yes.'

'Johnson and you will take the teams up for the guns; be ready to move off at midnight.'

'We shall be there about five, then, sir?'

'Yes.'

'It was a bit sticky at five the last two or three mornings, sir.'

'We shall have to risk that.'

The road was busy. We joined with long strings of horsed traffic going up in the darkness. A little past Voormezeele, Daddy sent a corporal ahead. The teams went up to the position two by two. It was quiet as we climbed through the wood. Rawley and Mac were waiting on the roadside. We got one section away and the others came up. Then without warning the shells began to rend the track at the bottom edge of the wood. The shoot increased towards us. It seemed to be even odds whether it was preferable to go on to OP or to stay with the teams. I started out. The sky was the colour of slate, and looking back I saw a tree trunk fling up from the bottom of Ravine Wood, turning over in the air.

It was afternoon when I was relieved from the OP. A captain came running in to the pillbox. 'I should get out and look slippy,' he said, 'there's a show coming off in ten minutes.'

'I don't intend to dally.'

I took the first mile and a half at a run and had to wait at the cutting and watch others trying to dodge the shells. The battery position was derelict and all our people had gone from the Tunnels. The Tunnels were full of men lying in exhaustion upon the muddy floor, their faces seamed with mud and pallid in the feeble glow of the carbon filament bulbs. It was forbidden that they should lie there, but at the corners the travellers stepped over them, infantrymen bent under their packs and rifles, swaying in the narrow space, still striding carefully to avoid sleepers who looked as though they could never be woken again.

When I emerged at the bottom end I could not find my horse, and set off in the twilight to walk the twelve-mile road. It was black night when I got near Vierstraat, seven miles from the OP with about seven still to do. Parties of wagons rolled forward, artillery, small arms, rations, baggage, water-carts, travelling kitchens alight and smoking, motor lorries, despatch riders. I saw a familiar head towering over me and the trot of hooves.

'Is that you, sir?'

'Is that Hampstead?'

'Yes, sir, been up before today but I got sent back. I chanced meeting you.'

'What a chance!'

'Yes sir. We're going out day after tomorrow, I believe, and you're billeting.'

'Do you know where?'

'Arras I think, but a quiet sector, anyway.'

'The horses will have to lie up all tomorrow.'

'Yes sir. They'll have done nearly fifty miles today, I reckon.'

Chapter 8

All the Happy Times

Arras – Auutumn 1917

W e rode in the fine October weather, southwards to Arras, and the Salient lay behind. The cavalcade travelled complete, man by man; washing kit, tobacco and other gear in the saddle wallets, coat rolled and strapped, a nosebag of corn on the off side of the saddle. Amazing freedom to ride in the dusty sunshine without fear, to sing and joke; sometimes on a grassy margin to put the horses to a stretching canter and feel them rocking smoothly between the thighs, while the wind swept the tears into the eyes! Amazing luxury, at night, after billeting was done, to find soup, omelette, chops, preserve, wine and coffee at an inn, to roll among sheets so orderly that Raven, for one, could not find his way into bed; to rise to hot shaving water and a cold sponge-down!

One morning I rose early and pushed on ahead. We were passing near the rest area of the Canadian Division in which my uncle served. It was near Houdain that I found Private Boyd drilling with his company. We talked hurriedly, explaining where we had been. And then, 'Do you remember how we used to fight and roll down the steps, uncle?' I asked.

'Don't I just! I've got a lump on my head still.'

'This is a pretty awful business, isn't it?'

'It certainly is, but our chaps are a fine lot.'

'Is there anything you want, uncle?'

'No, Donald, I guess not.'

'Are you short of cash at all? I get lashings, you know.'

'No, honest. We get better pay than your infantry.'

'Nothing at all?'

'If you could get hold of a pair of strong gloves I'd like those, it's so darned cold and muddy for the hands in the line. Look!'

129

His hands were chipped, cracked, grained with water and earth. Deep cuts ran down the sides of his thumbnails.

'I'll send for some tonight. Goodbye, uncle. I must go. I'm billeting. Goodbye.'

We shook hands. He watched me mount, saluting with a grin on his face. Then we waved.

We had planned to meet again, but that was the last time. He was killed at Vimy, ten days later. Looking over the waste highlands near Arras I could only feel that there was something to be said for death; better, perhaps, to be overtaken by death and be safely buried than to wait for it in an infantry battalion and feel, week by week, that the amplitude of courage was shrivelling and would leave some day soon, no more than a wrinkled husk of the 'I' that had rejoiced in its strength; better to be among the grasses on the windy hill, undisturbed for ever.

One of the first things I had to do was to write to Sam. 'Such a cushy place, dear Sam, where it simply isn't done to wear tin hats behind battalion headquarters, and where staff captains in lemon gloves and lemon canes come prancing up on horseback to the colonel's dugout in the line. ... I hope your toobs are better. Stay in England a long, long, time because I'm sweating on leave in a month.' It was like that, opposite Gavrelle and Oppy. After the last advance there the place was as quiet as a graveyard, and almost as melancholy. The grass had grown grey and long on the old front, with occasionally a poppy. The rain had followed us from the Salient, and my winter kit had arrived. It was so peaceful that one almost loved the place. Nevertheless we began to sink a deep dugout at once. My hands got hard again, and awkward with a pen. Stansfield went on leave with Mac and left Rawley in charge. A subaltern called Immingham joined us, and another called Spragg. Immingham was half French, tall, pale and thin. Spragg talked as if he had engaged in every sort of trade one could mention. He had a red face and a bluff manner. He always called Rawley 'Skipper.'

The night OP was in an ancient earthwork near Point du Jour and looked over a battery position of 5.9 howitzers captured in the battle. The dugout smelt strongly of wet earth. We untied our sacks and the telephonist made a little fire of wood and coke. Then we found we only had two tins with us, one smeared with butter, the other with jam. We tossed and Eldred won the jam tin. I had to drink tea with butter in it; while his bully tasted of gooseberry. We huddled over the fire coughing in the fumes and smoke. Someone called down the entrance shaft and there descended a short, benevolent figure with gleaming glasses, very much like Mr Pickwick. 'Glasgow,' he introduced himself, 'Divisional Infantry Observation Officer. I've got a good place here. Come see.'

There was a roaring stove in his dugout. 'Another stray,' he said, waving a hand at a tall man by the fire. 'Vail, by name. Corps Signals. Good chap. Novelist. Have a drink.' We roasted at the stove and talked of books. Vail spoke of magic and Sir Thomas Malory. Glasgow said he hated words and asked us to exercise our minds by calculating how many raindrops 1-500th of an inch in diameter it would take to fill a conical wine-glass with a radius of half an inch and a height of two inches.

Glasgow offered me a bunk. We went down the stairs.

'I always say my prayers,' he said. 'Good habit, praying. You pray, too.'

'Shall I?'

'Yes, do.'

I sat on the edge of the bunk and wondered as he knelt there, praying. There were no dry sandbags about. I wrapped my feet in my blanket and pulled my coat over my shoulders. The freezing wind blew down the shaft of the dugout on to my feet and prevented me from sleeping. The cold climbed up my body, and made it feel damp. I got up and went out. Glasgow snored. It was nice to be able to wear a soft cap again.

At daybreak we went walking above ground through fields in which turnips and lettuces struggled with weeds. Across the Arras-Gavrelle road was the day OP in some German gun pits on the Fampoux road. They were wonderful gun pits joined up by subterranean passages, full of sleeping galleries and ammunition stores. The superstructure was timbered and concreted and quite waterproof.

Our staff as usual wanted the war stirring up. We spotted a German working party near Fresnes and scattered it with shrapnel at long range. It was so peaceful our divisional infantry could quickly demand retaliatory fire for every sort of projectile. A single 'pineapple' bomb might earn eight rounds of HE. The front line was held by isolated posts, a sort of winter quarters easily discernible by the enemy. But it was still peaceful.

There were three days and three nights to be spent between the two OPs. It was very cold in the gun pit. There were two boxes to sit on. We stayed there from 8.0 in the morning till 4.30 in the afternoon, looking through the mouth of it to the German front. The rain drove in through the opening. It was too cold and wet to write letters. Glasgow's mess was very warm. Going out in the starlit morning, the cold fell on one like a blast, it embraced one like the touch of metal on the bare skin. In the gun pit we kept a full petrol tin of water. When the day was aired we shaved and washed in cold water from the tin. We were not clean.

It was so quiet that a social conscience awoke. I invited some infantry subalterns to the OP and telephoned to the battery for biscuits and a bottle of port. The whole idea tickled the infantrymen immensely. They knocked at the doorway of the gun pit and said in affected tones, 'Is the observation officer at home this morning?' We stood in the gun pit in British warms and mufflers, glasses slung round our necks, and drank port. They wanted to see the new thermite shell fired. It burst in a wonderful cloud of thick white smoke and incandescent flame. We put three or four rounds in Fresnes and set fire to a tree. It was an incendiary shell. The infantry were very contemptuous of the 'winter quarters' plan. In a show, they said, the Germans would just nip off the posts and smash them at leisure. We talked about the new gas projectors. Nobody knew exactly what they were.

One night, looking north, I saw a sudden flame billow over the line, an enormous golden hedge of fire. Then the sound of a confused explosion came. It was the gas projectors, seven hundred of them, all discharged at once. They were buried in rows in the earth, cylinders of gas each in their own mortar. The officer pushed a button and they all went over together.

Back at the battery I found there was another show on. The cupola dugout was finished. Like all cupola dugouts it was uncomfortable because the arch closed over one's head; there were no corners in which a man could lounge. In one angle we made a shaft of bent corrugated iron to the earth level, for a chimney, and put other sheets above it for a baffle-plate to diffuse the smoke. I had to stay up all night for the show. I chopped up ammunition boxes with a pickaxe to keep the fire going. The smoke blew back into the dugout. It was hard to keep awake. I wrote a letter. My hand dragged on the paper. I made some tea on the wood ashes, my eyes running with the wood smoke. At five the show was all over. I slept for two hours.

I went on to battalion headquarters. It was a deep dugout, walled with sawn timber. The upper half of the wall was white washed, the lower half covered with sacking. All over the wall were pictures of girls by Raphael Kirchner. The colonel's chair was an article of Empire fashion, covered in golden silk, its frame gilded and ornamented with rosebuds and cherubs in enamel. The chair had come out of the village. The dugout was most luxurious. When my tour was ended Backhouse came up to carry down my blankets, and brought up six letters, long overdue. It was early afternoon.

As we bumped down the long communication trench I read my mail in disconnected sentences between the traverses. It was four or five days since any letters had come for me.

There was a bucket of hot water waiting for me in my dugout at the battery. The dugout was nine feet long, three feet six wide and seven feet high. I let down the gas blanket to keep the steam in, and washed all over. I was going on leave. I packed *David Penstephen* and *The Song of Renny* in my rucksack and rode off to Arras. On the way I met C. riding up to meet me. He turned round and accompanied me to the station.

'By the way,' he said, 'you remember my row with that old general in the Ravine, about the gun position? You never heard how it finished; I hadn't a chance to see you. I was hauled up before the general in the Tunnels. There were two or three other tabs about, footling people. The old fool said I was guilty of insolence. Very politely I asked him whether he remembered asking me a question. He said he did. "I answered it in a respectful manner, sir." They argued about that a bit and then the general said I was guilty of conduct likely to cause despondency among the troops. That was a surprise! I got out of it, though. I pointed out that the nearest gunner was at least ten yards away, as I had particularly noticed, or so I said, and that unless the general was a troop I couldn't have caused despondency. They argued a bit about that, too. The general got very red and said at last, "You must accept a severe reprimand and we'll consider that the end of the matter." I say, what a nerve! "Sorry, sir," I said, "can't do that, sir. Sorry, sir, can't give a severe reprimand without a court martial. King's Regulations." You should have seen them. They knew it was true; the general wanted to save his face. He ordered me out and said he would report me to our general for inefficiency.'

'I say, he won't do that, will he?'

'What's the use of worrying? No, I don't suppose so. Look here, I must get back for stables. You might post this in town for me.'

Put it in the pocket of the rucksack with the others.'

'You do look clean and tidy – all dressed up and going on leave. Cheer-ho!'

When he saw me Sam cried out, '"Hey baloo, my own sweet Donal," come and have a drink; we are unobserved.' He was ill. He told me about Rheims Wood. . . .

'The bloodiest place, marching, you know, ugh-ugh-ugh-ugh, through tall broken trees on a roadway made of brushwood. French *poilu* for guide, frightfully windy, wanted us all to run. Nothing doing though. Then, plunk! four 5.9s in the next platoon. No bloody guide. NBG. Running away at a split-arse gallop. Hours of that. Then we got somewhere. I can't tell you what happened. The usual stuff, gas, shells, machine guns. Then there was me and Webster and eight men in two shell holes in hellish sunshine, and no water. Well, I don't know. I think it was on the fifth day – now, look here, am I really a coward?'

'Of course not, Sam.'

'Webster said I was a coward. "Who's a coward?" I said, drawing my revolver. "You are," he said, drawing his. "I am?" "Yes, you are!" " – you, I'll show you, you bastard, I'll race you to that wood." So we ran like maniacs to the wood, in and out of shell holes, through the ditch, into the trees, screaming at the top of our voices. Then . . . Christ! ... we saw a bloody great German machine gunner waiting for us behind a steel shield. We dropped like dead 'uns. "Go back, you maniac," I said to Webster. We crawled back to the ditch and lay there till it was dark enough to risk. And all the time I waited for the Hun to crawl up and bomb us.'

'Where did you get that *Croix de Guerre avec palme*?'

'The damned liars said I captured two machine guns with *"beaucoup de mordant"*'

'Didn't you?'

'Not that I know of. I did have to absorb two kisses from a French general. Perhaps they give medals to anyone they think will stand being kissed. . . . Think of it! In front of the whole bloody battalion!'

Sam coughed incessantly and his face became a deep red. His eyes had recovered but his lungs were injured by gas, and his back was covered with marks of burning like boils and long red wheals.

'Come up to the tarn. Three years ago we skated.'

'I always looked damned foolish on skates.'

We sat at the edge of the water to recover breath. Sam's fingers turned blue.

'As cold as charity, and that's very chilly But not so cold as poor bloody Willy,' Sam said. 'Don't you think our garden suburb is about the last word?'

'Why?'

'Lousy with Wesleyans and other simps.'

'It is a bit bad.'

We walked round the tarn. Sam coughed, all crouched up. 'I like that Wesleyan hymn,' he said,

'Whatever, Lord, we lend to Thee, Repaid a thousandfold will be —'

He managed to insert a laugh between his gasps. 'Listen! —

'Then *gladly* will we lend to Thee.'

'Do you remember walking to the "White Swan" at Middleham?'

'I wish we could go there now.'

'Feet is in Egypt. Where's Islay?'

'Islay's got killed.'

'Oh, blast it! Is he really? The damned nice lad.'

'Pip's in the Field Artillery, and Monty in the Garrison gunners.'

'I know; I met him at le Havre. Sixty-pounders.'

'I can't stand this. Let's go to the Wheatley for a drink.'

Sam kept playing with a phrase on the way down, when he could fetch his breath. 'A squad of winsome Wesleyan wenches will parade for duty with white feathers. ... A bevy of Wesleyan vestals will parade for feather pickets at the Great Lamp ... if it weren't for the family I'd never stay in this Godforsaken hole,' he said, 'I know the most perfect darling of a girl in Nottingham. God, you never saw such lips for kissing.'

We went along arm in arm.

'We shall be stopped by this fool – Good morning, Mr Crabshaw.'

'You'll be back from the front?'

'Yes, Mr Crabshaw, back from the front, Mr Crabshaw,' Sam said politely.

'Not sorry to be back either, I suppose?'

'Not at all sorry,' Sam said, bowing.

'And I suppose it's not always very comfortable?'

'Not always.'

'Ah, well, you chaps'll have to keep it up. We're doing all we can at home. A fight to a finish, you know.'

'We do all we can for you, Mr Crabshaw, we do all we can.'

'Come on.'

'It is heartening to think we are fighting for Mr Crabshaw,' Sam said, ordering a drink. 'Here's to Islay, wherever he is.'

'Might as well include the others; Feet, Monty, Pip –'

'Not out of one glass. To do them justice we'd have to get blindo-blithero. It simply can't be done.'

'It's good to see a Christian soul in this Goddamned place,' he said. 'Being at home makes me puke. It's true all the youngish decent people are in France.'

'Oh, well, away with melancholy.'

'Remember – ?'

All the happy times were in the past.

The sheets in my own bed at home were cool and luxurious. There was a fire in the room. I slept badly. In the middle of the night I heard my mother come in to see if I were really there.

I went to see Edward. We were quite strange to each other. It wasn't any good.

Soon, very soon, I returned. At Folkestone I met two men with whom I had crossed. We went into the dining room of the big hotel by the landing stage. We ordered a bottle of Burgundy. The waiter handed each one of us a ticket, 'if you want wine, beer, or spirits, sir.'

'Officers returning to France are not allowed to drink intoxicating liquor. Others are requested to sign the following certificate – "I certify on my honour I am not returning to duty with the BEF."' The officer of the Buffs read it out.

'Blast their bloody impertinence. What shall we do?'

'Sign it; sign anything.'

We signed the cards.

At Boulogne we raced to the Louvre and booked rooms. Then we went to the Monet for soles and Chablis. Our train left in the morning.

Chapter 9

Hymn to Saturn

Flesquières – Winter 1917–18

W e went to see C Battery's billet.

'Here,' said Coleman impolitely, 'enter Counts Durti and Morzo, looking for a drink.'

'To whom do you apply these disgusting appellations?' Mac asked. 'We utterly refute them. We killed all our lice on the feast of Septuagesima. Anyway we are going to Italy. Explain to Morzo that we are going to Italy.'

'We're not going to Italy,' I said.

'Why in God's name shouldn't we go?'

'Because we should never have the luck.'

'You're a nice sort of optimist!'

'I say my prayers to Saturn and I'm never disappointed. Besides, think how delightful it will be for me if we do go. You fellows will have had all your fun.'

'Down with drink.'

'Success to crime.'

'Morzo, my love, we depart for Italy within ten days.'

'Divine Durti, I bet you twenty francs that before the end of those ten days we are going into action within fifty miles of this village.'

'Done.'

That was 18 November. I had found the brigade at rest. On the 22nd we had news of a great surprise attack towards Cambrai. Numbers of tanks had gone through leading the infantry. The same day we marched off towards the zone of the new battle. The newspapers told us that the joy-bells had been rung in York Minster and everyone was amused and shocked at this levity. Mac handed over his twenty francs and we were both disappointed.

We marched in the rain. It came down in brownish sheets as we went eastward. At nightfall we halted in some broken village of the Somme. The white ruins crawled up the hill on our right hand. There were huts to sleep in, and there we had just eaten when Spragg's face, shining with cordiality and rain, appeared in the door. He did a double shuffle. 'Come aboard, sir,' he said, 'attached for duty on the line of march.' He had been detached during the last fortnight.

'And in the nick of time, sir,' he said, a moment later, 'trust an old sailor to smell things out.'

'What have you smelt out, Spragg?' the major said.

'Needn't be a trouble to you, sir.' He put his finger to his nose. 'I just want my dear pal Immingham to step outside for a moment.'

The three of us went out together. It was true that we were short of a sound set of wheel harness. Spragg secretly unfolded his plan to the sergeant major, who sniggered and said cunningly, 'Trust an old sailor, sir!'

'Trust an old sailor!' Spragg said thickly, 'now where's the driver?'

The wind blew noisily among the ruins and the rain drummed on the corrugated roofs. I followed the party up the hill a few hundred yards. Spragg disappeared into some horse lines and the driver discreetly followed. Five minutes later they appeared carrying a set of wheel harness in a blanket.

'I thought so!' Spragg said, 'they'd just dumped the harness in the lines in horse-blankets. I had a few words with the stable picket and meantime, hey presto! a set of harness disappears. Nothing to do with me, my dear old friend. I know nothing about it!'

In the morning the rain continued. We passed through the battlefield which the Germans had evacuated because it had become useless. Farther ahead lay the belt of country their army had wasted to make our living difficult and uncomfortable. The whole countryside had been destroyed. We marched through Bapaume by night and at last came to the bones of a village called Bus. Two days later Immingham and I were marching to a shooting range in the old front line, with two guns which had to be calibrated in haste. It was a very dark night as we made towards Péronne. The land on the west was so convulsed that there was no road across it till we came to Rancourt. The earth made banks of darkness on either hand, fringed with tussocks of grass. We passed through the ruins of Combles and between Guillemont and Montauban we came upon the huts of a salvage camp and halted there. The roads were hard with frost. The salvage officers heard the section and asked us to have a drink. We went in and they told us they had now almost finished tidying up Trônes Wood, taking out bodies, shells, wire and timber. An Indian NCO came in and spoke to the OC, and went out again.

'Good fellow that,' he said. 'Spotted some deserters in High Wood the other day. Damn queer how they lived. This fellow was near Bazentin le Grand, with a pair of field glasses. Saw something move on the edge of High Wood. Two, three men. Mind you, there's no track of any kind there, now, not for three or four miles. Absolute desert now. Next evening we both went. I saw them too, coming above ground at dusk. I suppose they were going out to look for food among the corpses. Next morning I armed the NCOs and we went down there and tracked them to their dugout. Seven or eight surrendered.'

'What about the rest?'

'They tried to shoot.'

'You had to shoot back, sir?'

'Couple of bombs. Dugout timbers collapsed. All buried.'

'Good God! Immingham said. 'Where did they get food?'

'Off the corpses, I suppose. I didn't ask them. But once or twice queer things have happened. We found an empty mess cart by Mametz; no driver, no food in it. If you're starving you'll do most things. The driver never was found.'

'What would they get, the others?'

'There's only one thing you could do with them.'

'Shoot them!'

'I believe some of those fellows had been there since the line moved forward a year ago. You know, they'd rather face that than go and fight.'

As we went over the hill and down to Mametz we talked of those lost men in the wilderness. The horses walked on through the dark with a quickened step. The lead-driver bent over to me.

'These horses, sir, are remembering the old wagon line; watch them take the turning at Fricourt.'

I rode by him. He dropped his reins. Without a touch the horses swung round.

'More'n a year ago, sir.'

We found the hut at Bécourt, a shack of corrugated iron. The rain had made great puddles on the floor. The place was deserted like the whole of the old battlefield; it was nearly twenty miles eastward before there was life above ground. We tended the horses and slept. Major Stansfield arrived in the morning. The two guns were placed on the markers to shoot upon the target in our old position on Pepperbox Hill. The long grass was growing over the shell holes now and the road up the Valley of Death had been smoothed over by the rain. The grass was growing over its edges. This was where Conrad and I had walked.

We hurried back as quickly as we had come. There had been continuous fighting up by Bourlon Wood where we tried to hold the German counter-attack. Raven told me about it. He had just got a cushy job looking after small-arms ammunition in an enormous dump when he got orders to arrange and deliver a supply of ammunition in the Wood. So there he was in the middle of the battle with his mules, looking for people to take the ammunition, and there was such a strafe going on he could find nobody. At last he unloaded the boxes from the mules, dead or alive, and sent the living ones back, and himself ploughed round till he could find someone. He was very shaken up. 'Fifty times I said *na poo,* standing about with those mules right in the line; no guides, no unloading party. Anyway they got the stuff. And do you know, I believe it saved us.'

The battle came nearer. At half past nine a staff car came running into the village. The major said, 'That looks like business. Harness up. I'm going to brigade.'

Before ten we were in the gun park ready to move off. People were running about all over the village. The major trotted up to me.

'I've reported us ready to move off,' he said, 'is that right?'

'Yes sir.'

'Very well. I shall take Mac ahead. Bring the battery to Metz en Couture by Neuville Bourjonval. If I'm not at Metz bring the guns into action there, on Gonnelieu, and stand by.'

'Very good, sir.'

'Bring them along as quickly as you can.'

'May we trot, sir?'

'On the level, if the road's clear. We're first.'

'Yes, sir.'

The battery was waiting. 'Walk march!' I shouted. We turned out of the field and entered the road. Nobody knew what was happening in front. We turned south towards Metz. An ASC (Army Service Corps) officer came trotting round the corner in front, and when he saw the guns he stood up in his stirrups and shouted, 'Are you the guns going forward?' I shouted 'Yes!' Then he turned round and I heard him bawling out to his column of heavy wagons, 'ASC! make way for the guns, make way for the guns.' This was so unusual I felt bound to honour him; we broke into a trot and I gave the order for the ceremonious 'eyes right'—for he was on the right of the road – and he stood to receive it like a general, saluting each team with rigid courtesy. Metz now came into view. The road was full of small parties without arms, marching between Guardsmen with fixed bayonets. But they all marched the wrong way; they all faced us. Then on the roadside there came a procession of artillery men, carrying dial-sights. It struck me abruptly that the infantry and artillery in front had been driven in. They were under arrest, these parties, deserters in the face of the enemy. A colonel of artillery galloped past on the grass margin. As he met me he waved his arms and shouted, 'It's hell up there. I've lost all my guns and men.'

'This,' I said to myself, 'is very encouraging.'

There was a block in Metz. We halted. On the roadside a subaltern was sitting, leaning his chin on his hand. We stared at each other.

'Hallo! Aren't you Hugo?' I called. 'I haven't seen you since school!

'Yes. How are you? I am glad to see you.'

'Not so bad. But this isn't very nice, is it?'

'I don't know what the hell to do. I'm Heavy Machine Guns; tanks, you know. All my fellows have bunked. I suppose they'll all be arrested and shot.'

'What's happened?'

'The Boche has swept through. The line was only thin. He's retaken the front up to Gouzeaucourt, just over the hill there. If he gets on the Queen's Cross Ridge – that's it, there – he can see right down here. I wish I knew what to do.'

'Come with us.'

'I better go and report to someone.'

We shook hands and said goodbye.

The battery moved on. Mac was standing in a field with his arms up like a fat scarecrow. I brought the guns into action at the trot as though it were a drill parade. The battery was much amused and laughed. Mac laid out a line of fire. We fired a short barrage. It sounded very thin. There were only eighteen guns and six howitzers. Nothing else happened till nightfall. Then Stansfield sent me up to make liaison with the Guards Brigade in front. I found the general on the Queen's Cross Ridge, sheltering under a tarpaulin sheet with his staff. He was a fierce little man.

'Where's your telephone?' he said.

'There, sir,' I said, pointing to the cart. 'The telephone will be through in three or four minutes, and also a signalling lamp.' The mules' ears bobbing on the track seemed comic at that moment.

'Very well. You will fire a barrage in the morning. The orders will be given direct to the battery.'

'Yes sir.'

There was nothing to do. The telephonist and I dug a deep hole for ourselves and covered it with a mackintosh sheet. It was very cold and smelt like frost. The Guards in front had armed people with anything they could find; even shovels and picks. They attacked and re-took Gouzeaucourt with the help of our small barrage. In the morning the major took me forward to look at the front. There was a solitary British field gun on the far crest. It was surrounded by empty cartridge cases and shell holes.

'That must be the one that mopped up some thousands of Huns yesterday,' the major said. 'They fired shrapnel over open sights until the gun was put out of action by combined shellfire and riflefire. The subaltern is in for the Victoria Cross. He fired the gun himself when everyone else was laid out.'

'He must have been damned courageous.'

'It's not unlikely. Look at it; right in the open facing the enemy. But what a target! The Germans came down the road on the right. Exciting work, what?'

'Very exciting.'

We walked along the crest. On our left there was a depression, and in it the guns of our companion brigade were aligned, eighteen of them. The colonel and his staff stood up midway between the flanks; then in three smaller groups the battery commanders, and after these, kneeling between pairs of guns, the section commanders. The shells were falling among them. It was a surprising sight; exactly like a barrack square. Stansfield said, 'Well, I'm damned! That's their new colonel, Bowes; look! He won't take cover or kneel and he won't let Captain Wilson, either! They won't stay there very long!'

We shifted the guns forward to the protection of an earthen bank. The frost bit deep into the ground and made it hard digging for cover. We came to rock chalk a foot down. Meanwhile we lived in tents and stuffed the ventilators with sandbags to keep the cold out. We put on all the warm clothing we could. My seaboots were warm. Under my helmet I wore a knitted cap ending in a long muffler and under my British warm a goatskin. The men wore goatskins over five or six layers of wool, and wound their necks with mufflers.

HYMN TO SATURN

We had a spell in the digging. 'What price a game of cricket!' Gunner Barrett shouted. He and his mate arranged themselves on an imaginary pitch. Barrett sought centre with an imaginary bat. Sergeant Wilson dropped his pick and swaggered in at the other end of the wicket. The bowler delivered an imaginary ball. Barrett hit a boundary and ran it for four. His next stroke was even more impressive. 'That's hit Jerry,' the umpire said, nodding towards the line. Apparently Barrett was set. The next ball made a terrific racket in the wicketkeeper's leather mittens. 'How's that, umpire?' he shouted. Everyone shouted, 'Well held, sir!' Barrett walked doggedly to long field. The light was fading. I served out the rum ration to the sergeants. There was tinned herring and roast beef for dinner, with a sort of trifle made of army biscuits soaked in water and buried under a layer of custard made of tinned milk and custard powder. There was whisky and port. The night air was like cold iron. Spragg, Immingham and myself slept in one tent. Spragg went to bed early.

As soon as we turned in he began to moan. 'Oh, will nobody help me, what on earth shall I do?'

'What's the matter, Spragg?' Immingham asked. He had stripped off his coats.

'Will nobody fetch me a drink of water? What on earth shall I do?'

Immingham crawled under the tent brailing, shivering audibly, and went to the water butt. I heard him hammering on the ice with an entrenching tool. He gave Spragg a mug of water.

'Thank you, Boyd, for all you've done for me,' Spragg quavered, 'I'll never forget it.'

'*Mon dieu*!' Immingham said. 'Listen to that! And me blue with cold. You're drunk Spragg, disgustingly drunk. This is Immingham, not Boyd.'

'No, no, it's ague, honestly, it's ague.'

He went sick in the morning and became the colonel's orderly officer.

With him went Immingham's pet cooking set.

The wagon line stayed at Metz until it was shelled out. The weather had broken. We set out for Vick-six-ack, (V6A) a map square near Fins, in rain which continued all the way, and at the journey's end we found that the place the staff had chosen was an empty down with no blade of shelter. The rain swept across it in slanting columns.

'How many tarpaulins have we?'

'I managed to "buy" a few, sir,' QMS Wills said.

'I think we have rights to the best part of the rum ration. The guns are far better off than we.'

'I've told the cooks to make tea and a rum punch.'

It was dark now. In the panic of the retreat from Gouzeaucourt someone had slashed the canvas water tanks on the top of the down. We watered the horses slowly from folds. The horses cowered in the rain and would not drink, playing with their loose lips in the pools. After feed the men slung the tarpaulins between pairs of wagons and lay on their waterproof sheets. The rain ran across the groundsheets and blew into the bivouacs. We had two tents and packed them full. The rum was dished out. It was after nine o'clock and I walked round the lines. The men were singing. They were singing 'Water Melons,' 'The Good Ship Yacka-hickey-doola,' and a song called 'Section Commanders and their Sins'. The sergeants' tent was very rowdy. In the other the men were lying across each other on the floor. I would have to get up at half-past three to take ammunition to Wild Boar Valley and I stepped across the sleepers to my camp bed.

Late at night someone crawled into the tent shouting for me. It was C, drunk. He had found the sergeants' tent and spent an hour with them. He turned his electric torch on my face.

'D'no how I got here, d'no where I am,' he said.

'You look too sober to be true, you damned semi-teetotaller. Gimme a drink.'

'I haven't a drop of any kind.'

I was angry with him because he had drunk so much while I had drunk nothing, not even a cup of punch.

'Serves you jolly well right.'

The men on the floor made a bit of room for him.

The rain ran under the brailing and the tent stank of wet wool and close breathing.

There were tinned sausages for breakfast at the battery, thin, like fingers with the ends chopped off. I got to bed at two in the afternoon, feeling ill, and slept till seven in the morning. The rain had stopped and the frost was back again. Soon the ground became hard, like iron. The colonel and the major stood near the battery talking. A 5.9 came down. The major heard it first and flung himself down. His skull was fractured. The colonel was killed. The Guards' Division had just recommended him for promotion to brigadier general. The major, as he lay on a stretcher with a crimson trickle running down his face, sent for Immingham. Immingham was much upset.

'Don't panic, Immingham,' the major said. 'Take down these instructions in writing . . .'

Rawley became major. We were at Havrincourt. He unwrapped the photograph of his girl and spent hours studying the women's underwear advertisements of Messrs Venn. Messrs Venn's special trade was to prepare sets of underwear ornamented with regimental colours and badges for dispatch to best girls, at the order of their boys in the field. You simply specified set so-and-so and sent a cheque. Mr Venn did the rest. So 'Venn's Undies' became a household word in the army. Rawley eventually chose black satin.

'I reely think black satin would suit the little darling,' he said, twisting his miniature moustache. 'Think so, Mac?'

'She would be the sweetest yums, major.'

'If only she were here, I could eat her,' Rawley said, shutting his eyes.

'Ah,' Mac said, very cunningly.

'No naughty thoughts, Mac,' Rawley said coyly, with a lifted finger.

There was a large room in Bus and six or seven of us lived in it. An orderly came down from the guns. 'You are ordered to report at the gun position at 18.00 on Christmas day for dinner, bed and breakfast,' the message ran, 'bunk provided AAA.' Underneath was written, in Mac's hand, 'Be sure to come. The doings will be monumental. Christmas costumes by WD and Moses Moss. Rum by SRD. Benediction by Sergeant Peace.' It was Christmas Eve and the snow was falling from a grey sky. We took some bottles of whisky across to the sergeants' mess and returned to drink gin and vermouth by the fire. Gerald and C. were there. We sat together, opposite the two Colemans and drank healths to each other in whisky. The new Scottish-Canadian vet was a small, merry man of about fifty, and when he smiled his face disappeared in creases. He danced a Highland fling. Clarence, our French interpreter, smiled fatly and played a trick with currants out of the plum pudding. 'See!' he said, 'I make him fly through the air. Now he stick on the roof! Bing! Anuzzer one!' The Colemans, sons of a parson, sang carols. The sergeants came to wish us a happy Christmas and begged the favour of a return visit. On the way through the yard two or three officers fell out to be sick. We drank with the sergeants. Then Clarence and I sat up to write home upon Christmas morning.

The party was wakened about nine by the doctor, who beat people with his stick. He was very angry because the room was not cleared for breakfast. He refused breakfast. He raved at us from the door, and said he would spend the day in Bapaume at the Officers' Club. We went after him in gum-boots, pyjamas and overcoats. The ground was covered with snow.

'Don't be silly, Doc, don't go to that Godforsaken hole.'

'Dammit, it's Christmas morning.'

'Be a Christian, Doc'

His irascible eyes seemed to start out of his face. 'I'll go where the air is clean enough for a human being to breathe,' he said. 'Do you think I'm going to spend Christmas Day with such a set of pigs?' He trotted off in the snow.

We had got two barrels of beer for the men, pork, cabbage, Christmas pudding, apples, oranges and nuts. These things had taken us three weeks to collect.

I was glad to think that after midday dinner I should begin my journey to the guns. I told Hampstead I should not ride. Nothing could be more pleasant on Christmas Day than to have this sort of a holiday, to walk through the snow alone and undisturbed, and at the end of the journey to be greeted by friends. It was almost as good as though one walked out of the station at Grassington, leaving the village behind, and strode out on the road up to the cottage at Starbottom, knowing that the fires would be lit and the house full of merry people. Upon the dresser there would stand the enormous double-handled funnel which someone had presented as a challenge cup, standing in a treacle tin painted ebony black, and perhaps they might have pushed a cork into the funnel and turned it into a loving cup. Meantime I plodded in the silent snow. The rucksack, full of late parcels, clung comfortably to my back. My box respirator bumped a little on my left side, my steel helmet on my right shoulder, and I swung my long Malacca trench stick at my side. I wished the guns were even more than ten or twelve miles away as I walked along the empty road.

In front the black trunks of Havrincourt Wood rose from the snow, sheltering small corrugated huts, livid in the winter evening. The curls of grey smoke rose among the straight, bare timber to the darker sky. The huts were propped and patched in all manner of ways, draped raggedly with frosted sacking. I pursued my way on a ride through the wood as night fell, and after a little while a brilliant moon rose and threw upon the snow at either hand the grey shadows of the trees. A couple of infantrymen met me, walking with the rapid shuffling gait which seemed to be induced by life in trenches; shoulders bent, chins forward, steel helmets inclined to the ground, the feet at an angle of ninety degrees, and the rifle slung upon the right shoulder and rising above it in the air.

HYMN TO SATURN

They must have come from some camp nearby, for when I came to the clearing the snow in front of me was undisturbed. Between the walls of timber the snow shone with soft and brilliant whiteness, a field of spectral purity. The track was untrodden, the night entirely still, and I stood for a moment to listen to the strange unanimity of silence which had fallen on the armies. On my right hand a high bank was pierced with niches leading to dugouts, and from one of them a splinter of candlelight broke into the blue night, and I heard someone singing a line from a Christmas carol. In another mile or two the wood ended and disclosed at a little distance the hill of Havrincourt and the roofs upon it shining in the moonlight where they emerged from trees. Over the dry ditch by which I walked, the larches in the chateau grounds were lightly rimed with snow. I followed the road through the village to the eastern wall of the chateau where it stood as a mark upon the edge of the front. The shallow valley leading up to Ribécourt slept under the snow, strangely lighter than the sky, and across it, in monstrous black zig-zags, the captured Hindenberg Line leaped from one crest to another.

Immediately at hand the guns lay under their shelters and behind them the trees of the plantation marked the ditch from which the dugout descended. As I skirted the position the sentry called wishes for a happy Christmas. Besides ourselves not a soul stirred. The candles glimmered in the lamps on the aiming posts and the moon shone among stars. I walked up the dry ditch among the relics of the German retreat, cowskin packs, water bottles, bundles of sandbags made of twisted paper thread, bayonets and a machine gun. For a moment I stood under the bare trees and stared over the snow towards the enemy and then put aside the gas-blanket and descended the dugout shaft, forty steps below ground, as safe and stuffy a hide as anyone could desire. I stood at the foot of the stairs, smiling at the warmth as they shouted at me, and Mac tried to kiss me with fairylike leapings. A sprig of mistletoe had come from England, and he had stuck it in a crack of the roof timbers.

The dugout was one gallery about thirty feet long and four feet wide, with two transepts running off it, large enough for bunks. The servants occupied the northern half and the officers the other.

The table was laid. There were three bottles of champagne standing on a cloth of newspaper. A case of whisky was open on the floor. There was even a Christmas tree cut from the plantation.

'My hat, this is luxury!'

'Not 'arf, sir,' Tanner said, 'but it's nothing to what's coming.'

Tanner had made *hors d'oeuvre* from two olives, a tin of sardines and the scrapings of a tin of bloater paste. Then there was turkey garnished with ham. After dinner the sergeants came down and settled in with the whisky.

'Dear Sam,' I wrote, 'so much water, so to speak, has passed beneath the bridge I haven't had time to catch the scintillating drops of pleasure and turn them into ink. That's real good, I think, when there's hell's own noise going on in this cellar. A party of much shelled subalterns is trying to play bridge, also the gram, is going. Mud, 4.2s and horses are the real trouble. Will you let me try again to persuade you not to chase over here a fourth time? If you have a decent chance of staying, don't hesitate. I work like hell trying to wangle something, but I'm one of those for whom things don't wang properly. I hear Geoffrey has an adjutant's job somewhere; love to him. Glad to hear of your success with the girl. There aren't any within forty miles of us. More noise outside. Must go. Three cheers.'

The Flesquières Salient was gloomy. The long grass growing on the wasted fields was depressing in its monotony and made the earth itself dark coloured. All the villages had been blown up where they stood, and the army lived, at best, among the ruins. Even shattered Albert was over thirty kilometres away and Amiens, the nearest centre of civil life, was over sixty. The weather held to about ten degrees of frost and the ground was so hard that even the big HE shells burst on impact instead of burying themselves before detonation, and the fids of metal sometimes travelled as far as eight hundred yards by measure. Thus on the road up to the OP, in the outer wall of a gardener's lodge in Flesquières, we met sunburst patterns in the snow, bare to the earth at the centre, where shells had emptied their metal over the landscape; and every journey became more hazardous.

The water ran out at OP and Eldred came to me one evening with his mess tin piled high with snow. He punctured a Cafay-O-Lay tin and spelled out 'Happy New Year' on the cake top before putting it on the tiny fire of wood chips.

In January and February we were sick alternately. Either one or the other would have a queasy stomach and a splitting headache. Starvation was the cure. Some blamed the rich tinned Maconochie ration or cooked meat and vegetables, but the sickness went about, like influenza, indifferently. The substantial reports of a German attack made the staff restless. One day they announced that we were to have a fish ration. A crowd gathered to see what it was. It turned out to be sardines. This was such a laughing stock of a fish ration that nobody turned out to see the rabbits arrive, but they did arrive, frozen rabbits, as stiff as sticks, but quite good to eat.

Each battery was divided; four guns went into a position from which they did not fire; the two remaining did the shooting for six. Sergeant Peace was in charge when Backhouse and I arrived at this active section. He wished to lay before me a complaint concerning the morality of attracting fire deliberately to this German dugout, which faced the wrong way and was therefore vulnerable. But life continued quietly for a few days. Then Peace became troubled about Backhouse's gun drill.

'An officer's servant, sir, is an anachronism in a citizen army,' he said.

'I shouldn't call this a citizen army, Sergeant Peace.'

'Nor I, sir. But he ought to know his gun drill. There's his proficiency pay to consider.'

Then Backhouse came along and said solemnly that there were many difficulties, but he ought to do some work on the guns. Would lunchtime do?

'Certainly; give me something cold. I shall be quite happy.'

Backhouse gave me a contemptuous look.

'How do you think I should have the face to give you a cold lunch, sir? It's ridiculous! I'll arrange it.'

There was no compromise in either.

The dugout was pervaded with dirt. My hairbrushes showed a daily advance in blackness. 'I am clean for thirty seconds every day,' I told Sam, 'immediately after the hot wash a.m., and I dare not take off my clothes for fear of getting dirtier.' The place was dark and slumbrous. I slept for hours with the section in this deep grave. We fired by night and by day. They shelled a little for they knew exactly where we were. Then we made them angry by bursts of rapid fire. We were all down below when the first reply fell over our heads, like blows with a stick on the ground. They went on for an hour and began on the dugout. The first crash blew all the candles out on the bottom tunnel. This was more exciting. Sergeant Peace came stumbling along. 'They've blown in our doorway, sir,' he said, excitedly.

'There's still another.'

'Shooting like that they'll soon hit it.' As he spoke a shell landed on the other entrance. We jumped, and then looked up the long shaft to the patch of sky veiled by drifting smoke.

'It's all right, look!'

'You take it calmly, sir, but what if both are stopped up?'

'Dig ourselves out.'

'We haven't any spades, sir.'

'Well, we'll use forks then.'

Backhouse snorted.

Peace stamped away angrily. The telephone wire had gone. We sat on our bunks and waited till it was over. Then at night we repaired the damage. Rawley and Mac came over to tell me what a fine sight the strafe had made.

Up there they were digging galleries underground from the bottom of a large crater. The galleries themselves were made, and now the working parties were turning towards each other, to join them up. Day by day they dug and knocked and heard each other distinctly. The sandbags of earth were emptied to protect the entrances. Then suddenly the whistle blew and everyone sank down where they stood until the enemy plane had passed over us and out of sight. Everything was covered with camouflage wire on poles as if we were in a birdcage, and when the sun shone, the knots of canvas on the wire cast flecks of shadows in our faces. There was not much sun. It was still cold. Before the tunnels were made to join we had to borrow an Engineer officer. The diggers were working parallel.

The snow fell again. The nights were clear, with a moon. I was at OP I had been shooting on our zero line, on the edge of Orival Wood. A new division of infantry was in the line and I went along to spend the night with them. They had been out a few months and the colonel was still aggressive. He thought nothing of artillerymen. To satisfy him I had to go out in front with his observation officer, a nice young man. After dinner we went out of Flesquières by sandbagged passages, till we stood on the snowfield sloping towards the German line. The infantryman breathed deeply and looked up to the brilliant moon. He led the way past the skeleton of one of our planes. At last we came to his night OP, perched high up in the bank of a sunken road, which ran towards the Germans. We could see nothing but the shadow of the wood on the snow. The front was silent at the moment. At last we turned to go, and walked out on the road. A machine gun suddenly whipped out at us; we dropped and sheltered behind the snowdrifts. When I got up again I saw the crust in the centre of the road was furrowed by the bullets. We hurried out of sight, bending double and running. 'Wasn't that exciting!' the infantryman said. The sandbagged alley through the houses was blown in just as we came to it and a sentry was hit. The colonel was highly excited and full of accusations. He refused us space to lie down.

'You gunners are always in the way,' he said.

'We only come to battalion headquarters to put the guns at your disposal, sir.'

He laughed. 'You come for a free meal and a drink, I think.'

'It has been the custom ever since I came out in May 1915, for an artillery subaltern to spend the night with the infantry, sir, but I've no doubt, if you wish it, you could do without. Our subalterns would not object. We have wire beds at our OP, I am quite ready to go back there; in fact I'll go as soon as I have sent a message. Any observations you wish I will willingly report to my colonel.' I went out and dictated, loudly: 'Returning to OP for night at request infantry CO. AAA.'

'If you want me tomorrow, sir, perhaps you will ask my brigade for me.'

We put on our kit, shouldered our sandbags of food and went out into the trench behind the village. It was about two in the morning and the mud on the duckboards had frozen. It was like treading on sticks of toffee. The declining moon lighted the gully and the stars shone brilliantly before us.

'At first they wouldn't let me connect up, sir,' Eldred said. 'The adjutant said I had no business there. Do you know anything about them?'

'Probably the second line to the — ty-worst Division.'

We dropped into our dugout at OP and slept till daybreak. The morning was black, and so cold we crouched as we went into the concrete chamber to look at the line. Eldred lit a cigarette and coughed and coughed, his six feet of length jerking about like a marionette. Then I lit a cigarette and coughed too, and the warm breath condensed on our mufflers. Eldred woke the junior telephonist and told him to make breakfast. Soon the wood smoke rose in the morning air, mixed with the delicious smell of bacon. The water boiled. Eldred emptied the screwed newspaper of mixed tea and sugar into the boiling water and we ate and drank.

During the day orders came from brigade to return to the infantry at night. They were much more polite, and Eldred winked at me discreetly. The third day we were relieved. On the way back we had to do much running to dodge the shells. When we got to a bit of cover the young telephonist said he could not go on without a rest. Eldred produced a flask of rum and poured a stiff tot down his throat. We all had a drink and went on warmed by the spirit. Other times we slept with the infantry headquarters in Ribécourt, where the Naval Division occupied the brewery. The ground floor was one enormous hall open to the sky, ruined, like some monastic building, and in the corner there was a shaft which looked as large as a mousehole. A ladder went down into the cellars. Here the battalion headquarters lived and worked. Part of the vaults was occupied by a wooden staging of wire bunks, three decks high. At night we slept while telephones and the infantry maintained a rapidly intermittent buzzing and the orderlies pushed in and out through the ragged blankets at the lower doorway; it was like sleeping in a dream to be roused by the low-toned turbulence which went on there, where the conflicting candles threw enormous shadows on the shadowy brick walls and the adjutant's acetylene flare at times appeared, encircling his figure in an arc of white and violet.

Early in February there came a spring day. The mist cleared before the sun and the birds sang in the hedge under the OP. Through the soft air came the sounds of a man working on a wall, the ring of the trowel on the brickwork and then the tap of the wooden handle. The clouds floating under the sun threw cold shadows on the golden earth. Backhouse met me at the section dugout and said he was going to do some spring cleaning. We hammered some lumps of chalk into powder and mixed them with water. Then we smeared the whitening on the timbers of the dugout with a folded sandbag. I told Backhouse that Glasgow was coming to lunch.

'There's nothing that's really worth eating, sir.'

'Have another look round. There must be.'

After a while he came back with an unripe Camembert cheese.

'There's this!'

'It's too firm.'

'It'll be quite ripe when I've finished with it.'

Glasgow came, and we ate the Camembert with tea spoons, it was so soft. Then we sat on the bank outside, in the mild open air. The roofs of Havrincourt shone in the sun. Glasgow told me that Daddy Johnson had been given a comfortable job at Corps Headquarters. He also told me that the German attack was expected in the third week of March. He thought we ought to learn by heart the relevant parts of the Defence Plan, 'although,' he added, 'it's not sure that they will attack according to our plan; or even that they are so intelligent that they can understand it, assuming they have a copy.' When he went he borrowed President Wilson's new book, which I had received from home.

'Backhouse,' I said, 'what did you do to the Camembert?'

'I put it on the brazier for a few minutes, sir, experimentally. The experiment went further than I meant it to. That's all, sir.'

At Bus there was no time to rest. Wherever we went in the back country we rode in pairs for company. Gerald rode with me to the canteen at Ytres and then to the Field Cashier's office at Villiers-au-Flos, and was depressing about the war; not that we should lose, but that it would simply go on. In fact we had the best positions, now. But as I had just come to the conclusion that war was useless as a missionary enterprise and could only punish, and then not those acutely responsible, we came to the fullest and most dismal agreement. 'For,' Gerald said, 'it isn't this war but war itself; quite blind and unable to think except in its own terms. One comes to think,' he said, 'that there's no way out of it for any of us; that it just goes on. We're done, finished, and what we've done is quite worthless.'

'We remain for the duration.'

'Oh, yes, we're in it. There's no back door. Either we're *na poo'd* or we go on. Think of a hundred years war on this scale. A filthy, rotten business – with squits like our precious leaders thinking it's theirs to turn off and on, or patting us on the back and pretending they're only holding on till the right moment. Why, good God, it's GOT them.'

'I wonder if they could stop it if they wanted.'

'They don't want to. They think it's right and every bloody politician agrees; everyone thinks himself made in the image of God to punish Germany and believes he is so god-like that twenty thousand, a hundred thousand deaths aren't worth his stinking conscience. It makes you weep blood. They talk about Jesus Christ's death. They put some poor bloody Christ to death about a thousand times a day. "Greater love hath no man than this" surely applies to every miserable human being? Haven't their deaths the same value? Then why don't they stop it? But no, by God, they haven't, not to them. They've got such hellish good ideals that there's nothing on earth fit to touch them or restrain them. Think of the way they stamped on Lansdowne.'

'And they said Sassoon was insane.'

'The churches at least – ', I said.

'Whoever expected anything of the churches?'

'I did, at one time.'

'You're sentimental. Nobody else but an imbecile would have expected the churches to do anything but rat at the first opportunity.'

'But surely, even now they might?'

'Oh, no, they've funked too long, and Lloyd George has pocketed the Nonconformist conscience and eats a slice or so when he's hungry. Sweetbread!'

We rode along slowly, in silent gloom, through the yellow-grey evening. A few flakes of snow fell. Our uncouth village came in sight, and Gaby, my liver chestnut, pricked her ears forward and neighed.

'What's she like to ride?'

'Lovely. So well schooled, though I say it myself as shouldn't – though, in fact, Hampstead did most of it, didn't you Hampstead?'

I told him that the mare was a treasure and could be ridden without reins and he checked his horse at the crossroads to let me show him. She hesitated a moment and shook her head, but turned as I directed, away from home. I recalled the day on which Hampstead and I had picked her; a cold, blustering day, so harsh that the coats of all the twenty remounts were staring, and their backs tucked up in misery. The chestnut which we liked looked liverish and wicked, but still we chose her and led her away rather proud, to inspect her more carefully than had been possible before. Day by day she improved her coat and her manners and her muscle. Her mane had been cut and her tail pulled. She never was a beautiful animal; her quarters sloped a shade too much for that, but she was elegant and full of fire, sensitive and intelligent. Her legs were slim, muscular and springing; her forelegs grew into her chest with a fine balance. Hampstead and I kept her strictly to ourselves; nobody else in the battery rode her. If there was any need to lend a horse, Hampstead rode Gaby and offered the enormous strawberry, who pulled like a traction engine, but for all that was an excellent leaper. The strawberry had over three years' service to her credit, a fine looking animal who would have figured well in a picture book as a cavalry charger.

I had to pay out the men with money from the cashier. Sergeant Major Burnett was a short, redheaded man with a weakness for drink; but since his promotion he had become unusually smart and clean. His blue eyes blazed in his creamy face. The men lined up in the darkness by the corrugated shack in which Burnett slept with the office books. One by one they came forward and saluted. Forsyth, I noticed, showed his bare skin through the button holes of his tunic.

'What's happened to your underwear, Forsyth?'

'In the kip, sir.'

'Why? You can't go about in this weather without underwear.'

'Can't wear it, sir, too lousy.'

'Too lousy?'

'Crawling, sir, all over.'

'Have you been to the QMS?'

'Yes, sir.'

'Come back after pay and bring the stuff along.'

Quartermaster Sergeant Wills was faintly Jewish in appearance. He had pink cheeks and brown eyes, a hooked nose and a long brown moustache. But the most conspicuous thing about him was the thin gold chain which dangled from his gold eyeglass.

'Gunner Forsyth says his vest, shirt and cardigan are so lousy he can't wear them. Is that so?'

'I really don't know, sir.'

'Would you mind finding out at once, then, and issuing clean underwear to him if they are?'

'I couldn't issue him clean underwear, sir.'

'Why not?'

'The whole battery would want it.'

Wills was very obstinate and it was necessary to fight him step by step. At length I said:

'If you find such difficulty in getting clean stuff, and if, as you suggest, the whole of the wagon line is as lousy as Forsyth, we will walk down to the staff captain's office at once. We can just catch him before dinner, I think. I won't have the men going about with nothing under their tunics in this weather. If every man's not equipped by tomorrow I shall make a report for the general, quoting you as evidence.'

Wills turned his face away from the candle and hit his leg with his whip.

'I'll just go along and see what we have, sir,' he said. 'I might just be able to fix up Gunner Forsyth.'

'Yes; bring him back with you in a quarter of an hour or so and tell me what you can do.' It was exhausting. 'Sergeant Major,' I said, when he had gone, 'this is bad, and you should have reported it.'

'There shouldn't be any shortage at all, sir. I don't know why QMS Wills hasn't got it and issued it.'

'I suppose it's the nature of quartermasters to hoard stuff. Anyway, we'll have this settled. Put down on battery orders for the wagon line tomorrow, after evening stables, all Numbers One are to bring men short of underwear to the stores.'

In fact Forsyth's underclothing glistened with lice as though they were woven in with the material.

'Now these damned accounts.'

I had charge of the accounts. The major had kept them, and he was a stockbroker. There was the imprest account from which the men were paid, the battery fund, an official fund useful for individual purchases, and the canteen fund. The imprest account books clearly showed that we should have held about a thousand francs, the property of His Majesty. But the cashbox was almost empty. It was a nightmare to struggle with the books. Researches showed that when the major wanted half a dozen Primus stoves for the telephonists he took the money from the box, whether the appropriate fund could stand it or not. I lived in dread of an audit, and every night turned over page after page, to discover where the thousand francs had gone.

At last I packed up the books and went to dinner in the new hut. Clarence, as mess secretary, was expostulating with Morley because he found him, before dinner, eating pieces of Gruyère cheese which he had procured at some difficulty in Albert.

Richards crouched by the stove, gloomily, and refused to drink. On the side table, five or six hundred letters were waiting to be censored. We cheered up a little over dinner. Clarence went to play bridge at a franc a hundred, and the rest of us sat down to the letters with a dish of water and a rag before us. That was better than licking. Some of the handwriting I knew. I took out a letter or so to read. Here was that damned grocer complaining about the food again. 'Pigs would be better fed,' he said, 'and I don't mind who knows it.'

'Don't you,' I replied to myself, sticking the letter into my pocket. 'You will tomorrow.'

'Here's a good one,' Morley interrupted, 'I ticked the fellow off yesterday, good and proper, and he writes: "Our officers are the best in the whole British army. You might think they had come from heaven straight down to earth." That deserves to go, I say!'

We finished at last. It was ten. Richards followed me out.

'I say,' he said, 'will you do me a favour? I'm going away. Will you send my stuff on to Number — Hospital?'

'Why, yes, Number —? Bad luck. I'm awfully sorry.'

'Isn't it bloody? I was a bloody fool. I copped out in England on leave. I'm going now.'

'Good luck! and let's know how – let's have a word.'

'Thanks!'

He walked off. Everybody knew that Number — was one of the hospitals treating nothing but venereal disease. Clarence looked in to say goodnight.

'Richards has gone?' he asked in a whisper. I nodded. He sucked in his breath and shrugged his shoulders 'These young men, they will not take care. It's bad news. He is a nice young man, it will upset him very much. You think so, too?'

'I do.'

Clarence went into his hut next door. I could hear him muttering to himself about the cold. He slept in his underwear and washed in the morning wearing his British warm collar turned up. Everyone was fond of him, excepting, at the moment, Morley. Clarence wrote innumerable letters with green ink, in a minuscule hand. He was a middle-aged Frenchman from the Riviera and played bridge as accurately as a machine. When people became irritated with his accuracy he explained that he only got half the pay of our subalterns and must meet his mess bills as best he could.

I slept for a while. Then Morley called me. He was dragging some clothes from the foot of his bed. 'Bombers,' he said. We could hear them plainly, four or five of them roaring just overhead. The moon was shining brightly. We walked up to the horse standings. The first three bombs fell with terrific crashes a little distance away. The planes circled above our heads, searching for their next target, their engines drumming with the harsh pulsation of the Gothas. Six more bombs fell the other side, and a bright crimson light flared up. 'That's a bit of poor old Raven's dump,' I said, laughing. Then they dropped one quite close. The air shook. We fell to the ground. Then the next and the next followed, shaking the earth beneath us. We were lucky. No horses were hit. Then we went to bed again. Life was full of exasperations.

I had not seen C. for some days. Probably he was at the gun line. One morning he came into the office looking unusually clean. 'Can you come to Ytres with me before midday stables?'

'Yes; I have to buy some stuff for the mess.'

'I've got to see the Major General.'

'Good Lord! What for?'

'D'no. Probably our friend in the Ravine.'

I left C. at the door of the divisional office and went across the road to the canteen. I bought tinned herrings, sardines, soups, asparagus (one tin), Bath Olivers, groceries and condiments, one dozen whisky, as much as they would let me have, a box of Punch cigars, a pound of tobacco for Rawley, Mac and Immingham, and a hundred fat club Turkish cigarettes in a cedar box for myself. Also two hundred various Virginia cigarettes. They had just opened a sort of bar at the back of the marquee. I went in and shared half a bottle of port with an infantry subaltern. The stuff was loaded up into the mess cart at the back entrance. Then I had to go to the CRE's office to try and get some rolls of camouflage wire, dugout frames and cement. I got authority for four rolls of wire and half a dozen dugout frames. There was the usual long argument with the clerk over the number of frames. At length he asked me to return the day after.

C. was looking cheerful when I found him on the road. But the situation wasn't pleasant. The general of the Ravine had complained; he had done more. He had canvassed the battery commander who hid in the Tunnels and all the others he could; they were not of our brigade though in the division.

'But the colonel knows you, damn it!'

'Yes, but he's dead.'

'Dammit, yes! What did they say, the other BCs?'

'Three said I was inefficient, the general told me. He showed me all the reports, of course.'

'What did you say?'

'I was very amused. I said I could answer any specific charge of inefficiency any of them could bring, and that I was certain they couldn't bring one. The general interrupted; he said I'd been charged with using bad language to an NCO. It was when I was taking up ammunition and getting shelled. I said "Yes, sir, I did use bad language." The general grinned. "Shall I answer that charge, sir?" I asked. "How would you answer it, C?" – "I should recall the passage in King's Regulations placing upon any officer in an emergency the responsibility for doing whatever might be necessary for the best conduct of the situation." — "It was necessary to use bad language to the NCO?" – "It was, sir, he was a frightful blighter – " '

'Well isn't that all right then?'

'No. I'm afraid they're thinking of something else. The general said he would give them a week to produce concrete evidence of inefficiency. It's astonishing they're so vindictive when I'm all for a quiet life.'

'A quiet life! You're always too rude and too truthful.'

'I wasn't rude to Conrad.'

'No.'

We rode along in silence.

'I'll write to Conrad tonight and ask him to send the general a character for you.'

'Will you?'

'Yes. It's a sound scheme.'

'Oh, jolly good. It might help a bit.'

The divisional general had a sudden visitation of battery cookhouses. Hurriedly I prepared some diet sheets with the help of the cook. They were in the form of charts and they went back a fortnight without one day repeating another. The cook smeared them artificially with his fingers to make them look old, and put them on a spike over his hearth. We rehearsed some of the recipes.

'Steak pudding sir, well it's not really steak pudding; we puts the steak in the dixie lid with fat, covers it with soaked biscuit, puts another dixie lid on top and simmers gently. Then there's boiled jam roll, biscuits and jam boiled in a cloth; rissoles, that's bully mashed up with biscuit, onion and cheese, fried and rolled together.'

'Could you make any of them?'

'If there was any necessity, sir.'

Then the general came, after due warning, and walked into the cookhouse, newly lime-washed for the occasion; and he saw the sheaf of diet papers and read them. He sent for his staff captain.

'B Battery seems to have good ideas,' he said. 'I think we'll have a copy made of this dietary and circulated to all units.'

'Very good, sir.'

'Saying that the general would like to see all units provide such a variation as this.'

'How do you make this soup?' the general said, turning to the cook.

'We 'ave a stock pot, sir, but just now it's empty. We 'ad soup yesterday.'

'Where do you get all the dixies?'

'It does take rather a lot, sir,' the cook said, with an expression of guile. Everyone laughed cheerfully.

'Excellent fellow!'

The general moved on a pace and turned suddenly upon a stray gunner suspiciously hanging about the cookhouse. 'How do you like the food here?' the general asked. 'Best in the division, sir,' the man answered promptly.

'Well, that's excellent!'

The procession departed. Cook admitted the man had been posted in the way of the general. 'I thought 'e might save a lot of trouble,' he said.

Then the adjutant came and cursed me for overdoing it. 'Everybody will have to try and imitate these fakes of yours, now,' he said.

It was worrying to think of C. I saw our brigadier general on the road. He had such a gentle manner that he was called 'Softly, softly, catchee monkey' and his ADC, who was so much older than he, we called 'Softly's Uncle.' Softly was coming out of the veterinary lines. I begged leave to speak to him.

'It's about C. sir. I understand some adverse reports have been made against him by battery commanders. I wished to report that I was his battery commander on la Rutoire in the absence of Captain Conrad, and worked with him on the Somme during an awkward time after Captain Conrad's departure; he was a most efficient officer, and very courageous. He volunteered to do forward OP on 15 September.'

The general received this kindly.

'But all this was before he went sick on the Somme, wasn't it?'

'Yes, sir. Captain Conrad had a high opinion of C, sir.'

'You see,' Softly continued, 'it is a difficult matter; but the accepted view, after careful consideration, is that the undoubted hardships of the Somme had a lasting effect on C.'

He looked at me gravely through his half-moon glasses.

'I don't quite understand, sir.'

'The only conclusion we can come to is that C. has been not quite sane since then.'

'Not quite sane, sir?'

'The doctor agrees. I have considered it best,' Softly continued, across my amazement, 'to recommend his transfer to England for permanent home duty. He is a friend of yours, I think?'

'Yes, sir.'

'I expect you will agree with me then. I am obliged to you for speaking upon the subject.'

'Thank you, sir.'

I saluted and withdrew.

C. came to see me as I sat in the office, with a candle at each hand, trying to add up columns of figures.

'What a lark. I say, field officers and staff so inefficient they can't manage a second loot!'

'Are you insane, C?'.

'Of course I'm insane. Anybody can see that. I join the rest of the imbeciles at home. Did you know I was saying cheer-ho and goodbye, now, at once?'

'What about a spot of dinner first?'

'Damn dinner, anyway a drink first.'

'Righto!'

'You will? None of your tricks?'

'In Scotch.'

So an hour later I stood on the road in the darkness while he mounted. He leaned from his saddle and shook hands.

'Goodbye. Why don't you become insane, too?'

'Goodbye! I'm not clever enough. My sort of insanity is the sort that gets shot.'

'I say, I'll see you again,' C. said, turning his silhouette towards me.

'I wonder if we shall?'

'Oh yes, *après la guerre fini.*' 'Perhaps there won't be any *"après".*' 'Don't you believe it, there will.' 'Have a drink for me in town. Cheer-ho!' Then he trotted slowly down the road and I stared after him.

The reports of the expected attack became more precise. The brigade was withdrawn from the line and joined the wagon line at Bus, to re-train. Almost at once the weather became black again. Every morning at six the officers turned out for riding school. Gaby trod the ice with an expression of distaste, and stood tucked up with cold as I mounted. Our statuesque pose became at once pure motion-picture. Gaby bucked, kicked, slid, backed, side-jumped and cat-jumped. Twice she threw me off and I sprawled. She cocked an eye at me full of malicious pleasure. One might imagine she calculated the bruises. By the third time I had learned her new tricks, and then she gave them up. After the ride we breakfasted on bacon and eggs, and my latest gift from home, an enormous veal and ham pie. Breakfast was comfortable now; but we could not get enough sleep. The day was occupied with stables, gun drill, signalling instruction, harness cleaning, gas drill, inspections, accounts, censoring letters, preparation for visits by colonels and generals. Dinner was served at 8.15; we could not begin to go to bed until eleven. Life sped towards fever, and everyone seemed tired. Three young officers joined from home. Two were dental students and the other medical. They stayed a fortnight and then somehow managed to go back to England. Spragg got into trouble for taking money from brigade funds and not replacing it.

Before the frost ended there was a brigade church parade ordered for 8.30 in the morning. Every battery had to send fifty men.

We marched to markers on the frozen prairie. First the major inspected us and ordered half a dozen haircuts; then the adjutant came to look round unofficially. They took about half an hour. When the adjutant had reported to the colonel, he came and stared at all the buttons and the box respirators. Finally the general and Softly's Uncle came on parade and inspected us as we stood to attention. It was nearly half-past nine, and we were very cold. In front of me Sergeant Wilson stood as stiff as a post and as I glared at his back I saw a large louse crawl slowly out of his tight collar and make its way upwards. The general had got to D Battery by now, making good time, and soon he told the chaplain to carry on, and the chaplain announced that we would sing 'Fight the Good Fight'. We stood at ease and beat our clenched hands on our thighs. The chaplain's voice came from an immense distance reciting prayers. The louse had disappeared under Wilson's cap during the prayers. It must be an adventurous creature, I thought; head lice were different from body lice, but then this one was not very full of blood, as one could see from the transparency of his hind part; presumably he did not like the taste of Sergeant Wilson's back, and was searching elsewhere; a freebooting louse. There was a short sermon. Keep your armour bright. Then we sang 'The Church's one Foundation'. Rawley turned round to march us off. 'B Battery, shun,' he shouted. 'In column of fours from the right, quick march . . . Form half sections.' As soon as we moved we felt even colder, and wanted to run. We went straight into stables. In the afternoon there was a rugby match.

It was so desolate there that we had to make amusements. The batteries were encouraged to be up and doing. The major general inspected cookhouses again. Now that the frost had gone he was preoccupied with the manifold uses of mud. He stood in our new cookhouse among an admiring throng of staff officers, officers, NCOs and men. 'Mud!' he said. 'Excellent stuff, mud! Now, you need a chimney. Make it of mud, build it up, allow it to dry, piece by piece. Right up! Up to the roof! There's a chimney for you! Or an oven; mud in buckets, lay foundations with stones in it, work it upwards in a semi-circle, bit by bit; there's an oven! Do anything with mud! Think of the manure dump! You know it, don't you, Sergeant Major? Yes, four hundred yards long, all covered with mud; sealed, no flies, no bluebottles, all rotting internally! Excellent stuff, mud. With a few moulds, make bricks of it. I should think a brick – oh, about, er, this size, would be best, don't you think so?'

'We might make some experiments, I think,' Softly said, beaming.

'I'll have a mould made, sir,' said Rawley.

'Ah, excellent idea. D'no how you'd make it, though. Ha'ever, very

interesting. Excellent stuff, mud. Try make a chimney today, hey, Rawley?'
'Yes, sir.'

I looked at the cook. His eyes gleamed brilliantly in his black face, with an expression of bewilderment and awe.

They departed. Then I found Rawley in the office, laughing himself silly. 'Haw!' he said. 'Excellent stuff, mud!'

He had got two barrels of beer with great difficulty. It was poor thin stuff, but still beer. We were to have a concert in a big hut. The men came in carrying their mess tins very carefully. Rawley sang 'Let the Great Big World Keep Turning' in a thin and piercing tenor. Mac recited a number of indecent jokes. Captain Dodd, newly posted to us from A Battery, politely refused to perform. I sang a song I had heard in Harry Weldon's pantomime and felt acutely ashamed. It was the only thing I could remember.

I always sleeps so cold in bed
It's that what made me wed,
And every morn at half-past five
I kicks the old girl out of bed,
It don't do her no harm,
Then I creeps into her place, where,
She's left it nice and waarm.

I wished I had been Tom Brown, who sang 'The Leather Bottel' so well on a comparable occasion. Immingham was the great success of the officers. He sang 'Madelon' in French.

We had built a number of cupola huts to accommodate the strength of the battery. The officers had one, whitewashed inside and out. I went into Albert for the day and brought back some pink cotton. We draped it in the windows and Rawley had the battery artificer paint the words *Mon Boudoir* over the door. I begged half a bag of cement and made an ornamental pool in the 'garden,' modelling a dolphin on the side. Immingham got leave from Rawley to go to Albert and extended the trip to Amiens in one lucky lorry-hop. His horses waited in Bapaume. It was late when he got back, still merry; in one hand he carried a bowl of six goldfish and on his back was tied a cage of two canaries. We put the goldfish in the little pool. Hearing of this the adjutant persuaded the colonel to take the necessary action, and one evening the brigade orderly brought us an order. 'OC B Battery will note,' it ran, 'that goldfish and canaries will be grazed daily. Canaries will wear box respirators at all times, fish will be muzzled. Rations will be drawn on the following scales:

Fish   ... 10lbs hay
Canaries   ... 20lbs corn

Canaries are not to be allowed to sing between the hours of 11 p.m. and 8 a.m. nightly.'

Day by day the goldfish in the pool became inert and died.

At night the whisky went round freely. Even a gymkhana could not make Bus attractive. Dodd showed no pleasure in Rawley and his new captaincy, and went to England for a course. My supply of dark Virginia had not come and I was forced to smoke the ration tobacco. There was plenty of that. Nobody wanted it. Mac and I went about a good deal to the other messes. Then one night Rawley drank more than usual. We were all tired of the black winter, but I was on duty and had drunk less. Rawley suddenly ordered horses for himself and Mac and stared round in a disdainful way. 'Mac and I are going to Paris,' he said. We laughed. Rawley hiccoughed and pulled himself together, slewing his eyes round from Immingham to myself, with an expression which was meant to be commanding. 'Laugh when you're invited,' he said. Then his face dropped forward and relaxed into smiles.

'You boys look after the battery properly while I'm away, and I'll bring you back the prettiest little girl in silk stockings and a pink silk camisole. Mac and I are going to Paris.'

Mac said, thickly: 'Are you sure it's all right, major, without passes?'

'Are we to remain segregated here forever? I will provide myself with passes, signed by myself, acting-colonel.' He sniggered and put on his belt.

I said: 'Not really sir?'

Rawley said: 'Why not, Boyd?'

'Suppose there's an inspection?'

Rawley gave me a grossly detailed description of what I might say he had gone to do. Then Tanner came and said the horses were ready. Rawley got up and put on his coat.

'Really, sir – ' I began.

'Don't be silly.'

'I say, Mac, this is sheer bloody lunacy.'

Mac goggled at me and grinned. He was drunk, too. They went out and struggled into their saddles. The Colemans were on the road.

'My major's blotto, I fear,' I said.

'He's going to Paris,' Immingham added.

'I think your major is the biggest cad in the brigade,' the elder Coleman said. 'Whenever I hear his accent or whenever I see knock-knees and New-market boots a mile off, I go into the nearest shell hole and vomit.'

'He's a tout,' the younger Coleman said, 'and how you can live with him, I don't know. Probably diseased, too.

'He's quite decent to me,' I said. 'But he takes the biscuit, going off to Paris.'

'You don't mean you like him?'

'He's no passes or anything; and God knows when he'll come back.'

'I say, you don't like Rawley, do you?'

'Oh, damn Rawley; he's a swipe, but he's all right as a swipe, so why worry? I think he's decenter than lots of so-called gentlemen. His habits are really disgusting, that's the only thing one has reason to object to. I find them amusing, too.'

'Anyway you think he's a swipe and that his habits are disgusting. That's a relief. We thought you liked him.'

'Oh, we're very fond of our major,' Immingham said, 'he brings a delightfully feminine influence into our lives.'

'Let's have a drink. Come inside.'

Rawley and Mac did not come back that night. They did not turn up for morning stables. We dodged questions about the major, and lied where necessary. The major remained somewhere else at teatime. They did not appear for dinner. Immingham and I ate in solitude, and went to bed without a sight or sound of them.

In the night someone shook me, and I woke. It was Mac.

'Has anything happened?' he asked.

'No. Nobody spotted it. Sleep in peace.'

'What a game. What big sillies we were, *hein*?'

'Without a doubt, *hein*! How far did you get?'

'Amiens. We stopped in Bapaume for a drink; then caught a lorry to Albert and a train to Amiens. The major wanted to go on, but I was getting sober. I pulled him off the train. Besides the military police were getting suspicious —'

'Those stinkers!'

'Rawley sobered up after a bath in Amiens.'

'Well, sleep sweetly.'

'God bless!'

When I saw Rawley he was smoking a Turkish cigarette. He tilted back his chair, lifted his nose and let the smoke trickle out of his nostrils. Then he waved the cigarette slowly in front of my face. I saw he was defiant.

'Have a good time, sir?'

'Excellent time. A peach in fact.'

'Would you mind if I went into Albert to-morrow, sir?'

'Do you want a peach, too?'

'No, sir, nothing like that about me. But Mac might be wanting a peach.'

'Seeing that you've been such good boys and not let your uncle down, it might be considered.'

'Thank you, sir.'

Mac and I rode into Bapaume in the morning and had a bath at the club. It was cold and raining. The bath sheds were of corrugated iron and very draughty. After lunch we lorry-hopped to Albert. The rain was falling heavily. The town was still in ruins and almost deserted. A few shops had opened in wooden booths. We found a shop selling notepaper and ink. Under a pile of music I discovered a copy of *Jardins sous la pluie*. The ironmonger's shop was full of the silk postcards which the army loved. There I bought a new knife, a poor cheap thing of the kind whose blade locks. The words *L'avenir est à nous* were stamped on the blade. The officers' hotel was extemporised in ruined houses, and outside the rain lashed down on the cobbles. There seemed to be nobody in the hotel. We tried to get cheerful over dinner, but it was difficult. Yet we tried so hard it was late when we walked on to the Bapaume road to look for a lorry or a car that would take us back. Two staff cars flashed past with the rain driving in golden beads across their lamps. Mac did not want to go back. He said it was no use and that it was too late. We returned to the hotel to sleep. Early in the morning I awoke with a feeling of guilt and depression. The household was not up. It was about seven o'clock when we got on the road. The day was grey and cold, with gusts of hard rain. An empty staff car came into sight and drew up by us. It belonged to the DADMS, the medical commander. The driver promised for a consideration to take us as far as Barastre, only two miles from Bus. The grey road ran shining between the miles of shattered earth.

'That's the Butte de Warlencourt.'

'Why be gloomy? There are others.'

'Not even a woman in the place.'

'What a place!'

'I think I'll resign.'

The driver made good time and took us straight to Bus. Outside the hut two pairs of horses were standing. Hampstead told us hurriedly he had orders to bring us on. The brigade had gone out for a field day near Vélu. We cantered along the prairie. Hampstead pointed out Rawley to Mac. 'You're to report to the major, sir; Mr Boyd to take centre section commander. Dismount here, sir, they won't spot us then.'

Sergeant Wilson said, 'Supposed to be firing enfilade on the road between Haplincourt and Villers au Flos, searching from 4,500 up to 5,500.'

'Thanks very much.'

I knelt behind the right hand gun. The colonel trotted down on us, checked a moment and went on.

'Has anybody wanted us?'

'Only the major, sir.'

The day went on as usual. After dinner there were a lot of letters to censor. It was 20 March 1918.

Chapter 10

Poor Bloody Horses

The Retreat – Spring 1918

What time the bombardment woke me I do not know. The persistent rumble had long since penetrated my sleep, diluting it so far that my mind hung uncomfortably suspended between the dream of the gunfire, which I could not shake off, and the real awakening from which I withdrew as long as possible. Somebody burst open the door and shouted, 'Stand to!' We rose immediately from our bunks and dressed. The attack had begun.

Everyone was stirring. In the orchard the drivers hurried to take down harness from the trees on which it hung. Rawley told Burnett to send the men for breakfast a section at a time; to dump all the spare kit and stores in the farm, under two men. We went to *Mon Boudoir* to go over the defence plan. To the north and the east the gunfire increased and in the middle of the morning the shells began to fall in Ytres and Bertincourt, our neighbours. Mac clutched me in affected terror.

'Me chee-ild,' he said, 'hark to the storm outside! How it howls!'

A few minutes before eleven we marched. We followed our companion brigade towards Barastre, and stood halted upon the road which traversed the prairie, while the site of the village went up in smoke. We were halted for ten minutes, and then we reversed and went back to Bus. It seemed that only one brigade was needed. The two colonels met at the head of the column, and tossed for it. Ours won. The other led his brigade through the steel fountains which played on the road in Barastre.

It was in the afternoon that we marched again. There was a hollow between Vélu and Lebucquière, and there we stood as night fell. The mist billowed up thickly from the ground. Only machine guns continued the fight northwards, where we faced, but far south the gloomy rumble continued, and we waited for something to turn up, while the men made little fires in shelters of ammunition boxes roofed with corrugated iron. Thus the first day ended.

It was 4.30 a.m. before any order came. The battery turned north again and went into action facing across a shallow trench a mile east of Beugny. As the mist cleared, the trees on the Cambrai-Bapaume road came into sight, two hundred yards away on our left, and in front a camouflage screen on telegraph poles marked the near crest. Rawley sent Mac forward to reconnoitre. I saw him disappear on his dun horse under the screen. Tanner had made some breakfast in the trench. Rawley handed me a fried egg on a piece of bread and gave me charge of the wagon line; it was to withdraw to Bancourt, near Bapaume. We left ammunition and drew off, refilled in a strange dump, and waited for orders.

The battle had begun again. A Scottish division was in front of us and I went to their artillery headquarters with a mess cart to try to find two or three tents. The staff was in an underground dugout at Fremicourt. People rushed about in great excitement. I stopped the staff captain. 'Tents?' he said, 'Good God! What do you want tents for? We're at war!' He rushed away. I waited a few minutes for him and then demanded tents from the regimental sergeant major. 'We're retiring; everyone's gone,' he said, wildly. 'Look, there's the last.' A big car hurtled out of the yard, throwing up showers of stones and grit. I got on my bicycle and rode up the Cambrai road towards Beugny, with an increased distaste for the war. The shellfire in front was intense and the German planes hung over us. There was a crucifix in Beugny village, enclosed in a shrine. The iron gate was broken; a shell had burst on the brick work. As I cycled past I saw the doctor and Clarence inside, sitting below the cross eating sandwiches. Clarence was doleful, he missed his meals, but the doctor uttered explosive bursts of laughter. 'I've been in this war for about eighteen months now, and this is the first bit of real war I've seen,' he said. He gave me a sandwich.

'Have you had many wounded?'

'Oh, so-so. I'll do you as soon as you come in.'

'Thanks!' I got on the bicycle and went down to the battery.

They had a telephone working on a short line to an OP over the crest. The guns fired a slow barrage and the Germans threw a sprinkling of light shells upon us, not very accurately. Rawley sat on the edge of the trench.

'I've sent orders to the wagon line to rendezvous at Mill Cross,' he said. 'That's much nearer. Then I can get the gun teams in a hurry.'

I cycled to Mill Cross and met the column. The light was already fading and the shelling seemed heavier. Many enemy planes flew above us, dropping balls of silver light into the bars of darkness rising from the earth. The wagons filed on to the open land behind the huts and spread at wide intervals to avoid the danger of shellfire. An aeroplane hovered just above us. Scarcely had the teams halted when a flight of shells fell upon them. They were light, instantaneous-action shells, throwing their metal along the ground level. I signalled the teams to retire over the hill; they reversed and trotted in perfect order, but even as they went, as I watched the six files retreating, the next salvo caught them. Three teams vanished in shellbursts, struggled out pitching and falling, and halted. The smoke still wavered over the field as the drivers dropped the wounded and followed at a crippled trot. Now I was alone with the wounded horses, which must be shot at once. The shells fell all about as I crawled from one to another, despatching them, whilst my hand grew so unsteady that I had to rest the Webley on my left forearm to level the barrel firmly over the brainpan. The horses stared and tried to rise, and the blood gushed out upon my coat covering it from collar to hem. As I reloaded to shoot the last three, a man came galloping over the prairie. He had come for the gun limbers, and I sent him over the hill. The last horse kicked and relaxed with a groan and as I watched him, feeling as though my inner creature had been emptied out, I saw the kind, confiding light in his eyes die, as if a dirty cloud had flowed into them.

I walked to the battery. The day was closing with a deep orange sunset which needed no imagination to make it sinister. I sat down on the edge of the trench and talked to the major between the explosions of the guns. I had forgotten the blood on my coat.

'We got shelled at Mill Cross,' I said.

'This is going to be a fight to a finish,' he said. 'To the end.'

I looked up to the camouflage screens expecting to see the files of German helmets passing the skyline. Behind the guns, the drivers stood to the limber teams. The shells were falling about them.

'You get back to the wagon line,' Rawley said. 'We may get away; it's just possible.'

I felt ashamed that I was not courageous. 'No,' I said. 'I'll stay here.'

'No, there are enough here; you must go back.'

'No, I'll stay here.'

'I order you to go back.'

I sat still for a moment, absently staring at the puffs of smoke exploding among the teams.

'There are only four!' I said.

Rawley shouted, 'Go back!'

I got up and hurried away, running and stumbling over the grass in my heavy equipment. It was a mile and a half to the wagon line and by the time I got to Mill Cross my breath was almost gone. There I saw the sergeant major of the howitzer battery on his enormous light bay horse, a severe and excellent soldier.

'Can you lend me a horse?' I gasped. 'I want two limbers,' and pointed over the hill.

'I'll go,' he said, wheeled, putting spurs to his horse, and bounded up the slope. In two minutes the limbers came trotting towards me. I swung on the rear one as it passed. We went across country, over the ridge and into the southern end of the depression in which the guns had lain. At the top two 4.5 howitzers still stood. Else there was nothing in the valley. The light was almost gone but overhead the aeroplanes were watching, dropping brilliant silver balls which burned in the sky for a few seconds. We had another half-mile to go to the light railway embankment. The first team suddenly plunged and stopped. 'Wire!' the drivers shouted. The railway telephone posts were down. I sawed through the wire with my French knife and then we charged the embankment, bumped across the ditch and came to the two deserted guns. The spades had sunk deep in the ground with much firing, and the bombardier strained with me at the steel trail. We shifted it a fragment, rocked the wheels forward and got her up. Then the team would not stand for us to drop the eye on the limber hook, until the centre and wheel drivers dismounted to climb on the wheels. The second gun was ballasted with sandbags. We hauled at it as the sweat poured off our faces and the wind whistled in our throats. At last she shifted, limbered and we went away. The rifle fire was loud across the Cambrai road, and now it was dark except for a deep glow which covered the face of the earth with deceptive shadows. We cantered past the crucifix and drove through the infantry digging in on the Red Line. At the corner a battery of 6-inch howitzers had left a pile of fused shells lying on the road; we drove over them. Two salvos of light high explosive burst on the bank, and drove us on to the prairie, but there again the swift 77s whistled down; the first team must have been destroyed, I thought, as we turned to the road again; and hardly had we entered it when a man hailed us. It was the major's servant who was trying, with a friend, to carry Rawley's overloaded valise. They loaded the thing on the gun and we pursued our way, while the German batteries put down the shells about the road. We passed our dead horses. The quartermaster sergeant's dun trotted up to us as we breasted the slope. It was fully saddled and had a great hole in its side. We caught up the first team and each in surprise shouted 'Are you all right?' to the other. We walked now upon the grassy crest of the prairie and dropped beyond it into a hollow where the rest of the wagon line was assembled. Soon the moon rose, at first red in the low lying mist, and then, as it climbed, it lit the hollow with white light.

I found Burnett rearranging the teams with the NCOs. We went round the horses.

'Is the QMS dead?' I asked.

'I don't know, sir. I haven't seen him for a long time. He may be.'

'Send a man to strip his horse there. It's got a hole in its side. Somebody must shoot it. Here's my revolver. I'm sick of shooting horses.'

Then, as we sat on the grass we saw a man coming along, peering into the faces of the moonlit groups. As he came nearer we could hear him.

'Can you lend me two pairs of horses?' he kept saying. The drivers passed him on to us. It was young Danvers of A Battery.

'Can you lend me two pairs of horses? I've only six horses for two guns and one wagon.

Burnett looked at me and shook his head.

'Can't you lend me one pair. I can't get them away without, not over this rough stuff.'

'Couldn't we lend one pair, as far as Riencourt?'

'Where are you going to put them, sir?'

'Wherever you like, sergeant major.'

'If you put them in the lead of the gun – we can't have them used alone.'

'No, no. Thank you very much.'

'Where are you going?' I asked.

'I thought I'd come with you; I haven't an idea. I'm quite lost. I was staggered when I found I was in B Battery's lines.'

'The position of assembly last mentioned was near Riencourt. I'm making for there. You're feeding, I suppose?'

'I haven't any corn.'

'We can't spare any corn.'

'No.'

We sat side by side on a mound in the moonlight while the sergeant major finished arranging the teams. Danvers went back to his party. Burnett and I went round the teams. The men ate biscuits and bully. Hampstead came up to tell me that Gaby and Strawberry were unhurt. It took about an hour to get straight, to feed the teams and rest them. Meantime the moon sailed high in the sky, a brilliant silver piece which cast haloes upon the dark, moving bodies. We moved towards the Riencourt road.

There was a certain sergeant with the guns, Roberts by name, who had a husky, laborious voice, and now as I turned Gaby on to the road, with only the faintest hope of finding the battery, I heard Roberts's voice across the road. I called and he answered; we filed into the field and took up our positions with the rest of the brigade.

Rawley was talking to the colonel.

'I've got the guns,' I said.

'You've got the guns?'

'Yes, we went back and fetched them.'

'How many?'

'We've got them all, haven't we?'

'How many have you actually with you?'

'They're in the gunpark with the rest. I thought there were six.'

'Listen. How many did you go and get?'

'Two.'

'Then there's only one lost, sir,' Rawley said.

Mac was near. 'There were six guns,' I said, stupidly. 'I've got two, you had four; how many does that make?'

'It makes five. One of the teams got a direct hit; the pole was smashed as well. We had to leave it behind the crucifix in Beugny.'

'I could have got it if I'd known.'

'Well, you didn't know.'

'This can't go on very much longer, like today,' I said.

'Of course it can,' Mac said, angrily. 'This is only the beginning.'

Immingham came up. 'Come and have a bit of sleep, you bloody fools; there's a hut here.'

We went in and lay down. For long I turned about and then fell into a nightmare in which the events of the day repeated themselves, grossly. Immingham woke me and begged me not to shout so much. After an hour we got up again. It was one o'clock in the morning. The guns went into action in the hollow in which the wagon line had assembled. Orderlies were sent out to find ammunition. The moon had gone down. For an hour we collected and delivered ammunition. A procession of retreating tanks blundered across our track and tried to reverse on the narrow road between the trees. Everyone swore heartily at each other. Thus ended the second day of the retreat.

When morning came, I dispersed the wagons under the shelter of a tall bank in which the roots of pollards and hazels had made niches. The spring shoots of the pollards were scarlet and stood up stiffly in the sunshine. Backhouse had gone to serve his gun and Hampstead had both myself and the horses on his hands. When I had settled the wagons, he appeared on the tall strawberry carrying a sack.

'Boots, shirts, socks, sir,' he said. 'I've been to Bus.'

'You ought to have a medal, Hampstead.'

'Well, sir, I think you ought to have a wash and a change, covered with blood like that.'

I was asleep on the bank when he returned with a bucket of water. While I stripped in the sun he wiped the blood from my old coat. I splashed the water over my body. We repacked the saddlebag and wallets and ate bully, biscuits and tea. The morning was very fine.

When I had filled my pipe, I spread the map on the ground. The position of the battle in which we were concerned was that contained within the angle of two great roads leading to Bapaume; the Cambrai road running from the east, the Péronne road from the south-east. Bapaume also controlled the roads westward to Albert, Amiens and Doullens; northward to Arras; southward to Péronne, with the valleys of the Ancre, Somme and Canche, which lay in our hands. The Germans pressed the attack on Bapaume from the north-east, driving us towards the wilderness west of the Bapaume-Péronne road.

By the late afternoon the wagons had crossed that road and stood upon a spit of land running westward by the side of the corduroy road which traversed the crater-field from Beaulencourt to Thilloy. It was the only practicable road west for some miles. The guns were at Villers au Flos. I found Mac playing with a motorcycle looted out of the deserted village; but he could not get it to go. He had also brought away a small brown puppy, which he tucked under my arm as I mounted my bicycle. I carried it back to the wagon line and tied it up with the canary cage.

An hour or two later we tried to rescue some of the spare kit from Bus. The enemy were flattening the line out rapidly. The mess cart went off. Then an orderly arrived with a message to say that Raven's big ammunition dump was to be blown up by the Royal Engineers. All details must be withdrawn. A bicycle orderly followed the mess cart with instructions to find our two guards and send the mess cart back. I rode up again to the guns to find out what they were doing. They were gone from Villers and I could not discover them. It was quite dark when I reached the wagons. Two gunners had arrived with Rawley's compliments, a looted gramophone, a box of discs and a request for a bottle of whisky. It was the last bottle, as I explained when I took it back.

Burnett stood with me on the low whaleback of land staring towards Bus. We were worried for our men and the mess cart. At length they arrived. They had been turned back without the two guards. They had heard that the guards had gone.

'The Huns are in Bus,' the driver said.

'In Bus?' we ejaculated.

'Yes, sir. The Engineers said so. They're going to blow them up with the dump. It's due now.'

We stared into the darkness. Quite slowly a cloud of pink smoke rose, like some exotic growth. It expanded as it grew tree-like in the air, towering in the night. But we heard no noise from it among the noises of the firing front.

'Who was there, on the kit?'

'A lad called Cope and that Evans.'

'The grocer?'

'Yes, sir. He's that silly he couldn't get out of the way of a traction engine.'

The guns were quite near now. I crossed the road and reported the story of the men, that Bus was in the enemy's hands and that the last of the kit had been lost, books, whisky, gramophone, records, clothes and blankets.

'They've got my best clothes,' Immingham said, 'unless they've gone sky high together, clothes and Huns.'

'And mine.'

'And mine.'

'Here's the last bottle.' I put it between the major's legs. We were sitting on a plank under a tarpaulin which was thrown over a small-arms ammunition cart.

'Do you know when and where we are retiring, sir?'

'No idea; but the general line of retirement is north-west.'

'Did you get much shooting done today?'

'Not a lot. Haven't too much ammunition. But we did scrounge a hundred rounds from Villers.'

'I've four orderlies missing so far today,' I said, 'all looking for refilling point. I have a little forage and rations, of course. You know the QMS is missing? I must go back.'

A small ration of food and forage had arrived from Bapaume. The teams stood in harness, as I had left them. They had worn harness since the morning of the 21st, nearly three days ago. I decided to risk it. We put up lines, groomed the horses and blanketed them. The canary cage and the puppy were wrapped up in sacks and put under my tarpaulin. The puppy wriggled out and came under my blanket. We slept together. So ended the third day of the retreat.

The night passed like a shot. At five o'clock in the morning, in the darkness, the puppy woke me, whimpering and licking my face. I started up, listening intently. The attack had not yet begun. As I lit a candle I saw that the canaries were dead with the cold, their feathers fluffed enormously, and still gripping the perch. I called for the sergeant major, who was asleep. Giving orders to him I felt prophetically inspired, and in the most definite way. 'Get breakfast on at once,' I said, 'send the horses to water, harness up as soon as possible on return. Then we'll shift the lines a quarter of a mile back and feed up; we can send the men for breakfast if it isn't ready by then. I don't like the smell of this place. Make the men double; see the water cart is filled.'

We filed down to water at the pumping station on the Bapaume road. On the way back there was a fine smell of woodsmoke in the air. I played the looted gramophone as night broadened into day. I played 'Tambour Chinois' and 'Caprice Viennoise' and then 'Raggin' through the rye'. The music sounded strange in the open air at that time of day. The men in the neighbouring lines stopped work to cheer.

The morning had the grey quality of an aquatint. The gunfire had begun and big solitary shells were falling on the pumping station. There were a lot of horses there now, which disappeared in the smoke, and many bodies were left on the ground. But we were all safe. One by one the teams went back along the spit of land. The last to come was the water cart. It was not a minute too soon. The 5.9s spread over our resting place and hastened the old wall-eyed bay to an ursine gallop. Slowly the barrage crept forward and I withdrew again, and fixed signboards in our deserted position as pointers for messengers. We had now come almost to the limit of the plateau, where it sank to the level of the plank road. A canvas hospital stood off the road a few yards north. They were bringing out the lightly wounded and arming them with rifles and as I watched a shell dropped through the roof and exploded inside, inflating the canvas for a moment and then dropping it limp and broken. A string of ambulance cars appeared; the hospital swarmed with people carrying out stretchers to the cars. Then they moved off to the road. In front of the teams a party of oldish men began digging a trench. The lightly wounded from the hospital came along and helped, and one of them said that le Transloy had fallen. It was only two miles south of us. He repeated the news. The Uhlans were there. I lifted my binoculars and searched the land thereabouts, and handed them to Burnett, but we could see nothing. There was still no message from the guns.

The trench was getting deeper, and it was apparent that we must cross. Burnett took the wagons over while I returned on foot to search for the guns. On the open land I met a staff captain, mounted. He asked for news of le Transloy, and I for news of ammunition. He pointed westward to a smoky column some miles behind. 'That's the railway bridge,' he said. 'They've blown it up for safety; I'm frightfully afraid there won't be any more until you get behind that – but there's a splendid dump at Riencourt.' 'Yes; but that was empty yesterday.' 'Oh, well, I can't help you, I'm afraid.' The guns had gone. I hurried back. Hampstead was waiting by the trench with the news that the battery had come past and the wagons had followed. By now the plank road was full of retreating traffic; every team followed hard upon every wagon and the faint dust rose in the bright sunshine, marking the movement so far as the eye could see. A mile or so away the long caterpillar bent left up the hill to the ruins of Guedecourt, silhouetted against the blue heaven. I looked up into the sky, expecting to see the flight of German aeroplanes, shining like honesty seeds as they pursued the slow column with bombs and machine guns. But not a single plane did I see. The column moved back at about two miles an hour with irritating halts every half mile. At length I left Hampstead with the horses and made direct for Guedecourt on foot, across the old battlefield which fringed the road.

It was about noon on a warm spring day. The grasses growing round the shell holes moved a little with the faint breeze. The wind, sun and rain had covered the blast marks in the earth, and the earth, undisturbed for over a year, was light and crumbled under foot. I climbed in and out among the shell holes and the old barbed wire up to the village. There a faint wind was blowing and the sun was warm. It smelt clean and sweet. The column rumbled patiently along the road. I found the battery halted at Factory Corner. We were hungry and thirsty, and some drank cautiously and secretly from the water in the shell holes. Hampstead said he had 'found' some sand-wiches of corned meat. They were wrapped in dirty old newspaper. We shared them out and chewed at the stale dry bread. The men were sharing out what they had.

In the afternoon we fired from Thilloy on to the sugar factory near Bapaume and the wagons waited by the roadside in le Barque. The place was empty, and at intervals streams of traffic moved backwards. It became cold. Backhouse arrived with his long, slouching walk and serious face and gave me a pair of pyjamas. 'I found these, sir,' he said. 'You've none at all now and when we stop somewhere you will need them.'

I rode up to the guns in the growing dusk. We were about to retire again. I was to go ahead and choose a battery position immediately by Loupart Wood. On the way out of the position an overloaded wagon lay with a broken axle. Its owners had been too hurried to take the stuff away. A small leather case lay among other wreckage on the bank. I took it and gave it to Backhouse. 'That will do for the pyjamas,' I said. 'Bring it along on the limber.'

As Gaby trotted to le Barque I looked at the map. We were now cutting across the apex of a second angle, between two great roads. We went westward with the Bapaume-Péronne road behind; shortly in front lay the symmetrical leg going from Bapaume south-west to Albert and Amiens. When we crossed that we should enter the northern half of the old Somme battlefield at a point two and a half miles from Bapaume. Upon the crossing we met an infantryman, wounded in the arm and leg, limping towards Albert in hopes of a lift. He said Bapaume had fallen.

The way to Loupart Wood was the roughest of tracks, full of old shell holes bridged with loose timbers from German dugouts. If this were the only way in and out, I thought, it seemed likely we should get into action but never out again. The moon rose as we gained the plateau and showed us the shadowed edge of the broken trees. Hampstead held the horses while Eldred and I surveyed the ground which was everywhere deeply pitted. We staked out the positions for five guns and looked round for tools to make platforms. They had been cutting timber in the wood and there we found axes and a spade. We spent an hour levelling the earth and bridging the shell holes with rough sawn timber, so that the guns could get in easily. We rehearsed the manoeuvre for each team and then looked round the ground. Westwards, in the direction we should retire, the ground was more deeply pitted than any place I had seen, or seemed so in the moonlight. The earth was honeycombed, convulsed, sown with stakes from which barbed wire trailed and coiled about the feet. The track disappeared on the edge of the wood into a wilderness of shell holes. Eastwards it was as bad. Eldred reported the same of the terrain on the lower flanks of the track. We got into a shell hole to light pipes and stood in the moonlight looking towards Bapaume, listening in silence. There was a faint noise behind and someone whispered 'Halt!' We turned round, and upon that followed the rattle of rifle bolts, and a voice shouted sharply, 'Who goes there?'

'Artillery!'

'Put your hands up and keep still.' Three men came up to us. Two carried rifles at the ready. The other was an officer with an automatic pistol. We exchanged compliments and apologies. They did not know where they were. The officer blew his whistle and a company of men rose out of the earth and passed forward in open order. The moon shone on their steel helmets.

'Our orders are to go forward until we make contact with the enemy,' the officer said.

'Good luck!'

'Cheerio!'

They passed out of sight. Some hundreds of yards down the track there had been another small group like our own. But the sounds we had heard from them seemed to have stopped. Now I began to fear something had gone wrong. More than two hours had passed since we arrived. While we wondered what to do the figure of a horseman rose in the moonlight haze far away down the track and stood, and raised his arm and called, a doubtful wavering cry. Then he turned away and disappeared.

'And what does that mean?' I said, uneasily, 'is it for us? At least they can't come any other way.' We decided to go back.

We picked our way carefully down to the ruins of Warlencourt-Eaucourt, and stood in the mouth of the track watching the endless stream of traffic pass across a piece of whitewashed wall on which the moon threw hurrying shadows. 'There's the major, sir!' Eldred said suddenly. He rode past us, huddled forward on his horse. The teams followed him, traces tight, muzzles swaying a little to their steps as though they were part of a machine of perpetual motion. About that time of night the fourth day ended.

The retreat continued westward on the Miraumont road. A succession of lorries of the heavy artillery broke out of the column and passed the horsed transport, double-banking on the road. For an hour we moved forward in short jerks until at last we came to a standstill. The night was still brilliant and calm but no bombers came over us. It was very cold. The lorries had jammed the crossing in Miraumont. After half an hour we moved on through Pys and halted again. The men dismounted and smoked by the roadside. I walked up and down the battery, up and down again. On the north bank, at a little distance were the huts of some camp. The night glistened with frost. I thought I would wrap the pyjamas round my neck, and called to Backhouse to bring the little bag. It contained a chalice, a metal bottle, a box of holy wafer and a dirty celluloid collar with a black dickey.

'Well, where the hell are those pyjamas, Backhouse?'

'In the mess cart, sir.'

'Why didn't you say so before?'

'I thought you might want these too, sir,' he said, grinning.

'Well, is there anything in the bottle?'

'Not a drop, sir. But perhaps you'd like a drop of this, sir.' He slung up his water bottle. It smelt strongly of rum.

'It smells of rum,' I said, doubtfully.

'It is rum,' Backhouse replied.

I drank a little. The neat spirit ran round my empty stomach.

'You found it, I suppose?'

'Yes, sir.'

'Did you happen to find a few mufflers as well?'

'Yes, sir, two, one thick and one thin.'

'Lend me the thin one, then.'

There was no sound of movement on the road, but I heard a sort of quiet singing forward. Then I saw a most remarkable group in the middle of the moonlit road, dwarfs playing 'Ring o' Roses'. They were dressed in Chinese hats, wide shiny jackets, like candle extinguishers, and short, shiny trousers. I leaned against a gun wheel and stared with astonishment. Then the leader sang 'Acha, Acha, all fall down', and they all fell on the road and laughed. As the lights struck their faces I saw they were my drivers, Todd, Parkinson, Shields and a few others. Sergeant Wilson slipped between the wagons and said quietly, 'Oilskins, sir – they've been in the Labour battalion camp there. All sorts of stuff there, sir. Would you care for a drink?' He swung his water bottle forward and took a small mug from his pocket.

'It smells remarkably like rum,' I said.

'Yes, sir.'

I drank a little. 'It is rum,' I said, 'neat rum.'

'Oh, yes, sir,' Wilson replied eagerly, 'it is rum, sir. Let me give you some more. My canteen is full.'

'Where did you get all this rum?'

Wilson had an even smile on his face; it was a trifle fixed.

'There was a little in the camp, sir, and I thought I better draw it off myself.'

'Certainly.'

We began to walk up the section, talking about the horses, and looking at the casualties.

Todd's brown mare was a bit lame in the morning. It was out of draught with the spare pair. We stopped to see how it was. Todd appeared, beaming under his sou'wester, and explained. He had bandaged the pastern. It was a strain. Wilson moved to speak to another driver. Todd smiled ingratiatingly. He slung his water bottle forward. 'Like a drink, sir?' he said, huskily.

'It smells like rum,' I said.

'It's rum all right, sir. There was lashings in the camp. Not an empty water bottle in the section – centre section's got the whole bloody issher! Some of them's selling it; but I'm keeping mine.'

'Has everybody got some?'

'Oh yes, sir, everybody's had a few. But there's no food there.'

I strolled to the head of the column where the mess cart stood, and looked under the tilt. Inside four bodies lay, and groaned in their sleep. I recognised Mac's boots and the major's boots and felt very indignant that they should not have told me of their bright idea. As I bent over them it was certain that there was rum here also. The major stirred. I began a long report. 'Oh, God!' he said; and then, 'What's the time?'

'About three, sir.'

He leaned on his elbow, wiping the tears from his eyes, and shook the figure on his left. 'Oh, no,' Rawley said laboriously, 'that's the infantryman. He says he's the only officer left in his battalion. Which is Immy?'

'The far one, sir, I think.'

Rawley hit Immingham until he woke up, and flashed a torch in his eyes. Immingham looked very dishevelled and shaggy.

'Didn't I tell you to relieve Boyd at two o'clock? What do you mean sleeping there like a beast?'

'No, sir,' Immingham said.

'I'm all right,' I said. 'Quite all right.'

'Immingham,' Rawley said, gravely, 'consider yourself under arrest. I'll see you are properly relieved, Boyd.' On the very word both sank back to sleep again. I wandered down the road and had some more of the rum, which was circulating freely. Half an hour later the major and Immingham came. The major walked straight enough, but paused every few yards to pull himself up, and whenever he stopped Immingham stopped alongside, all hunched up. I leaned on the gun wheel and watched them indifferently, feeling enormous fatigue in my legs. Then I was aware that the major had halted and was assuming a baleful glare.

'You will consider yourself under arrest, Boyd, for not springing to attention and saluting.'

'Very good, sir.'

'You will also accompany me on an inspection of your section.'

'Very good, sir.'

Some of the men were lying on the road asleep, and some were draped over the limbers. Others were shouting and laughing in the ditch. Rawley put two, and then three, under arrest. This tired him. He sent for the sergeant major and ordered him to put the whole battery under arrest. 'And you're drunk, too, sergeant major!'

'Oh, no, sir,' Burnett replied, and added in morose tones, 'the effects of rum on an empty stomach.'

'Oh, the effects of rum on an empty stomach!' Rawley gave a falsetto giggle and took my arm. 'We'll go sleep now, dear boy.'

When I awoke the column was moving again. I got up and walked along for warmth, tucking the ends of the cheap cotton muffler well down my chest. The wind was bitterly cold and piercing just before daybreak, and although I wrapped the pyjama trousers round my neck as well, I could not keep warm. Every few minutes my hand scraped for crumbs of biscuit in my pockets, but it was long since that the last fragment had gone. We passed through Miraumont on the military road, black like glass, and turned north to Achiet le Petit. Light had now broken and the sky was overcast by dark shapeless shadows between which gleamed the neutral colour of day. We were passing through a camp astir and packing; a row of dixies smoked over a fire by the road. Without a thought I jumped Gaby over the ditch and accepted a cup of tea. It was only when I had drunk it that I realized my greed.

POOR BLOODY HORSES

In a little time we were in Achiet. The wagons turned off the road and halted. The major received orders to take the guns into action three-quarters of a mile south-east. Four men were put on to chop hay with billhooks on billets of wood, while the storeman and the sergeant major measured out the remaining corn. The horses were hurriedly watered, groomed and fed. There was some breakfast, but only little. I got one slice of bully and two biscuits. We stood ready to march. A brigade orderly passing said he carried orders to the guns to withdraw. I wasted no time in waiting but ordered the wagon line away. As the first team left the field the first shell arrived in the ruins. I stared with astonishment at the black smoke crawling up the sky in front of us. The enemy must be very near to have brought his 8-inch howitzers up so soon. The column walked on towards the corner and the second shell burst actually on the crossing. One after another, at regular intervals, they fell with precise accuracy upon our course. There was no other way out; it was quite certain that one part of the column or another must be hit. As I got to the one arm of the corner a big shell howled down and burst in the other. I turned and saw there was room to trot past the wreckage of horses and wagons. The column came rattling along; wagon after wagon, in unwavering line, they came through the gut and passed on to the open down, while I counted the seconds. The interval seemed longer. Even the clumsy GS wagon had cleared the corner, with the water cart splashing after it; and then, hypersensitive, I heard one distant explosion, and another; and a duet of roaring shells growing momentarily louder and more savage. They had delayed to lengthen the range. I saw Sergeant Edwards throw up his arm and vanish with the wagon in the upthrowing of the shell; and a second later another fell into the blast and obliterated the water cart. When the smoke cleared there was not a sign of either on the plain. Behind them the mess cart had met the explosion full in face; horse and man were killed, the cart trampled into pieces.

At Bucquoy we assembled the wagons and guns and marched on south-west. In a valley below the village the guns went into action, waiting to fire on Achiet, 4,000 yards away. Our lines were in an ammunition dump from which we refilled; and on the slope were the huts of a labour camp. Some men found bread and jam there. Before the enemy got to Achiet we had fired 150 rounds and received orders to withdraw. Again I went on a futile reconnaissance to the scarred ground west of Puisieux au Mont. It was too rough even for a saddle horse and I returned at once. Rawley sat on the roadside, with dark rings round his eyes. A dirty golden stubble of long sparse stalks spread round Mac's chin. Immingham's face was grey all over.

His body drooped about his Sam Browne belt as though he were suspended by it. As for myself, when I called the wagon line to attention and tried to think of the best way out of the position, the only things I could think of were articles of food and drink, the crudest food and drink. Vivid images of liver and bacon and of roast goose confused me as I sat on Gaby shouting orders, and as soon as the wagons had begun to move my mind reverted to its vision of smoking dishes and bowls of punch. It was not the first time this had happened.

We marched on the Fonquevillers road, north-west again, towards the ruins of Gommecourt, sown with graves. Night overtook us on the way and the moon rose. A few bare masts of trees stood where Gommecourt had stood, among mounds of bricks, and the bare earth was tufted with grass. The moonlight gave the earth the powdery brown colour of the owl's plumage. We climbed the last slope and dropped to the plain. On the left of the road there gleamed like a mirage piles of hay, corn in abundance, boxes of bully, biscuits and cheese. A lonely sentry, armed with a rifle, marched up and down in front of the dump. His bayonet shone blue. Our divisional train had long since been lost to us; the food could not be for us. Nevertheless I turned Gaby to the ditch to ask whose it was, but as I did so a score of men broke from the column and I saw the sentry disappear among them, and heard him cry piteously, 'You musn't, it's for the —th Division! It's for another division, get out!' But all to no purpose, for in an instant the sacks of corn and trusses of compressed hay were on the limbers; the storeman as he rode along was arranging four bright tin biscuit boxes and two boxes of bully tins so that they would ride easily, and others too —

What should be done? Our horses were starving and tired out, as much as theirs; and I did not know whether Rawley had surreptitiously given orders for the theft. I rode on as the cries of the sentry became more distant and then ceased.

When we came to Fonquevillers we found that the houses were whole and that some trees were in leaf. I heard French voices talking excitedly and thought at first that French troops had come up. The moon shone on a gable end and a tiny casement opened in which a nightcap and face appeared, asking in God's name what we were doing here, and I heard Immingham's voice reply that we were simply reculing to *mieux sauter*. There were no French troops. We had come to the edge of civilization again. On the far side of the village we halted, put up lines and unharnessed. The stolen forage was shared out and while we looked round the horses, the cooks made fires and brewed tea. As soon as we had arrived Immingham had dismounted and disappeared, and now I saw him laughing as he talked to Rawley. The camp was strewn with twinkling fires; the beef tins were hacked open and emptied into dixie lids over the flames. The men squatted round the flames, eyeing the bubbling mess and sipping the scalding tea from their mess tins. Then Mac came and pointed to the major and Immingham, walking to the village, and put his arm in mine and said, as we followed, 'We're going to eat, drink and be merry. What a joy!' Still the moon was bright, the night calm; and still no Gotha came upon us. We mounted the steps of a house. 'There!' Immingham said with pride. We stared at the table. There were veal cutlets, fried potatoes, bread, butter and three bottles of wine. We sat down and ate.

'I'm told this is the only meat in the village,' Immingham said, with his mouth full. 'There is omelette to follow.'

It was one in the morning.

'This is the most wonderful moment in my life,' Mac said, swilling down the hard white wine. After that he took a packet from his pocket and unwrapped four cigars. 'I've been saving these for a festal day,' he said, and handed them round.

The woman smiled at our speeches of thanks, but with constraint, and when Immingham paid her she said something to him, low and earnest. 'There can scarcely be need to go at once,' he answered, 'but all the same it is my advice to you that you do not sleep but pack your goods.'

'Then you think there may be need? I have no horse.'

Immingham shrugged his shoulders.

'Come to us in the morning,' he said, 'perhaps, who knows? we might be able to lend a horse. But come early if you wish help.'

We went back to the bivouac and lay in one long shot of sleep till reveille at 5.30. Thus the fifth day ended.

Upon the broad plain in the full light of day everyone appeared to be running away. Rawley looked round with his mouth open. North and south of us everywhere the artillery was running away. The six-horse teams, three pairs of coupled horses with their square boxes of ammunition behind, ran with a merry appearance of haste over the grass, over thinly growing green, bumping in and out of ditches, falling into holes, took the corners off earthen pies; and the GS wagons lumbered after, great swollen wagons, groaning horribly as the flimsy carriages bent and swayed behind the tug of the heavy draught horses.

'Where's that bloody staff officer?' Rawley said, lifting his glasses again. 'I've lost him now. I bet he's a Boche, telling the troops to quit!'

The rout converged on the Souastre road, already full of heavy transport. An ammunition wagon came askew at the ditch and overturned. 'My God! What bloody bad driving, what a funk, what a bloody rout! There's a GS wagon gone, smashed up on the fore-carriage.' The batteries which remained fired furiously into Hébuterne, which lay about three-quarters of a mile in front of us on the crest. Our guns lay pointed up at Hebuterne, but silent. Mac was up there somewhere reconnoitring.

Rawley shouted. He had seen the staff officer galloping away from a battery nearby. Almost at once their guns opened rapid fire. 'No,' Rawley said to himself, 'I don't believe it.'

Along the road an officer came at full gallop, tossing loosely in his saddle, and in a flash I recognized him. I shouted sharply at him and he drew up

'Well,' I said, 'what do you think of the war now, Whitfall? You do remember me at Newcastle?'

He stared at me and put spurs to his horse. 'It's bloody hell!' he shouted.

An inexplicable panic had seized the plain. Men ran as if for their lives, with nothing in pursuit. Half a dozen batteries blazed away at Hébuterne and we stood silently to our guns and waited. Then a messenger arrived, running from our nearest neighbour.

'Staff officer says the enemy are in Hébuterne,' he said.

'Run back to your battery commander with my compliments,' said Rawley, 'tell him that staff officer is a Boche. I have an observation officer up there. Be off. Quick!'

'There's Mac,' Immingham cried, from his limber.

We saw Mac hurrying down the hill. 'Cease fire!' he shouted, waving to the batteries.

Mac's horse was streaked darkly with sweat.

'They're shooting our fellows in the back!' he said. He had been over the hill and had met machine-gun fire from the little woods five hundred yards beyond. Rawley sent out three mounted men to stop the batteries from killing our own infantry.

About noon I took the wagon line back. We marched sedately to Souastre crossroads. A Guards officer with one arm was trying to bring sense into a mob of fugitives. I hurriedly addressed a field postcard and erased the superfluous words. 'I am quite well,' it said, in italics, '26 March.' The Army

Post Office at the corner was in such panic its staff almost refused to take the card.

I walked back to Gaby. The Guardee wiped his head with a silk handkerchief.

'Any news?' he said.

'The Boche is being held beyond Hébuterne. The Australians are coming up.'

He held up his hand in tribute to the Australians.

We made a temporary wagon line through the village. The sun was brilliant, and all the afternoon the old people from Hébuterne and Fonquevillers toiled up the hill with barrows and handcarts. Sometimes an overloaded cart passed, its load awry, mattresses, beds and chairs lumping into the sky. Two pigs were fastened behind the cart, and went unwillingly.

The rout was stopped. The wagons went back to the guns, and all night we waited in the frosty road, feeling the air cold and sharp. Immingham was in front. Mac walked up and down with me for a time and told me how the afternoon had gone. For the first time the German planes had got through the concentration of our machines, hanging in wait over their aerodromes. 'God bless the RFC,' we said in unison. Seven Germans came over and killed two horses before our machine guns drove them back again. That was the ending of the sixth day.

The morning came up fine. The line seemed stable. Rawley and Mac promised to have dinner with me in Souastre. I took the wagons to the village. The steel tyres of our steel wagons cut deep into the rich sod and broke down the yellow daffodils where they stood under the trees in the orchard. The sap ran out and smelled strongly.

Dinner was a failure. We sat down in the farm and then a roll of shellfire came from the front. Rawley and Mac mounted and went away, shouting to me that I was to keep the fowl hot; but they did not return. The bird was extremely tough.

I went up to see the guns the second day after. They were in a field of long green shoots, like winter oats, and the men had dug holes in the soft earth for cover from the shellfire. They were shelling as I rode up and I dropped my bicycle on the track of beaten green stalks and went up on foot. There I found them all, sheltering in a hole. Rawley was much like himself, but Mac and Immingham were getting worn. The retreat had not been comfortable or easy for them. Now Mac was irritable and even angry about things, and would not try to show the least geniality, and Immingham walked

187

about the position with a slow exhausted step, as though he held his courage in his hands and was afraid of spilling it all to the last drop, and so have nothing left. I had seen such movements before at Bus, while the bombardment surged round us, and knew them well, for they were my own, too. It was as if one's body were cramped and would not expand.

On the 28th the enemy increased his shellfire on the batteries and attacked the Anzacs. But the New Zealanders refused our help when we offered it. 'New Zealand's machine guns can manage them alone, thanks,' they telegraphed. We were still in the open. The battery fired south of Hébuterne while the men knelt behind the steel shields serving their guns. Sergeant Wilson was kneeling at the trail of Number Three when a 5.9 landed on the piece and threw the whole thing in the air. The bombardier and one gunner were blown to pieces, but Wilson was not hurt. He came to the wagon line for a rest. The sergeant major went sick; his skin had broken out in eruption all over. Thus I was still worse off; there was neither quartermaster nor sergeant major.

The stragglers came in one by one, the men began to send letters home again. I wrote to Sam. 'I've been a bit above my luck lately,' I said, 'largely due to my invariable policy of moving from point to point by the largest shell holes, irrespective of their position. I'm very glad you're still at Moffat. It's a very good place to be at and I wish you a long, long stay. We're fairly well off where we are, though the overture was a little *basso sostenuto* while it lasted. We left a lot of hares behind. My own heels looked just like Cherry Blossom. The army is in very good heart indeed and the *morale* has never wavered for a minute, but I won't say we were delighted.' It was 3 April when the first English mail arrived. Immingham sat with me in the light of a paraffin lamp which Madame had lent, and we read in silence, and then re-read. He went back in the morning with Willoughby, an old member of the brigade who had just rejoined us. The front was uneasy. I woke on the 5th to the sound of heavy shelling and decided to clear out of Souastre. It was too near the line; only 7,000 yards from the actual front. Wilson rode out with me to find a better place. Near Hénu we discovered a deep, wooded valley, so small that it was unconsiderable on the map. Nevertheless, lying immediately by the road, there was a delta of flat meadow large enough for the wagons. The men's bivouacs could go into the light shelter of the birch trees, the horses in front and between them, the tents on the terraces of the hillside. By the meadow a clear brook ran over gleaming sand, and the bank of the stream was bordered with cowslips. It was an ideal place, giving water, shelter and space. We trotted back to Souastre, and as we descended the hill we saw four shells fall in the village. One made a hole in our orchard. The biting vapour of high explosive still hung about the place. The wagons were ready to march. We moved off.

At the gate the woman of the house cried into her apron.

'My husband lost a leg in the war; he was also shellshocked; we have scraped this little farm together again, must we now go?'

It was hard to comfort her.

We pitched tents in the dell. Water, food, ammunition, tobacco and whisky were all in reach. The year had turned; again I ordered a new tunic and new riding breeches. Mac came down for a rest. He told me about the 5th, how brigade headquarters had been shelled out of the Chateau de la Haie, several men killed, and how the guns had been plastered all day long. But there was something further in his mind which he did not add. We rode into Doullens to buy things. Someone said there was a good eating place a mile south, on the roadside. We passed among the pretty white houses in the sunshine, up the hill through the fortifications, enamelled with fresh grass, and came at last to an inn. It scarcely looked like an eating place. We pushed inside the bar. An old woman said 'This way, sirs,' and showed us into a room. There were eight or nine officers sitting there in silence with glasses in front of them. They looked like people in a dentist's waiting room. A girl appeared, half dressed.

'Darling Donald,' Mac whispered, 'I fear this is a brothel. Let us flee.'

We were late for lunch in Doullens, but made up for it with a bottle and a half of Burgundy and several glasses of mild cherry brandy.

Mac said: 'There's not a spot of leave on the horizon.'

'It was 2 November I got home, five months and four days ago.'

'They told me, leave every three months when I joined the army. They lie so nastily.'

'Mac, what do you do on leave? Go and see your people or fritter away the precious moments in carousing?'

'You wouldn't ask me to tell you that. Oh, no! It wouldn't be nice!'

'I see!'

'Tell you what; last time it was thumbs, oh, absolute thumbs! A pal lent me his flat— I usually live at the club – and he filled it, Morzo, with foodings and winings and smokings. Then I came along with the sweetest little thing, and we went to a show every night and razzled and what-not. Straight for Piccadilly; that's my plan of campaign.'

'I feel like that too. But I don't know. I have got a family – I mean father, mother, brothers, and sister, you know. Being there, although I couldn't perhaps be anywhere else, you don't feel quite alive. Women say "We do understand all you're suffering" and men say, heartily, "Keep it up, my boy" or else they say "The home front is solid, in spite of the awful hardships of the sugar shortage." They make me absolutely boil with fury. But how can you make them see?'

'The women I meet say "*Mon petit coco*" or "Duckie" and the men say "Another little drink won't do us any harm." Arrayed in my black silk pyjamas, she bit me below the left ear! I haven't any people in England.'

'You don't really get away from the war on my sort of leave. Perhaps that's my fault. You're so full of it. If you haven't some absorbing sort of passion you won't forget for an hour that you're going back in ten days. You can't fit into civil life. You're not real. But I couldn't go anywhere else, all the same.'

'Hear, hear, passion! You forget the war in good old London town. Have a hell of a good time. Then you wake up at Victoria.'

'You don't feel real either. We don't either of us feel real on leave. We're only real in the line. But you choose ten Arabian nights' leave while I – I expect England to be pre-war.'

'Oh, hoots! hoots! Have a drink, lovey!'

Mac relieved me at the wagon line and I joined Rawley, Immingham and Willoughby at the guns. They had got into one of the old Somme positions, with dugouts. Willoughby was like Sam, so impulsive and comradely that he was charming for these things, even if there had been nothing else.

'I say,' he said, frowning, 'what do you think of Rawley?'

'I've found him very decent.'

'Yes. But on the fifth we had a dreadful time, as you can see.'

'Mac didn't say exactly.'

'He wouldn't. It was absolutely the most ber-loody strafe. I don't know how many guns he has, but they were all shooting on us. Immingham had been on duty in the battery and came back to the mess. There was MacVeagh and there was me. Then the strafe started twice as bad; all the next corps' guns, if you know, and in the middle of it – SOS!

'SOS!'

'Yes. Now I should have thought Rawley ought to have turned out to get the guns into action. He knew what the men had gratefully received earlier.

But he sent Immingham. I said it was my turn; but he sent Immingham. He has a down on Immingham and he favours Mac.'

'Damned good chap, Mac. Immingham, too.'

'Immingham crawled across between the bursts; the position was a perfect cloud of smoke, and of course the men were in their dugouts. He got into the first dugout and told the men to get out, and then to the second; and when he got out he saw Number Six wasn't firing; they hadn't got out. So he went back and said "Look here, this isn't playing the game. SOS. Get your gun into action." Nobody moved at all. Immingham ordered them out. They all stayed still. He drew his revolver. One of them said "Don't be a bloody fool, Immingham," just like that. He says he couldn't, couldn't shoot. He ran back to the mess like a madman and told Rawley. I heard him.'

'How awful! What a shocking show!'

'That's not the worst. Rawley told him to go back to the guns. And Rawley stayed here drinking whisky.'

'Did he go?'

'Yes. He was sitting in a shell hole, looking like death and swinging his revolver on his finger. I went after him. Now what would you have done?'

'I haven't an idea. Thank God it wasn't me. The only difference is, I should never have got even as far as the guns if the strafe was as bad as that.'

'It was, quite. But think of Rawley.'

'He has his own standards. He's not a strong, silent Englishman like you. He's a London b'hoy.'

'I think he's a —. Besides, Immingham's got a Military Cross; he's not a complete coward.'

'He got it near Hollebeke doing forward OP during a show, and what's more, he got it on the recommendation of an infantry brigadier.'

'Did he, by Jove!'

'He did. How filthy for him. He can't go and leave the war. He can't go sick.'

'There's one thing. I believe the men were very decent. They sort of rallied round almost immediately after the worst shelling and started firing. Perhaps there wasn't five minutes passed altogether. They were very much ashamed; but they're all so tired; all those had been out, as it happened, since April, '15, you know, three years and about two leaves.'

'Did Rawley do anything at all?'

'Not a bloody thing to anybody. Not to Immingham. Not even to the men.'

One night three men and the mess cart went up unofficially into Hébuterne to see what they could find. They got caught in a burst of shellfire. Two men were killed and the horse was wounded. We had to send the mess cart back to collect the bodies. A number of signallers working through Hébuterne had been killed in the same way by sudden bursts of fire. One of them was in my section, a young father who wrote fantastic and delightful letters to his children. I had read one the night he was killed, recognizing his handwriting in the pile, and I had to send it to his wife with the news. Now that I was going up to Hébuterne cemetery to do liaison with the Australians, Immingham and Willoughby advised me to circle the village by trenches. I dropped into the muddy gully from the roadside and made my way laboriously southward upon the forward slope of the hill. The trench had no duckboards and the rain had turned the bottom into clay. After a time I met a sergeant and asked him if my direction was correct. So far as I could make out his badges, half covered up, he was of the Essex Regiment. To my surprise he asked for my name and brigade. Then he went down the trench, begging me to sit on the firestep. In a moment he returned with an officer.

'Mr Borrow, this is Mr. Boyd of the —th Brigade, Royal Field Artillery.'
Thus introduced, we shook hands.

'Not a very charming place,' he said, 'and more than a little untidy, but we hope to make it passable for our visitors and ourselves, quite soon.'

'Not at all,' I murmured.

'It's been such good weather until the last few days; the war's been really much more tolerable; but the rain is so uncivilised. Now, if you want the cemetery, I can easily send a runner with you, and I would rather you were led through our sector; the trench scarcely exists in places. But better still, the major would be most pleased if you could stay to dinner.'

'I'm afraid I must get along to the Australians.'

'Excellent people. We are so unenterprising by comparison.'

'Will you express my regrets to your mess? It would have been pleasant. If you have any time to spare I hope you will call on us; we are at E.26.a.8.6.'

'Thank you. I will try. Now here's your route and a runner.'

We shook hands and crawled our various ways, and as I went I remarked again to myself on the difference between the regular army and the rest; not perhaps so much in fighting quality, though that might show, but in this rigorous parade. The idea that the sector was the private charge of a company had so far passed that I could remember scarcely another occasion which had suggested it since I had left the Rue du Bois, three years ago.

The Australian trenches ran along the outer boundary of the cemetery among and below the tombstones. The Australians were thin men with flat thighs and flattened convex noses, except when their noses were broken; and they had thin lips and bright indifferent eyes. Their pleated jackets were untidy, they were extremely dirty in their trenches, their manners were wholly careless; yet they were magnificent fighters and more tolerant of a stranger than one might have expected. The colonel gave me a corner of his dugout and the night passed peacefully. The morning brought my twenty-third birthday. Before the mist cleared, Baker, a new subaltern from C Battery came up to man the OP. It was in a corner of the cemetery; a shelter shaped like an up-ended coffin made of steel rails. At about ten a hurricane strafe fell on the cemetery.

'Would you like some retaliation, sir?' I asked.

'No, 'twouldn't do any good, much. You've only got pipsqueak guns, haven't you?'

A youth fell down the dugout steps. He was badly shellshocked and lay in a corner whimpering and groaning.

'To think this is my birthday!' I said.

'All the joy of the day to you, gunner,' the colonel said, 'you got your birthday presents outside.'

I went up the shaft to the doorway and looked along the trench. The great shells screamed down with the roar of a spinning world and burst upon the floor of the earth with a multiplying blast, so violent the fibres of one's nerves seemed to part. Gouts of smoke drifted across the gravestones on the bank above me. I lay on the steps staring up at the sky. I wanted to go into the trench to tell Baker to come into safety. In the trench the invisible metal fled past and stung the earth savagely. I went down to telephone but the wire was broken. Climbing the other shaft the smoke quivered like an animal in the blast of the shells. I crouched again on the upper steps. A man threw himself into the shaft, an Australian sergeant he was, and under his arm he carried a man's leg torn off at the groin. The thick red blood was still spouting from the stump and fell upon the stairs. The sergeant was laughing and shouted to the people in the dugout. 'Any feller missing a leg?' he said. The colonel was angry with him. I heard him say 'You something sergeant, you're frightening the lad here. Take that leg out and pitch it into the cemetery where it belongs. Go on, get out of it.' At the top of the shaft a soldier was lying without a head. His blood was flowing where it could among the intersecting footprints in the trench; it made lakes of bright scarlet, thick and gummy. There was no sign of the man missing a leg, but it was an Australian leg, not Baker's; I could tell that by the cloth upon it. The trench was empty of men and I still wished to find Baker, but the storm of shattering noises pressing inward drove me back, and in a few minutes Baker raced along, bent double, and threw himself down the shaft. Half an hour later we went to the OP and found that the two faces of the girders were smashed in together. The rest of the day was bright and clear.

My next tour was with the Australians on the right of the cemetery. The colonel lectured me, as an Englishman, upon the stupidity of the 'limited objective' battles of the Somme. 'If you are willing to spend ten thousand lives, you should get value for them in German lives and German territory. We did not get the equivalent either way. It was foolishness from start to end.' In the middle of his discourse two men came in out of the sunshine, lean, excited figures.

'Jerry's buzzed a bomb at Jake,' one said, 'and hit him in the guts. Kin we go out with a *carte de visite?*

'Go back like good boys and I'll come and see.'

'All right, we will.'

We went up and surveyed the place. It was high noon with a bright sun. The trench was excited at the idea of a raid; Jake's friend was flapping his hands in disgust at all the volunteers who wanted to come. 'Two dinkum babies can do this best,' he said. The colonel said kindly, 'He'll take you, though, gunner, if you like. Three's not too many is it, Pete?'

Pete looked downcast.

'I'll not spoil the party,' I said, heartily, 'leave me out of this.'

So they crawled over the parapet and dropped in a grassy ditch, running towards the German sap. Through periscopes we watched their hindquarters dragging along the gully. After half an hour a voice outside called 'Joel'. Joel disappeared. In a little while two bombs exploded in front. A few minutes after, Pete and his friend arrived with a prisoner, half-dead from strangulation. 'They was all kipped down,' said Pete, 'so we lifted the machine gun; it's in front there; then we took Joel back. There was one of them snoozing in the sap head. We slithered in and throttled him while Joel watched; then we dragged him out and told Joel to bomb their dugout when we got clear. Here we are; and here's Joel.' He leaped over the parapet as a machine gun traversed towards us. But the German line had awakened too late.

Soon I went back to the wagon line again. The line was firmly held. The usual stream of forms and orders flowed upon us again, and one day I found among them a message to myself. I was to go to a rest camp by the sea for three weeks. Gerald and Truscott came down to have a farewell party, and we all drank a great deal of whisky. Gerald kept on trying to explain why it was that one often felt more safe in one's own battery position, however exposed, than in a strange battery position, and so also in a familiar trench than in an unfamiliar one. But Truscott was not interested. He put his monocle in his eye and beamed upon everyone, and then we all went out and Truscott said he was a tank and climbed on his hands and knees up the grassy bank, growling as long as he could keep his breath. Then we all went back into the tent again, and Truscott became a tank between drinks, and growled horribly, while Gerald became sober, suddenly, and very sad.

Chapter 11

A Bottle and a Kind Landlady

St Valéry

Albert – Summer 1918

The ceiling had been covered with so many coats of varnish that it had become a deep ivory colour and on that ivory sky half a dozen paper swallows pursued one large bumble-bee and various small insects. Outside the inn windows the real swallows whistled and dived and the faintest breeze shook the curtains. I was so possessed by my bodily emptiness and cleanliness that I myself scarcely seemed to exist more than one of the unnumbered animals. We had been swimming nearly all the day from the hot sand at the mouth of the Somme and my body was cool and firm and dry. It felt as though it had been bleached; and my hair was still full of harsh salt. The salt water had flowed into my mouth and nose and scoured them to acute sensibility, and I was aware of the touch of my clothes, particularly the touch of the loose Indian khaki trousers on my legs. The feeling of the breath of the free air upon my skin had not gone. Above all things it seemed good to lie exposed to the water and the air, to eat and drink; to pursue these things with singleness and to be nothing but a hollow physical being.

We sat in silence for a long time. Fall's long thin fingers moved among the cutlery and pressed upon them with a caressing movement, as though he wished to impress upon himself the knowledge that they were there. The meats followed each other upon the table and were succeeded by a little dish of baked chocolate, fruit and coffee. Still without speech we took cigarettes. The bitter smoke of the French tobacco filled my nostrils. Fall poured the white wine and again we fell into abstraction. I was bemused by the feeling that I was like one of the little crabs long since dead on the shore, a carapace empty of the soft decaying meat, nothing but a bleached shell. This was the state of blessedness, to have emptied out the corruptible, the vulnerable, the treacherous inner thought and feeling, to have lost all memory and all past time, to be beyond conceits, humiliations, fear and shame. Then, I thought, I can live in this golden moment, wine-coloured, like the sleeping summer evening, then the moment will become life, and the moment will become always; I shall hear the whistling of the swallows forever. I shall hear, taste and feel and be nothing more upon this earth.

While I thus tasted the black coffee and sank deeper into my chrysanthous dream a piece of bread flew over my shoulder and hit Fall in the face. He looked up, puzzled, with a smile on his lips. There was a commercial traveller at the far end of the room, pursing red lips over an account book. There were only two other people in the room, two women dressed in black. My gaze was dropping to the cloth again when I heard a bar of laughter. Another piece of bread flew through the air, and then, as 1 turned, one of the women moved and I saw that the other was quite young. Under her mourning hat her hair shone golden, a fillet of gold cut squarely at the temples, and her eyes were blue; a Norman girl with wide, firm cheek bones. Fall lifted his glass and bowed to her, and she lifted her own wineglass and threw her head back so that her eyes seemed to darken and yet become more revealing, more piercing as the lids closed over them, but she still seemed to laugh. Then Fall rose to pay the bill, and we prepared to go. The girl rose with a swirl of her skirts, whose outflung pleats swept, as it seemed, the whole of the dusky room, and was gone. But she had delayed in the passage past the servery. She had taken off her hat, and her coarse hair was shaking loose upon her golden skin like the parallel dancing of the Northern Lights. She had waited for Fall, and took him by the hand. He gave me an apologetic smiling glance and went out of the inn with her.

The night was filled with such light airs that they seemed to carry me over the gleaming cobbles. I passed under a grove of trees and mounted the hill by the white cottages of the fishermen. The night air was warm and visible, as though its warm softness was embodied, tangible, and the sky was the velvety grey which sometimes follows great heat. I walked over the hill to the camp.

At the rest camp there were no shells, no bombs, no orders; no forms, returns, states, indents, accounts; there were no parades, no inspections, not a single parade, day or night. Instead there were hot baths every morning, golf, tennis, cricket, swimming, badminton, music, books, bowls. We could please ourselves and the breeze went lightly through the groves of silver birch trees. Upon the grassy cliff we slept in the sun and went to bathe again, dressed in shorts and shirt. In the long afternoon we moved lazily down the coast, stripping and bathing and drying in the sun till we came to the little harbour below, and waded across to the inn among the sand dunes. There we ate shrimps and looked at the pictures the artists had left behind, wonderful pictures of light on the long sands and heat quivering above the pebble ridge, penned in wicker fences. On the wall there was a glass case and in it their pipes, the artists' pipes; pipes of all curves and materials. 'Poor artists!' we said, 'they are all done for, now,' and the grizzled innkeeper with the long moustaches stared at us with contempt. We were barelegged and bareheaded, creasing our eyes against the upthrown dazzle from the sand, and he murmured to himself that a dead lion was worth a thousand live dogs. In the evening one of Miss Ashwell's parties came to the camp. There was a man who sang a song composed by a captain of the Warwicks. It was called 'The Ruddy Platoon', and pleased everyone, very much.

The mud in the trench is a bit of all right,
If you 'an't a tin 'at on you'd sink out of sight,
And what with the minnies and what with the crumps
A-strafing the rations and strafing the dumps –
We started with fifty odd non-coms and men
We started with fifty, but now we are ten,
And if this ruddy war doesn't end very soon,
There'll be nobody left in the ruddy platoon.

And there was another song going through the ranks of the battalion, but this was an unofficial song. The authorities did not quite approve.

If you want to find the officer,
I know where 'e is,
I know where 'e is,
I know where 'e is,
If you want to find the officer,
I know where 'e is,
'e's a scoffing of the swaddy's rum.
I seen him, I seen him,
Scoffing of the swaddy's rum I seen him,
Scoffing of the swaddy's rum.

A BOTTLE AND A KIND LANDLADY

Last verse serious, please.

If you want to find your sweetheart
I know where 'e is,
'E's a 'anging on the 'ole barbed wire.
I seen 'im, I seen 'im
'anging on the ole barbed wire I seen 'im,
'anging on the ole barbed wire.

MacVeagh and Rawley one afternoon came stalking through the camp looking for me. The brigade was at rest and they had lorry-hopped to St Valéry. It was a rousing evening, almost too rousing, for I did not wish to be roused. And at the inn, where the swallows flew upon the ceiling, we dined together.

Rawley said, after his fourth brandy, that he was deuced fed-up with the war. Very much too bored. Later I saw them out of the village. A grey French *camion* picked them up and left a wake of fine powder above the road.

As their lorry disappeared I thought of Mac's story of the blind the majors of the brigade had held at the Hôtel de France in Abbeville. Mac told it to me while the major was talking to someone at the rest camp. 'The colonel was there, too,' he said. 'After dinner they were all jolly well blotto. Rawley had his eye on a juicy little piece in black. So had Parkinson eyed the same piece. But when Parkinson wasn't looking, Rawley gave the girl the wink and snook out, and up to her room; and Parkinson, seeing they'd gone, pursued. It happened that a Waac had been at dinner in the hotel. She had just gone out after Rawley and his whore, and she went to her room. Parkinson was so blind he could only recognize a skirt. He saw the Waac disappear into a room and piled in after her and embraced her with passionate embraces. Now it happened that Lucas really had seen the Waac. He also prowled in the passages and he heard her screaming. Gallantly flung he open the door, nobly did he dispossess Parkinson. Then, alas! he realised that he was now a chivalrous white-headed boy. He apologised for his friend, and staggered sadly downstairs. Oh! Disillusionment! But what is this that approaches? A beauteous maiden with ripe red lips! "Com wis me," she whispered. "Can a duck swim," said Lucas. So they exited to a downy couch, leaving Parkinson alone on the stage. Dear Parks was actually pulling himself together in a corner of the corridor, preparing for a venture. He marches proudly along, listening for sounds of amorous levity. And who does he see but a girl with ripe red lips, as in a dream. That was Lucas and his girl. But they don't see him. He thinks it is the original piece of virtue ensconced with Rawley, fumes desperately to himself, straightens his tunic and barges right in. You know how Lucas loves Parks? Imagine the *furore*! Alas! Parks now has a black eye. I may say that the colonel did not participate in this part of the evening. But I will add that Rawley at length descended, very gloomy, said he was too drunk and offered me the key to the room he had left.'

That was Mac's story of the majors' blind.

A few days later Mac wrote two lines to say that Dodd had come back. 'Good-bye,' Mac scrawled, in his enormous hand, 'tootle-too, likewise farewell, and come back soon, you.' The letter came the day before the last. Upon the last night the camp seemed to flame up out of its sleep. Nearly everyone went to the little inn for dinner, and let the smooth wine run down his throat, and then in a troop the officers went across to the house under the trees. But the door was locked. Several hammered upon it till it was opened and Cunliffe argued noisily at the bottom of the staircase. He had arranged to see the brunette called Stephanie, he said, and at length he climbed up the stairs and put his shoulder to the door and would have broken it down had not an angry English voice shouted, 'Wait!' Then the door was flung open and he saw his own general in pyjamas on the landing, and the words choked in his throat. The general said to the men at the foot of the staircase, 'You must learn to behave like gentlemen even in a brothel,' and everyone then left the house quietly.

First of all the Railway Transport Officer sent me to Abbeville.

I had to spend a night there, after a long and fruitless argument.

The next morning the RTO at Abbeville sent me to Étaples. By this time I had a small party of strays in charge, all bound for the division. I had travelled so far about twenty kilometres southwest and fifty kilometres north.

We halted at Étaples. It was one enormous camp of reinforcements, thousands and thousands of them, camped in long black huts which encircled and jostled the hospital tents. I got my blankets and billeting order for one of the nameless lodging depots and carried my small kit into the mess. No servant came. I could not find one. Presently an officer entered.

'Isn't there a mess servant?' I said.

'They've all gone,' he said, offhanded.

'Where?'

'Gone to the woods for the night.'

'I don't understand; I want a spot of food. Surely there are servants?'

'Are there hell-as-like! They've bunked because they're windy. Last night they bombed us.'

'Do you mean the staff's bunked for the night? At eight o'clock?'

'I do. You'll find all the servants of all the camps camping out under the trees two miles away, scores of them.'

'This is the lousiest place in the whole war,' he said. 'Did you read the screams at home about the nurses in hospital being killed by bombs? Well, I was here. First place: I don't believe more than one nurse was injured. Second place: they painted red crosses on the canvas after the bombing, for propaganda photographs. Third place: how the hell do they imagine the bombers can miss the hospitals, when they're planted in the middle of the biggest railway centre and reinforcement camp in France?'

'No can do.'

'Anyway, what the hell! Dump your stuff in a tent. There are a dozen empty. You're too late for dinner at the club, but you'll be able to get something to eat.' I was too hungry to continue the conversation.

The Officers' Club was like a big golfhouse made of asbestos boarding and timber. It was a gift to the army in memory of two brothers, both killed in action. I got something to eat and then watched four subalterns keep a billiards table to themselves by putting down their names in rotation on the slate. Then I had a bath. There were little notices in the bath cubicles – 'Officers are requested not to use permanganate of potash in these baths as it stains them.'

In the morning the RTO confessed he had not any idea where the division was. I must spend another night and call again. I slowly got better of my annoyance in Paris-Plage, a tawdry resort of the staff.

After my return I sat in the club waiting for dinner, and drank a glass of sherry. There were hundreds of officers in the ante-room. About a quarter of an hour before dinner I saw a number gather about the glazed door of the mess, and stare through the glass at the tables. The number increased rapidly. Within ten minutes half the officers in the room were packed round the door, shoulder to shoulder. They were waiting for their food. When the mess waiter unlocked the doors they fought their way in. The next morning the RTO gave us movement orders for Watten, seventy kilometres northeast on the Canal de l'Aa. He sounded quite confident, but I had doubts of him.

The RTO at Watten said he hadn't the vaguest idea where the division lay but would find out. I put up at the Tête d'Or. The officers on the Inland Water Transport, who sent the barges gliding up and down with wounded and stores, came in to dinner and sang in the dining-room. For dinner we had soup, *hors d'oeuvre* of prawns, egg and lettuce-heart, asparagus, baked tench, a green salad, a salad of green figs and apricots, cheese and coffee. It was a meatless day.

By lunchtime the next day the RTO announced that nobody knew where the division was. For lunch we ate soup, shrimps, mackerel, roast beef, green salad, fruit salad and coffee. The inn was charging about *10s. 6d.* (52.5p) a day for my food and lodging. We were all tired of our homeless state.

We loafed at Watten five days before the RTO knew where to send us. Then we went about a hundred kilometres south towards Amiens and spent a night at Canaples in a mossy camp in the heart of a wood. From there we went thirty miles eastward. I finished the journey on horseback and found the wagon line among the tall trees of Bavelincourt. It had taken ten days to get back, and all the time the battery had been within eighty kilometres of St Valéry.

It was fine to be greeted by friends again, on every hand.

In a few days it was as if I had never been away. Gerald had a pair of howitzers on the raised chalk prairie south of the big road from Amiens to Albert, and our guns were quite close. I walked among the growing crops to see him. He unfolded his long body from a lump of chalk where he crouched writing a letter.

'You're back at last,' he said.

'I don't feel very different.'

'It's nice to be away, but when you come back it's just the same thing. If you were fed to the teeth, windy, you return the same; if you were on the edge of insanity you begin to get nearer again. If you loathed it all your loathing gets more powerful.'

'That's true. Still, you have to get back. I mean you want to, there's a sort of compulsion on you.'

'Yes, but you crave for leave, for any bit of time off. . . . The general's pinched a leave warrant two months before his time.'

'It's a day or two over seven months since you or I were home.'

'Oh, yes! I know that well enough. It was 2 November 1917. Now it's about 8 June 1918.'

A BOTTLE AND A KIND LANDLADY

Across the bare swell of the ground which accompanied the road to Albert, there were three or four terraces and upon one of the higher ones our guns stood. The men's shelters were cut from the bank below them. The sun scorched the unsheltered land, the grass was dry and brittle, and where we walked the ground became bare, exposing the white chalk dust. The field behind the position was full of clover, which we struggled to cut with an old scythe and a sickle. In the late afternoon the wagon took away one load, and returned long before we were ready with another. It was backbreaking work, swinging with the scythe and stooping with the sickle. Somehow the men in charge of the wagon got permission from Rawley to take it onwards, across the ridge, to the villages of the Ancre, Heilly, Ribemont and Buire, to see what they could find. There was a heat haze which made observation difficult at that hour. Dodd, Mac, Willoughby and I went on cutting the clover until there seemed enough. Then we piled it together and sat sweating in our shirtsleeves at the doorway of the tiny mess, drinking whisky and water as the dusk fell. The wagon came back, loaded the clover, and departed. There was a hush fell on the position. After a while we heard the sounds of a mouth organ playing amid subdued laughter. Rawley rose and stretched and then stood at gaze. We got up and joined him. On the terrace above a girl and a young man were approaching in the heavy dusk. The mouth organist followed them. All three wore civilian clothes of French cut. Rawley stood staring at them as they approached the half circle of gunners on the terrace. Then the mouth organ halted a moment and began another tune. The girl swayed her hips from side to side, taunting the man and broke off into an erotic cakewalk and the man followed with little sinuous rushes, thrusting out his hips and shaking his elbows backward. For a few seconds the illusion was sufficient.

Rawley at my elbow swore with startling fury. I took a hurried glance at his face. He was talking to himself passionately; I could see his lips moving and his eyes glisten. When he got control of himself he shouted in a high, cracked tone, 'Sergeant major, send those men here.' The party came trailing down the slope to us. I recognized the girl as a young gunner called Cruikshank, who was something of a pet among the telephonists. He held his skirts up piteously as he came to us.

'Where did you get those — things?' Rawley said, harshly.

'They came on the wagon, sir, from Buire, I think it was.'

'Take them off at once.'

Cruikshank fumbled with the strings of his skirt, which slowly fell down his breeches and puttees. He stood a moment in a striped cotton blouse and a flat straw hat, ornamented with artificial roses. Rawley stared at him thus half-clad, the skirt crumpled about his ankles, and burst out into hysterical laughter.

'All right,' he said, 'take your clothes away. You're the funniest girl I've ever seen.'

Cruikshank smiled uncertainly, and departed with his garments.

Our share of the loot was a mirror so large it filled the wall of the shelter. But there were also some tawdry candlesticks of brass. One of them had seven branches.

'They are obviously out of Buire church,' I said.

'I don't see that that need trouble us,' said Rawley.

'Isn't it sacrilege?'

I'm not sufficiently acquainted with religion to say.'

'We might send them back to the priest at Bavelincourt with your compliments, sir, as having been rescued from Buire?'

Dodd made an assenting noise.

'Oh, do what you like.'

Rawley went riding and pitched awkwardly from his horse. He said he believed he had either broken a collarbone or torn a muscle. 'Bye-bye, you fellows,' he said, 'going sick for a bit. And time, too.' So he departed and we saw him no more.

And still there was no chance of leave. I met Gerald at OP, but now leave had become a preoccupation with him, and so he kept his mouth shut, he said, sooner than talk, for fear the word might come into the conversation. The day was quiet and the hours crawled by with intolerable slowness as I waited for something to turn up. I stared at the front through my glasses. The OP was on low ground and there was nothing to be seen but the jungle of summer grasses and the low mounds of their front line. Leave and the boredom of war; these were the only things to think about. One could go on for hours saying how bored one was and still fail to reach the centre definition of that oceanic boredom which saturated every nerve and fibre. Boredom oppressed us, atmosphere upon atmosphere. We were fed-up, fed to the teeth, abso-bloody-lutely fed-up. By its usual miracle the day declined to dusk. The mist permeated the half-light and I packed up my scattered implements and departed to the shallow quarry in which the infantry battalion had their headquarters. Sitting in a corner of a dugout was a quiet man with an old-fashioned stiff collar to his tunic. His skin was inclined to grey, and it was very smooth. After a while he moved over and asked with great politeness what my duties were.

He was the first American I had met in the line. Later at night a shoot broke over us. I went up to the OP to watch.

The American came too. 'Aren't you going to do anything?' he said.

'No, nothing.'

'Won't you attack them?'

'No, please God, we won't attack. It's nothing, merely nothing. A few men killed, possibly, but nothing to report.'

He was so keen and willing to fight that he seemed terrifying.

The dawn came very slowly and it was raw and harsh. The trench was scarcely more than an alley between low walls of sandbags filled with earth, and they were cold and clammy to the touch, like marble. A few shells came over and a few rifle grenades, then the sky lightened perceptibly and I lit a cigarette which made me cough. One of the infantrymen offered me a sip of his tea and took a cigarette from my case

'When are the Americans coming into the line, sir?'

'There are a few already, I believe. A month or two, I suppose.'

'They ought to make a difference. They can have the war for all I care.'

'Oh, they'll have it all right!'

At night a sack of rations came up with a note from Mac about my relief. It was to be delayed a day, 'because our dear new major wants me to bring him up that day and show him round,' Mac said. 'He's got a blue chevron, to show he's here, that's nice for him, is not it? PS, he's rather a nice tick, really, a fat white one, about forty-four. Incinerate this, dearest of Ds.' I dropped it in the stove.

The new major was called Lettner. He had never been out before, and as Mac said, he wore a blue chevron on his sleeve showing that he had arrived. Major Lettner was a prosperous manufacturer from Birmingham, so far as we could gather. The first night we were together Immingham was on duty. An orderly brought orders for night firing. Immingham went to the mapboard and began to work out the lines and rates and times of fire.

'Why do you do that?' Lettner kept saying, 'we didn't do it like that at Shoeburyness,' and then Immingham had to halt and explain, and forget where he was and have to start again, till in despair he begged for a few minutes to get it done, first. Then when Lettner had gone to his dugout to sleep we asked each other why Captain Dodd and Truscott and Anson and

Peterson should not have got the battery, one of them or the other, for they were all good men who had been in the war since 1915. But there was no answer to that. And in that frame of mind we marched out to rest at St Sauveur, behind Amiens, and Dodd was with us, saying nothing, showing nothing. 'Perhaps he's even pure enough to think nothing,' Immingham said, 'or just too bored to care.'

At St Sauveur influenza sprang upon the brigade. In a few days Dodd, Immingham and our new subaltern, Farmer, fell ill. About twenty men went to the hospital which the doctors organized. An epidemic spread like fire and in the middle of it we were ordered to go up for an attack on the village of Hamel, which lay on the hill above the south bank of the Somme.

This attack was to be planned in a new way. No colossal railheads were to be built; no enormous dumps. No columns of lorries would beat up the dust of midday. The guns would not advertise themselves by firing on all the points beforehand. Not a man would show his head by daylight. It was to be a surprise attack by Australians and Americans, timed for 4 July, out of honour to Independence Day. The weather was brilliant. We rode out to reconnoitre positions at noon on the 27th, two officers from each battery. Lettner rode in front, bumping on his saddle, and Gerald, reconnoitring for his howitzers, rode with me. We trotted through the ruins of Corbie and turned north to the ridge between the Ancre and the Somme. Then we left the horses and went forward on foot, separating to our own positions. We had scarcely done so when a shoot of 5.9s fell about us. I dragged the major into a shell hole and lay upon the earth. The shooting persisted round us, and the bits of metal whirred into the crater and shot into the soil. 'Keep down, sir,' I said. Lettner turned a white face to me and shook his head. His lips moved and a strange sound came out of his throat. I saw he wanted to run. Then he started crawling up the side of the hole. I dragged him down to the centre of the crater and held him there. Then when it was over we went on and he never said a word, so I had no chance to explain how fashionable it was to be horribly frightened at first. I marked the place carefully in my mind so that we should not get the teams caught there, for it was clearly a registered target.

On the night of the 28th, the battery moved to Heilly, those who could move. Farmer was better and came with us, but Dodd and Immingham remained, and over a score of men. We spread the horses along the edge of a canal bordered with poplars, so that they should be well hidden from the air. We exercised and groomed them by night and early morning, and during the day watered them from buckets where they stood. It was a matter of luck that brought the bombers over. They killed two horses and left nothing but a hole. The guns went up by night and were spread along the grass ridge under camouflage netting, and not a spadeful of earth was turned up. Nearby some old dugouts in a bank gave us shelter.

Lettner was nervous about it all. First he put Mac in charge of the wagon line and brought Farmer to the guns. But Farmer was quite without experience. Then he sent Farmer back to the wagon line to help Mac. I protested that we must have at least three officers at the battery. Lettner said that there must be a senior officer at the wagon line. I suggested circuitously that perhaps he would take charge there himself and send Mac and Farmer up to the guns. He considered this for a time. I was obstinate. I persisted in arguing that there must be three officers at the battery, especially if he were one of them. For he was not likely to do OP. Someone had to do OP and I did not want to do it all. Lettner, moreover, was not fit to leave alone at the guns. He agreed at last, and said he must have Mac and myself at the guns. So Mac came up.

We sat together outside the shelters, grumbling softly while the major slept in the coolness of his dugout. We decided to make applications for leave to Trouville, since we could not get leave home. Mac was very keen. 'What times we could have,' he said, reverently.

'No good till this show's over. That looks like an orderly down below.'

'There's one thing certain,' Mac said, 'it's no use letting the major take the orders for fire. We should never get the barrage worked out in time.'

The messenger toiled up the hill, keeping to the shade of banks. Mac took out the orders, signed the envelope and handed it back. We went into the dugout and set to work. After a while the figure of Lettner blocked the light. 'Hell!' Mac said, under his breath. We waited. 'Would you mind, sir?' Mac said, 'we can't see.'

'What are you doing, MacVeagh?' Lettner said.

'Working out the barrage, sir.'

'I think you should have woken me.'

'Oh, I'm sorry, sir; I thought it would be quicker.'

'I shall never be able to do them if you don't let me start,' the major said petulantly, 'practice, of course, you know.'

'I thought you would wish to check them,' Mac said.

Then we had to start again at the beginning and halt at every step through the calculation, because the major had to do his own sums as well, so that an hour passed while we sat fuming with impatience, and the dusk increased so far that we feared the gunners would not get the fuses set in time. We had no cover in which a light could be shown sufficient for that work. At last we cut the major short, and sent for the Numbers One, and he did not seem to understand the need for haste. Each gun had fired two or three rounds on different days, and the calculations were based on the results of those rounds. Again we went through the sums to make sure of accuracy. We lay down for an hour or so.

In my sleep I had a vivid nightmare. I was standing in the doorway of the château garden in Heilly looking into the street, and my family appeared, every one of them. I could not persuade them to go away. They started across the Ancre marshes, from one of the birch islands to the other, while I floundered in the dried mud at the edge of the lagoons, imploring them to return. My feet were clogged with the mud, which smelled very strong in the sun. My father was behaving with genial gallantry. He kept waving his straw hat and saying, 'Oh, no, we came to see what it was like,' and my mother smiled and said, 'It seems rather nice here, really.' The small flies rose in swarms from the mud and my sister walked with the two children. At length we came to the road, and passed the spot where the water cart had been blown up the night before, and the horse plastered on the banks. 'What a funny smell,' my sister said, 'nasty, I think.' I besought them to go away, but they got to the battery position before I could push them back. 'Come along,' I said, 'this won't do,' and somebody came and helped me. 'Come along,' he said fiercely. Then, as they all went away, I woke in terror with sweat running down my face, to find Mac bending over me.

The night was still and peaceful, but somewhere in front the tanks and the Australians and Americans were waiting till our barrage should fall. A runner came with a watch timed by brigade headquarters, and another with the zero hour. Then two others, duplicating the information. The air was fresh and moist. Mac stood at the control, watching the minutes, holding a megaphone in his hand. At last he shouted 'Fire!'

The barrage broke widely over the front and lit the darkness with winking points. Mac still kept his eyes to the time, signalling the lifts in the barrage. The Germans were taken by surprise, the tanks crushed the wire entanglements and the infantry stormed up the hill to Hamel and swept through German gun positions, so that they were disorganized and defeated. When the line was secure we went back to St Sauveur.

Exhaustion had fallen upon the brigade. Day after day the influenza picked the men off and now the remainder had to do two men's work. It was over a mile of dusty road that led to the watering place among the banks of rushes in the Somme. The officers and NCOs and men took four horses apiece to water. Additionally each man had to clean harness and groom for two. There was a late feed to be given, pickets and guards to find. The mere watering took four hours out of the day, it was so far away. The men worked all the daylight hours and more, and had no time for a drink in the *estaminet*. Lettner moved through the scene with an air of disinterest, appearing from time to time at watering order or harness cleaning; one would say a man not perplexed, worried, involved. Yet at times when we passed the barns where the men were billeted we overheard remarks which were meant to be overheard, and Lettner pulled at one of the cigars out of the private box he kept in the mess, and said nothing. It was not simply that the men were tired, but the officers also were tired, and looked forward without pleasure from the years that lay behind to the years that lay before, but still with no thought of defeat. The years were a burden.

One day, when Lettner was in the lines, a driver swore at his corporal and struck at him, and ran away, dodging in and out of the horses, and at last out of camp, the corporal pursuing for a while, and Lettner saw it, but said nothing. Stables at last ended and the sub-sections lined up. I was orderly officer.

'All watered and fed, A?' I called, and so with the rest. I turned to the major and saluted.

'All watered and fed, sir.'

'Dismiss them, please.'

'Parade, dismiss.'

Several voices came from somewhere at the back, crying: 'And about bloody well time, too!' – 'Hear! hear!'

I looked at the major. He said nothing, but turned and walked away with Mac.

Then Sergeant Wilson came to me.

'Perhaps I ought not to say so, sir, and I hope you'll consider it confidential; there's going to be a mutiny. It isn't in your section, sir. But I know positively there's to be a mutiny tonight. I wanted you to look out. The ringleaders don't know I know. It's serious.'

'Is it the battery orders, times and so on?'

'Chiefly that, sir, and there being no leave. They say there's no time for a drink, even.'

'For the time being put back the time of harness-cleaning parade an hour and knock out the harness inspection.'

It was on my way to report to Lettner that I met Mac and told him. He flamed out in bitter anger at me so suddenly that I found nothing to answer. His face became hideously creased and his eyes bulged. The only thought in my mind was that he looked like a parrot when it ruffles its feathers and screams, so much had he changed. 'You think you can run this show,' he said rapidly, 'do you think it's yours because you're orderly officer? How dare you alter battery orders?'

I gaped at him in bewilderment.

He pushed his face forward and his words fell over each other. 'Yes, and I'll tell you something more. You're a coward, you're frightened. I've always known you were a coward.'

I walked away and left him still talking. It seemed to me I must go to Dodd, who had known us both so long. 'I suppose it's true that I'm a coward,' I said. 'Heaven knows I've no pretensions to bravery. But has Mac any right to say that?'

Dodd said no. 'Mac is overwrought,' he said, 'you all are. You'll both have to make it up. You've got to live together somehow or other.'

I sat in silence upon a hard wood chair in the tiled room and Dodd lay on the high bed, looking towards me. The evening was still and serene. We stayed silent for a long time.

'Don't let it worry you,' he said.

'No, it's not quite that, not all that. It's the whole war, getting us down. We shall never have any chance for ordinary living.' Dodd said nothing. I went to the gramophone, there on the chest, and wound it up. A book of borrowed records lay at its side. I put one on and let the needle drop into the groove. It grunted and jarred for a moment and then a few bars of music followed and someone singing —

Alas! that spring should vanish with the rose,
That youth's sweet scented manuscript should close,
The nightingale that in the garden sang —

I snatched the sound box from the disc. Dodd turned over in bed to face the little window and hot tears suddenly scalded my eyes. I was angry to be betrayed by that music and those words, and I walked out of the house. The mess was empty as I passed along the street. I went in and sat down, wondering what to do. The light faded, the swallows swooped low over the dust. Then Mac turned into the path. I waited till he was at the door and got up abruptly, to leave him. He began to say something.

'I don't sit or eat or sleep where you are,' I said, and then I saw the major had followed him, but I walked past the major and he called me back.

'I see there's some trouble between you boys,' he said, 'now what is it?' Mac laughed with hearty affectation.

'Oh, it's just nothing at all but a piece of foolery of mine,' he said. 'Quite foolish, sir. I'm sorry about it.'

I looked from one to the other. Neither of us would explain to Lettner.

'That's all right, then. I want us all to make a new start. We better make it now. Have a cigar —' he opened his box, ' – and be good boys.'

Mac laughed again, with acquiescence. 'Jolly good of you, sir,' he said. 'Thank you.'

Between them I was caught. I stood a moment considering my departure from the situation. But that would be an outrage upon the respect and civility I owed my commanding officer. In the moment, standing there and fingering the cloth, I was aware that he suspected that I was the ringleader in dissent from his view, an awkward one who would not be satisfied. He had put the cigar box diffidently between us on the table. Mac picked it up and offered it to me. He called me by my name. I dropped my hands to my side.

'Thank you, sir,' I said to the major. 'I should like one very much later on; but not just now, if you will excuse me,' but having said that I had to sit down with them and watch the major, still embarrassed, lumber about the room fidgeting with things. Then Mac jumped up from his seat by the window and said, 'Boyd and I will go down to see about hay-up, if you like, sir, and be back in ten minutes for dinner.' We went along the dusty road.

'What does all this mean?' I said.

'I don't know. Nothing. I'm sorry. I'm not a talking sort of fellow. I'm damned sorry. I didn't mean it. I was angry all of a sudden and couldn't stop.'

'I am so fed up to the teeth,' he said.

'Yes, well, all right,' I said. 'Let's leave it all. It's too sickening to think about.'

There were so many who were fed up. Gerald said that when he did get his leave he would go to some general he knew and persuade him to give him a job in Africa. His leave did come, and I rode with him in a French military car to Abbeville, and we sat in Charley's Bar drinking prairie oysters and glasses of Asti Spumante, and so got on to brandy, until it was time for the train. I returned with the French officer. He was gloomy and drove very fast; the car's exhaust throbbed in echo back from the trees on the road. We stopped in Flixecourt and drank absinthe in the back parlour of a small shop.

Two days later we marched out of St Sauveur at dusk. One sergeant, the storeman and the newly promoted QMS were drunk and the QMS rolled in his saddle. We arrived at Baizieux an hour or two later. Before we dismounted we heard the bombers coming across the valley. We sat still upon our horses and listened for the crashes. At regular intervals the bombs approached us, one, two, three, four – Now! But there was a pause. We listened to the beating of their engines. They passed over. Five and six fell beyond. It seemed better to be dead than to endure this.

Dodd was the mildest of men, in manner and in appetites.

'Personally,' I said, 'I'm very glad there's such a thing as whisky in the world. It was specially devised for the sinner. It soothes his troubles, calms his mind and wipes away his fears.'

We sat down to dinner. I poured out a whisky and put the bottle down by Dodd.

'It's a hellish life,' I said, after a pause. 'As soon as night falls you begin to expect the bombs. Now the moon is rising behind that hill like a snail shell. They'll be across soon.'

Dodd murmured, 'Yes,' and picked up the whisky bottle abstractedly.

'Backhouse! Is there anything else to eat?'

'Nothing else, sir.'

'Damn, there's nothing else.' I poured out another whisky.

'It has a curious taste,' Dodd said, emptying his glass.

'Like earth when you drink it and fire afterwards.'

'We ought to go and see the colicky horses.'

'Let's go now.'

The house overlooked the horse lines from a bank. We went down and saw the veterinary sergeant. One horse was dying in agony. That was not our fault. The corn ration was short and we were ordered to fill the horses up with green meat. The horse was distended and would not be moved, however its driver might try. They hit the horse with a stick and yet he would only move forward one stiff pace, groaning. They joined arms around his quarters and half lifted him, but still he would not move. Then as we watched, his legs trembled and he fell, his legs outstretched from his swollen barrel, and there, half an hour afterwards, he died.

We went back to the billet and censored letters. My pad lay before me but I could not bring myself to write to anyone. Sam was still hoping for a transfer to the RFC, but I could not write. I must write home; I wrote home nearly every day. 'This is a charming village,' I said, 'in a wide well-wooded part of the country. The land is divided by erratic valleys, and abrupt hills covered with trees rise between them. So I hope you don't picture me in the midst of barbarities. I feel very well and am enjoying the sunshine, hot and clear. Tomorrow Capt. Dodd and I go up to the guns for a spell – '

I was arrested by a faint noise in the distance. Dodd was listening too. He blew out the candle.

'— they are in a comfortable place,' I continued, moving to the moonlight at the window, 'safe and quiet. Forgive shortness, just got a small bit of work to do. Will write tomorrow.'

'Sounds like four of them,' Dodd said.

We stood by the window, listening. The machines rode over us and then some turned back, growing louder again. The first bomb slithered down like a ship launch and burst into a thousand screams. The crash shook the house and the pieces of metal knocked on the walls. Immediately another double crash fell over the horse lines and blinded the room with lightning. The planes circled and the pulsing drone diminished. We went down to the lines. The bombs had fallen at a little distance. We stood there and heard the planes casting back. Dodd sat on a heap of dried mud under a tree. The place smelled strongly of horse dung. He rested his chin on his hands and stared into the tree shadows cast by the moon. This time they dropped none upon us but went sailing on. Then we heard the rest.

'That's in the next parish,' Dodd murmured, 'might as well go to bed.'

'We might as well. We might get to sleep before they come back.'

We undressed and lay in our camp beds, as still as possible. The watch ticked on my wrist. Dodd turned over and coughed. Between the shutters the moon traced out a small arc on the floor, a brilliant silver arc. I could shut my eyes, but still my ears listened, acutely, and at last caught the first warning of the planes. Dodd coughed and swallowed.

'Are you awake, Dodd?'

'Yes, I'm awake. Are they coming back? I thought I heard them.'

'Yes. I think I'll have a drink, if you don't mind.'

'Not a bad idea.'

I brought the whisky bottle, a jar of water and two glasses and set them out in the alley between the beds. Dodd slewed his legs out of the sleeping bag. We drank. This time the bomber sowed his eggs in a straight line, two or three hundred yards to the west. One, two, three, four, five, six.

'Life gets rather uncomfortable at these times,' Dodd said, 'can't our planes do anything about it?'

'I suppose not. You can never see them at night, can you?'

We refilled our glasses, and sat drinking in silence.

'There they are again.'

This time they went straight past.

'Perhaps they've gone on to GHQ.'

There was a long pause before the next party arrived, and the moon was sinking.

'It sounds like the GHQ lot on their way home.'

'I hope they've dropped all their bombs,' I said, and then one fell, a large bomb which rattled the windows.

'I suppose they do this for moral effect more than damage,' Dodd said, 'of course if they do hit anything there's nothing left, but it's this sort of thing, keeping people awake and expecting the next lot, that counts.'

We waited half an hour and finished the bottle. It was nearly four in the morning. We slept.

Chapter 12

Old Soldiers Never Die

Aubers – Summer 1918

Coming back in the dawn was a weary business under all that equipment, with an empty belly, wanting sleep, and wary for the sound of the first shelling. The soft earth broke open, moreover, at every step, letting one's foot drop into the soil for an inch or two; and all the straps burdened one's chest. They made one feel like a wheezy old man. Then came the first lot, with a choric roar, more pervasive than time's winged chariot.

The sun was bright now, and the ground mist rose, to disclose a belt of wire. My ancient waterproof which had survived three winters' rains and seas of mud, received another tear in the skirt. Right in front there was a new shell hole. There was always something shocking in a new shell hole made where few had been before. Here was this untouched field, the clean, peaceable, orderly field, the virgin field, torn open by this shell, almost as though one had seen a murder committed, and might look round at the murderer. A warm, bittersweet smell hung round the hole. I struck off again to the right, stumbling sleepily among the lumps at the edge of the field.

The mess was empty. In the outhouse of the cottage the servants were asleep on old sacks. Their faces were grey and moist and they lay together like puppies, with their eyes screwed tight. It was full day now. Backhouse moved and groaned. I went inside the mess and shed my equipment on the floor, yawning so much that the tears came into my eyes. Since there was no cup of tea to be had I poured out a little whisky. The spirit made me feel sick. The birds were making a terrific noise in the gardens. I crawled into my sleeping bag and plunged into an extraordinarily deep sleep which oppressed me by its depth, so that when Backhouse woke me I felt exactly as though I had been baked, both hot and shivering. My clothes were stiff and clammy and the stale smell of the blankets was nauseous.

It was lunch time. Backhouse had made a cup of tea for me, and brought a mug of hot water for me to shave and wash with.

There was something I wanted to ask Dodd, but I could not remember what. A little bit of mirror was leaning against the broken bricks of the house wall. As I shaved I could see the line of the guns pointing towards Albert, and Dodd was standing there with Farmer, waiting for something. Number Three fired. Then Number Three was back. That was it, to ask whether Number Three, C Sub's gun, and the team, were all right. We had done a stunt; taken a gun up to the ridge looking into Albert. It squatted there in the noon sun, under a hawthorn, and waited for the colonel. We all waited for the colonel, Dodd, Farmer, a sergeant, three gunners and myself. He was to come up and watch us fire. We waited an hour. Then a message came asking Dodd to make the trials, first of myself and then of Farmer, just as we had done before, near Noulette Wood. There was a yellow building on the right of Albert. That was my first target. We lay on the grass, staring into Albert, and then, when I had given the orders, the gun fired one round. At the third round Dodd said, 'That'll do.' Then I switched on to another target. The front line was under us, 2,000 yards away. Then Farmer had his exercise.

Dodd was at my elbow now. 'C Sub got back all right,' he said, 'after dark. They had spotted us. The gun was surrounded with shell holes. They'll probably waste a lot of ammunition there during the next few days.'

'Then the infantry will bless us. It's one of their transport roads for the rations.'

'Yes. Lettner is shooting Number Three on zero line to make sure she's on the line again. It's almost his first shoot by himself.'

'You know the colonel's gone on a sort of a course?' Dodd continued. 'The major has been up at HQ the last three nights playing bridge with the new man.'

'New man?'

'Yes. Lucas isn't in charge.'

We went in to lunch.

'Mac's coming up tonight. Immingham will be in charge at the wagon line,' Dodd said, and looked to me.

'We do speak, you know,' I answered. He nodded. 'We're bosom friends

216

again,' I added. So Mac and I wandered through the deserted gardens of Henencourt, picking currants from the bushes, and when we came back to the garden of the mess there stood Farmer, so chubby he overflowed from his shorts and khaki shirt, cutting roses to put on to the dinner table. He walked inside through the hole in the wall. 'The roses are blooming in Picardy,' Mac sang, 'in the shade of the sheltering pine.' We joined him, lifting our voices in the still evening, and Glasgow wriggled through the fence and said he had come for dinner. Late that night the adjutant warned me to be ready for my leave warrant. It seemed incredible that it should come. It was nine months and one week, I reckoned, since my last leave, and at last I had the sacred green paper in my hand. And so through to Boulogne, where the cursed transport people stood on the platform picking out officers here and there to march with the men up that beastly hill to the leave camp. Just my luck to be caught, singled out. 'Captain Ash sends his love to you,' I said to the officer, 'but it's more than I do.'

'Damn it, are you one of the old brigade?'

'I am,' I said.

'Anyway,' he said, 'take them up and come down for a drink later. You'll be on the boat before the others and get a better place. It'll be absolutely crowded.'

The Pullman was waiting at Folkestone. We made a crowded rush for the armchairs and the tea. Then one was walking in London streets, stunned by the noise. After that another train to the north, which let the land slide past at a speed which was exciting and even confusing. The days went by in silence, as though one were deaf or numbed, a stranger.

The carriage door slammed again and the whistle blew. The local train jolted along the line for a while and halted by a platform on which some women ran excitedly searching for someone. 'Here he is,' they cried and came towards me, full of wishes, and handed through the window something to take back with me. Now that the train had gone on I looked at the parcel. It was a paper bag full of coarse-skinned purple gooseberries, like small footballs. One or two had burst and the juice was oozing on to the blue Melton cloth of the cushions. So I was back again at Henencourt.

The battery had gone under cover. They had shelled the village too often for safety. The rumour spread that a big attack was preparing; another surprise attack. Meantime the ordnance people had issued a new device for sighting guns, an arrangement of prisms and mirrors, by which the layer of the gun could see his front aiming posts and others behind at the same time, and so preserve his line with certainty. The mirrors were lying outside the mess dugout. Mac said he would pinch one to shave in. We put the mirrors in a row on the side of the trench and I wrote on them with soap our degrees from 'the great big bear' to 'the littlest bear of all'. The major was not pleased.

It seemed odd to me that I should be chosen for the gunnery course. Perhaps Lettner thought I needed bringing up to date. Perhaps it was kindheartedness. It meant, at least, another three weeks out of the line, at a small village west of Abbeville. It was like being at the rest camp again, but for the work, work from eight until four, all kinds of artillery work and of games, that made everyone hungry, so hungry there must, we said, be means to satisfy our hunger. It was only a day or two before we discovered that every course was hungry and that we could be fed out of hours. In the warm night we slipped from the line of huts under the great trees to a cottage barred and in darkness, and there knocked. They were waiting inside, and soon the cheap champagne frothed over, and the smell of frying eggs and chips filled the little room. Akeroyd came from Yorkshire, Lewis from New Zealand. We drank together and played hockey together. Akeroyd wanted some feminine company, and left us to find a Waac who waited in the mess. He went in his servant's clothes, because officers were forbidden to speak to Waacs. Then he returned and said she was a nice, decent girl who came from Ripon or someplace nearby, so they spent the evening talking about Yorkshire places. But a drunken Australian, called Fellows, had heard something and lounged over to us at the bar in the ante-room and used some filthy language to Akeroyd. Soon Akeroyd got up, very grim, and told Fellows he must fight or apologise in public. Fellows did not apologise so Akeroyd knocked him down. The next afternoon we went secretly to a clearing in the wood.

'Do you apologise?' Akeroyd said.

'I apologise to no dirty Imperial officer,'Fellows said, 'this is to be a fight to the bitter end.'

'Well, well!' Akeroyd said, lightly. 'Here are gloves, if you prefer them.'

'I do not prefer gloves, I am out to hurt.'

'Very good. But I shall wear gloves.'

They stripped to the waist and the sun threw flecks of brilliant biscuit white upon their skins, falling between the leaves. Fellows's skin was dusky, and Akeroyd's quite white.

'Remember we shall change positions each round,' Akeroyd said, 'because of the sun. I give you the advantage of the first round'.

The referee shouted 'Time!'

They came at once to blows and Fellows reeled backward. Akeroyd threw his chest up and breathed through his nose. Again they met, Fellows with his head down, Akeroyd bending over him and punching hard with his right, the muscles scarcely seeming to move under his shoulders. Fellows then fell forward on to his knees and his hair dropped over his face.

'Time,' Akeroyd said contemptuously.

When the space had passed, Fellows ran up. Akeroyd suddenly flung arm and body forward in a lunge and hit Fellows on the point. His body turned back in the air and fell with a thump which seemed very loud. Already the marks of Akeroyd's gloves were coming out in dull crimson patches on Fellows' chest, a strip-pling of pink upon the edge of each bruise. Akeroyd was untouched. He dressed and we went away.

It was the last night but two and we drank so heavily that I picked Lewis up from his bench and carried him a quarter of a mile to our hut, saying that he must go to bed; but as soon as I had left him on his bed he climbed out of the hut window. In the morning we were shaky and did not play the new army leapfrog game at our best. Akeroyd and Lewis and I were six feet high. As I pivoted on Akeroyd's shoulders, he standing almost erect, my nerve went and I landed on my wrist. Already Lewis had fallen out of the squad. In the afternoon a Scottish officer came and lectured upon the spirit of the bayonet and said how important it was to remember that ferocity would win the war quicker than anything else. To grunt and lunge, hating your enemy, to twist the blade making no mistake, to kick off the writhing body if it clung . . . so in gunnery, to land the man in the belly, to sweep the transport road with low shrapnel, which would pit them with the leaden balls, horses and men, to sweep the roads clear and leave them terrified of the unseen guns; that was war. Lewis drew designs in his army notebook and Akeroyd sighed, trying to keep awake. The man seemed fascinating to me.

We went to the cottage at night. It was our farewell. At two we all turned out, running along the great avenue of trees to the instructors' billet, and turned the German guns about so that they faced into their bedroom windows. We plastered the guns with lime; took the clock out of its housing . . . some had to stay behind the next day to clear off the mess, but Akeroyd came as far as Abbeville with me. He paused with one foot on the running board of his coach and said, 'That was a damned good ride we had when we lost ourselves accidentally in the wood and ate an omelette and drank Chablis, wasn't it?'

It was a good day, that one, the sun shining between the trees, over the vast spread of the park land upon which smaller woods rose like islands of dark marble. We had not been anxious to find the rest of the course, and when we returned no one had said anything to us. Now on our separation, I felt again the close presence of the front, to which my train was carrying me, the diminishing chances of life dragged out over so many years, and was depressed to think that neither my course nor my marks could renew a spirit of military enthusiasm. Moreover Gerald had sent a message of farewell. He had got his staff job in Nigeria and was gone.

In the small dark dugout the voices seemed to go on without end, and to be focussed in one black point. As if from the heart of darkness I could hear my own voice explaining again and again that it was all too bloody thick to put the dirty upstart in charge of the battery and let him muck it up. And now he had got me posted to A Battery and pinched both my horses. Perhaps he wouldn't have done it if the colonel had been back. Then at times Glasgow replied soothingly that these things couldn't be helped and that one was better away from a man like that, perhaps. Then he asked if I really wanted another drink of whisky and passed the bottle, and said that I ought to have some food, and indeed brought some food which appeared suddenly in a pause. After that the fog which seemed to fill the world receded a little and the pressure of useless anger in my mind relaxed, but still surrounded me, so that I could not get away from this envelopment. 'He sent me away so he could get me out of the battery, after I've been with it more than a year, he has pinched my horses and I lose my section, my servant and my groom. I suppose it doesn't matter.'

'It does matter,' Glasgow said, 'but it doesn't matter now, just now. Besides that the A chaps are an awfully decent lot. I like 'em much, what I've seen of them. In these new battles that are beginning you'll be better off with A.'

'I come back from this gunnery course and the first news I get is from my groom. Then the major is too funky to tell me, and Dodd has to do it. In one of those damned dark Nissen huts among the ruins. Most gloomy places, like the inside of a shell. Dodd couldn't do anything. And when I asked

Lettner for Gaby he said he couldn't spare her, unless I could get a charger in return. A charger! I ask you!'

'Yes,' Glasgow said, 'but you'll have Beecham, Peterson and Kerr to live with now. What did Dodd say?'

'He said he rather envied me.'

'Besides that you may be imagining it all. Didn't A lose a senior fellow on 5 April?'

'Yes. A man with a hatchet face, Smith, a good chap. He was badly smashed up. They were over strength then.'

'They've lost a junior now, I believe, someone sick or mildly wounded. So they need another man.'

I rose. I was going on to A Battery.

'I'll come with you part of the way,' Glasgow said. It was pitch dark outside. We moved along the grass track.

'It's damned decent of you to listen to all this grousing,' I said, 'to let people come in and mop up your food and whisky and then behave so badly!'

'No it isn't. I like it. I'm proud of my visitors.'

'You are a damned decent fellow.'

Glasgow laughed in the darkness and thrust his face upwards to the clouds. 'Give my love to those nice fellows in A,' he said.

It was the last day of September and the rain streamed down out of a grey sky in increasing sheets. We were out of action, waiting orders for Italy again. The artificer, with the help of some other tradesmen, was making wooden slats to go over the space between the seats of railway carriages, so that we could lie full length and sleep during the long journey. That night Hampstead came along to our billet to tell me that a new subaltern called Levy had taken Gaby and had been thrown three times in one half hour into the ditch on the line of march, and had thereupon given up Gaby to Hampstead and was riding the strawberry.

'She bolted with him, sir,' Hampstead added, 'with all the battery watching, and put him in the mud. He couldn't keep his heels out of her, trying to keep on. I don't think Mr Levy is pleased with Gaby.'

'Captain Dodd ought to ride her.'

'I think he will, sir.'

Mac came up also. He wanted to get back the money he had lost when he betted we should go to Italy a year ago. We booked the bet again. Within three days we were marching northeast towards the Aubers Ridge.

I crossed Pont Riqueul a few days later. M. Bourdon's brewery was in ruins. The village had been destroyed. There was scarcely a trace of the Vittus' house except white rubble, and the trees were all broken. The country looked as if an enormous adze had passed over it a few feet above ground; in all directions there was nothing to see but the shapes of ruins fallen between broken tree stumps. The canal in which I once fished was broken and the water stood in stagnant pools. The smell of the village, which had been filled with the sweetness of orchards and sometimes with the warm smell of the brewing, was rank and bitter. The broken and disordered road led over a shapeless crossroads towards Laventie. I was travelling a day or two in advance of the battery to take over a position from some artillery of the division we were to relieve. I found them on the side of the Fauquissart road. A captain was in charge, almost out of his mind with worry. 'The men are about Class B2,' he said, 'and I have only one officer, and he is an epileptic. Do you mind if I make you my senior subaltern until your crowd arrive?'

His men scarcely seemed to know the names of things. It seemed to take nearly all the afternoon to prepare one section to march out. At last they went. The captain took me into one of the empty gun pits. 'I've had to live in a hole in the mud,' he said, 'I daren't take one man away to dig; and not one knows how to roof a dugout. Where's the food?' he bellowed. There was no answer. He drew his revolver and put it on the box between us. 'I'll frighten the devils,' he said. He shouted for a servant. The man came into the pit.

'Food, sir!' he said, 'I sent it all away with the section.'

The captain jumped up with his revolver in his hand. 'Run after the cart and fetch it back,' he shouted, 'or I'll shoot you where you stand.' The man darted for the road and disappeared. The captain called me and led me to the cook's quarters, and there we got some beef. Alternately during the night we got up to check the night firing lines. Even the gunlayers were not reliable. With the first light we rose and drank tea.

'We'll take a day off and look at our infantry,' the captain said, 'they're even worse.' So it came about that we were among the first in Aubers. The Germans had been forced back by the new attacks and had to leave the Ridge. The poor exhausted infantry toiled in open order up the Ridge, oldish men, short of breath, and boys with staring eyes and pale faces. We went along the road on top and peered into the houses.

The cottages we had fired at for four years were simply skins lined with concrete, every one an OP and every one proof against big shells.

The farmhouse at the crossroads contained incomparable ranges of concrete chambers, with steel shutters inside to protect the back windows against splinters. The rooms used for observation were properly equipped with tables for maps and with louvered peepholes. Something had gone wrong with their demolition work. As we walked among the houses the captain called me. He was looking through the back window on to a charge of four 6-inch shells, with fuses leading into them. We found others in the houses, and in one a small crucifix was lying on the table. I took that away with me. As we returned the infantry of my own division passed over the Ridge, and Major Beecham was waiting for us at the battery.

'It's a new sort of war,' he said, 'we shall have to follow them up and keep on pushing them back.'

We moved the guns forward by the crossroads in Aubers and a few hundred yards in front. Beecham and I went riding on to reconnoitre until we were stopped by shellfire and machine guns.

A day or two later the wagon line came up to the fringe of Aubers village, and I went down to take charge. The days were dark and the nights sheer black. We heard rumours that the Germans had asked for an armistice, and when I wrote home I said 'We don't pay much attention to that. Haig's message means "Don't talk nonsense." Besides, it's my golden rule never to believe anything good unless I see it happen. "Blessed is he who expecteth nothing, for he shall never be disappointed." The tenth Beatitude ...'

For three nights now I had not slept. At minute intervals a 4.2 howitzer fired towards us. I could hear almost every part of its flight; its weary ascension and its violent descent. The pieces of metal clanged on the corrugated walls of my hut. I lay between the officers' valises for some protection against the nearer bursts, which threw hot razor-edged pieces whirring at the hut. A great clod of earth fell on the roof and shook the flimsy shelter. As the burst dissipated I fixed my eyes again on the print of the book, endeavouring to remain interested in Margaret Deland's views of the suffrage movement. The candle flame burned steadily at my head. A carton of cigarettes lay at my right hand. I lit another and went on reading. Another 4.2 began its journey and ended it as usual, upon the flank of the wagon line. It was one of the howitzers which fired upon us regularly at dusk. The first night we had led the horses out of the line for safety, but ran into another part of the shoot which drove us back. There was nothing to be done but to lie there and wait. Another 4.2 wailed down, rather nearer the hut, and sent a piece of metal through the wall. They were still far enough away to miss the horses. And now, while the NCOs and men slept soundly in concrete pillboxes built in the wood, I had to lie in this vulnerable box. *The Rising Tide* distracted me again for a minute. I had read a score of sentences before a 4.2 burst not far from the door and blew out the candle. My eyes were sore for want of sleep but yet I could not sleep. In another forty seconds another shell would arrive and shake the night. He probably thought he was shooting into Aubers, but he must be 200 yards plus, at least. Perhaps he was a fraction off the line, rather. 'Drop fifty, One-o minutes more left' might fetch the crossroads. If he would shoot there for ten minutes I could sink into so deep a sleep that nothing would waken me, short of a bomb at the door. I tried to persuade myself that the 4.2 was so faithful to this corner of the field that there was no danger, and to convince myself that the noise was pleasant. 'The noisy devil! There he is again!' Far away a noise that sounded like 'Pump' spoken quietly, then a long 'Wee' which broadened into a roar; the assertive 'CRASH' broke up into a chorus of whirrs, some of them sure to clatter on the corrugated iron of my hut. I lit the candle and put out my hand for my writing pad. 'Dear Sam,' I wrote, 'every minute the Hun makes a disgusting noise, so I cannot get to sleep. I hear great things of you with a job at GHQ. This is only a scrawl to send compliments on a category of B3, and congratulations to the appointments bloke, whoever he may be, for having saved you from the wreck—' My pencil scrawled across the sheet involuntarily as the shell burst. There was a brief commotion in the lines. I got up to see whether anyone had been wounded. The picket came towards me, saying that it was nothing but an affair of kicks. We walked up and down together, talking quietly. One of the horses was loose. It had gnawed through its green hide head rope, which now was all slimy with saliva. The picket said this horse could eat nearly a whole head rope a week.

For an hour I lay in darkness, trying to go to sleep, but at the end of it I lit a new candle, took a fresh cigarette and lifted the book above my head, where it wavered a little on my elbows. I said to myself that I would give it another night, and if then the howitzer went on, I must go to the guns, or shift the hut, or bag a corner in the pillboxes. But that seemed impossible. Soon after daybreak the howitzer stopped fire. About 8 o'clock I got up to begin the day.

In the morning I had a long and exhausting quarrel with the sergeant major, which only ended when I told him to do what he was told.

At dusk the German howitzers began their dreary shoot on the area.

At about 10 p.m. the minute gun began. This night again I tried first to sleep. The howitzer was not exactly on the same spot, but near enough. I spent a long time then with the candle alight, lying on my back staring at the roof and watching a long blade of hay which hung down from the two by two rafter under the corrugated iron. I finished *The Rising Tide* and turned to a book by no one in particular. My servant had borrowed it for me. It seemed even more baffling than the other; something about racing. When it became too difficult to lie still I got up and walked about the lines. Surprisingly one shell fell off the line. Then there was a longer pause. The layer had been changed, I thought, and had been careless with the sight, and now his Number One had checked it and was putting it straight. I reflected that the German gunners were so proud of their gunnery that they did not search and sweep as we did; they refused to vary line and distance in case they were a little off the target. It could be calculated that if they had searched and swept with that howitzer, two, if not three, out of nine shells, would have come into the wagon line. But the gunner was back on his old line. My legs felt tired. The sky was obscured by cloud. I went back to lie down again and promised myself that I would not give it another night. I would do something or other.

But the day was too full, too busy for fancies. By nightfall I had borrowed another book and replaced my candles. I lay on my back till two in the morning reading and smoking, and gazed up at the piece of hay which moved a little, stiffly. Every time I heard the far-off howitzer fire, my mind lost its attention. It seemed that the shell was coming a little closer, closing up the gap between the hut and the field. Every minute I expected to hear that a piece had shot over the hut and wounded a horse. The desire to escape became strong. I got up and walked slowly across the lines to the gate. It would be enormously pleasant, a tremendous relief, to open it and walk up the road to brigade headquarters and there surrender the charge of that wagon line in any way they wished. My hand was even on the top bar. Three times, I said, I had promised myself to do something about it. I turned back and walked about with the picket for a time and returned to my valise. My eyes closed, but had scarcely done so when my ears caught the 'Pump!' and I could not stop myself listening. Now I lay again in frigid attention. I repeated to myself Donne's lines, for diversion —

Death be not proud, though some have called thee Mighty and dreadful, for thou art not so –

It appeared to me that death, extinction, was nothing. There was a Salvation Army hymn, 'Oh to be nothing, nothing, only to lie at His feet.' Only to lie anywhere peaceful, to sleep! It was easy, to be dead. Getting so far was the difficulty.

My new book seemed more vapid than the last, but I must wait before I got up again; let the howitzer kill off another thirty minutes out of infinity. Thus we ascended the hour of three. A horse was lightly wounded then, but when it was dressed there was again nothing to do. It was difficult to lie still and quiet when the heart beat like a powerful engine and shook one with the desire to escape. Some people had to scream, I reflected. But that was forbidden by King's Regs. 'Conduct prejudicial to good order and military discipline.' Or would it be 'Causing despondency among the troops?' Or curse; the diminished seventh of screaming. I was suddenly in a nightmare sweat at the thought that if I had opened the gate and even taken one single step on the road I should have been deserting in the face of the enemy and liable to be shot. 'Deserting his post in the face of the enemy.' Shoot him first and then blow his brains out with a .45 short barrel revolver. Put the muzzle in his mouth and turn it upwards. The soft lead service bullet which mushroomed. I turned over in the sleeping bag alarmed by these thoughts. Perhaps I was gone stone potty already. I took a piece of paper and wrote on it 'You must see the doctor in the morning. Signed.' Reading it over it seemed ridiculous. I put it in the candle flame and lit another cigarette with it. A cooler air was coming through the doorway and I saw that the hedge was becoming brilliantly dark against the sky. It was time the German shut up shop. One minute passed silently, then two, and three. I was asleep.

In full daylight Wellington woke me. Getting out of bed I trod some piece of burnt paper into the earth. An hour later the detail of the day was all decided. I went to the gate and walked up the road. Beecham said in a worried voice, 'I can't understand; I'm too frightened of being afraid to let myself admit it.'

'Yes, sir. But I feel I'm so near making an exhibition of myself that it's better . . . for me ... to push off. And for the army. I might make a disgusting exhibition of myself. Scream and run. Or scrabble into the ground. I thought it was better to preserve a few threads of sanity. Self-defence I suppose. I can't help that. "A sheen'd veil, thin as the veil of sleep." Thinner than that.

I lie down at night never knowing whether I shall be mad in the morning.'

'Spend a night here.'

'Very good, sir, if you wish it.'

I walked away from the pillbox, angry at the line of poetry. A gun fired in the distance, and I had to listen for the flight of the shell. The day at last ended and I lay down on the pillbox floor. After a time I fell asleep, in confused dreams. A little after midnight an orderly woke me. Beecham slept upon his camp bed. 'Orders for fire,' the man said, handing me the envelope. I prepared the orders and went out, walking up and down behind the flashing guns. My hands were cold and moist, and between each pair of explosions I had to halt and listen for a reply. I slept no more that night and in the morning I went to the doctor.

Chapter 13

Living are the Dead

Le Havre – Autumn 1918

The casualty clearing station was at St Venant. The sky dripped rain upon the spoiled land. Sister sent two of us out to gather branches of autumn colours for the ward. On the broken railway line we found a small variety of yellow foxglove. The ground was very wet and the land deserted. In the hedges there were scarlet hips and haws and great sprays of blackberries. Curtis cut down arms of hawthorn upon which golden convolvulus was twined. I came nearby to the towpath on which we had often ridden in 1915 and we walked along in the dusk with the bundles of blazing leaves over our shoulders, talking about the old grey war which stretched to infinity behind us and about us.

In the morning they put us on a long, slim barge for Calais. The great poplars slid past the windows as if we were travelling in a dream. At night I read by candle light till Sister came and took away my book. She sat at her table at the head of two long ranks of beds, which vanished into darkness at the hatchway, and she read in the ellipse of light falling from a silver lamp with a shade like a bell. She had grey hair and a white mutch and upon her grey cape she wore the ribbons of the South African War and the Nurse's Cross. As she read she perpetually smoothed the material of her dress over her knees with her right hand, only raising it to put back the white linen of her cap. Far down the barge someone moved uneasily and she looked up, her glasses flashing the reflection of the light. Moving restlessly the dreamers threw up half sentences into the stillness, and even their words seemed part of the stillness, as though in the red glow of the nightlights nothing could fluctuate or change. Upon the white sheets of my paper I could see the black marks telling them at home how much I was enjoying this journey.

LIVING ARE THE DEAD

We lay all together, the acquaintances from St Venant, and in the morning Pond, who was badly wounded, begged me to shave him, and lay still under my hollow-ground blade as though he were in a barber's chair.

The journey to Calais took two days and now I was installed in a hospital made from a hotel or a casino on the front, where the grey seadrift came billowing up against the windows. The sick officers in the hospital seemed to be mad, walking in and out of the ward with dark suspicious glances, whispering perpetually in corners. They behaved as though there might be some conspiracy which they must defeat, in secret. Two of them came to me as I put my small kit into my locker, to ask, to interrogate me. One said he was senior man in that ward ... he had been in some months. 'He's well in with, you know, Lady who runs the place,' the other man said, 'can make it cushy, if you, you know . . .' Then they both went away to another new man.

I asked that I could have a medical board as soon as possible, so that I might get some work to do. They sent two of us up the hill to one of the camps on the top and on the way the other man pointed out a hospital camp to me and said, 'That's the venereal hospital where they had the mutiny; they stopped it with machine guns.'

We sat in an open porch naked, with our clothes on our knees. It was very cold. At last my name was called. There were three doctors and they made many tests. I lay on an American leather bed and one of them scratched the ball of my foot with a broken match. I looked up at the skylight, wondering with interest what they were going to do with me. The match man still went on scratching, as though he were trying to wear his match away. One of them had a stopwatch. I had no idea what they wanted me to do. At length I grew tired of the scratching and curled my toes over. The man with the watch showed it to the other and said, 'Extraordinary!' They put me in the B3 category and sent me to le Havre. A letter from Peterson caught me before I left. He gave me news of the brigade. 'Thank the Lord,' he said, 'we moved when we did. I spent three nights with that 4.2 of yours. It was more than enough.'

In the mess a subaltern was playing 'Madame Butterfly'. He was a very small man with green eyes and a face the colour of flour, and he played well. Some of the subalterns were rather drunk and when he finished they called to him mockingly, 'Emmenthal, here's a fellow says you can't hypnotise at all, he says you're an absolute dud at it.' Emmenthal shook his head and said 'No, I do not care.'

'Oh, but you must,' they said, 'you really must!'

'No. I will not do anything.' The little Jew looked almost frightened. They gathered round him in a ring and pushed him into a chair opposite the other. Emmenthal objected. He said he was too tired. They held him down. At last he consented. He put the other man's palms together. 'You shall not be able to move them apart till I let you,' he said, and then he shook his own long fingers criss-cross in front of his victim's eyes, with great rapidity. The group stood silent. Emmenthal chanted, in a ferocious voice, 'You can't move your hands, move them! Move them! You can't move your hands, can't move them, try and move them,' and the subject expressed the violence of the attempt in his face, while his fingers were white down the ridges with the effort of pressing his hands together. After a moment Emmenthal stopped his movement and lay back in his chair exhausted, while sweat broke out on his forehead, and the other man sat as still as a corpse till Emmenthal roused himself to release him. The trick brought much applause. Emmenthal seemed exotic in that company, no less than his performance. He took me to his hut one night. We had talked about books and music. 'This is some of my writing,' he said, handing me a bundle of manuscript.

'It seems highly coloured.'

'It is madness, if you like.'

'Madness?'

'Thus —' He had a glass ampoule in his hand, and filled a syringe from it. This he pressed into the loose skin of his forearm.

'Is it necessary?'

'Yes – now, I must have two a day; sometimes three.'

'If the war ever ends how will you get all that cocaine?'

'We will not discuss that, if you please.'

He was telling me about the hideousness of army life, the lack of art and of privacy. I heard him say, 'She is a most fascinating girl, quite kittenish in fact. I call her Pussy – in French, of course – I have lived all my life in France. She will be at my apartment in town, soon. Come down and eat a meal. We'll go out together.'

'You see,' he said, opening the door of the room, 'here is the Pussy with the stove going, everything is here; a bottle of wine, glasses, a large bed!' She was a French girl, neat and pleasant, as big or bigger than Emmenthal

We dined in the town and caught the last tram up to the camp. Emmenthal was anxious I should rent the room next to his. 'Think of it; you have privacy for the first time in years, you could wear your own clothes, a dressing gown, and write or read! You're only on light duty, why not? Then we could dine in town every night; or if not, get a *consommation* from the girl and picnic in my bigger room. And since you have French acquaintances in the town, think how easy to go and see them. Besides Pussy has a sister. We could be four when you felt like it.'

My friends, whom I had visited whenever I passed through the town, lived not far from the apartment. They showed the most charming hospitality. The man played Brahms on his grand piano. His house seemed so attractive and so dainty that I felt shy of it. So Emmenthal persuaded me. I took the room. We went to a big store to buy things. One of his purchases was a pink silk dressing-gown.

In the afternoon he met Pussy at the lodging and when I came in out of the rain she had made tea, straw-coloured tea, with soft sponge biscuits and toast. Then her sister came in. To drink tea with people and to look out of a house window was like the relief one finds when some aching tooth has stopped. It was full of unexpected pleasures, the warmth, the cleanliness, the electric light. Pussy called me. 'You shall be Charles, he Willy, and my sister Negro, because her hair is so dark.'

'Or Blanche because her skin is so white!'

'I shall call her the White nigger!' Pussy said, laughing.

The stove was glowing with balls of coal dust shaped like eggs. Emmenthal began to look exhausted, as he lay on the settee. He drew off into a corner of the room and busied himself with his hypodermic syringe. We went out to dine at a small restaurant in the square. The sisters went home. Emmenthal wanted to sleep at the lodging. He said we could get into camp before the morning parade, by a way he knew. When morning came I had to drag him out of bed and stand over him while he dressed. There was nothing left of him but a body. We got into camp successfully. Again we went down and dined, but this time alone, in the little restaurant. Emmenthal spoke to a woman sitting there. She was a Spaniard. After dinner we walked back to the rooms and the woman came with us. When I entered his room to look for a book she was sitting on the settee wrapped in the pink silk *peignoir*, and in the night she woke me with some long story of Emmenthal's coldness. He didn't love her, she said, but love was necessary to her above all things. I took her back to Emmenthal, whom I found fully dressed, pacing the floor with his hand in his tunic, like Napoleon. In the morning again I had to drag him out of bed and push him into life and order a taxi to get us back in time. On the ground floor of the house the old soldier who was servant to an officer on the staff of the Assistant Provost Marshal, was cleaning the boots of his officer and his officer's mistress. She was a lively girl.

The following afternoon I found Emmenthal in the apartment alone. He was fingering the pink silk dressing-gown and weeping over it, his face working in the most fantastic way. 'What is the matter?' I asked. He said thickly that it was treacherous to let the Spanish woman wear Pussy's dressing-gown. He ought to burn it sooner than let it fall on Pussy's lovely shoulders again. At length he said, 'I will put it in the press, and if that woman should dare to come again she must sit without it.' He also said he must atone for his wrong by giving everyone – except the Spaniard, of course – dinner at the Petit Vatel in a private room.

Day after day drifted by in the slack duties of the camp, and the rumours of an armistice became more frequent and more assertive.

One day Emmenthal handed me orders to take a draft of men to Abbeville. We marched down to the goods yard below the camp before it was light. No one was there, and we spent three-quarters of an hour walking up and down under the stars, draped in our blankets, for it was cold. At last an officer appeared and showed us our trucks. The men clambered in and I went into the brake van and spread some dirty straw on the floor. Another long wait followed before we started.

We got to Rouen. It was about 10 o'clock in the morning. The conduct of the Railway Transport Officer was unusual enough to be noticeable. He ran in and out of his office in the most genial way, speaking to all sorts of people. The sergeant observed that we should be getting kisses from the military police next. As we marched off to the other station the RTO suddenly called to us and ran after. He shook me warmly by the hand and said the armistice would be signed that morning. I expressed some doubts. 'God bless you,' he said, 'it's to be done in a railway carriage; shouldn't I know?'

We marched towards the quay. It was a quarter to eleven. All the years that had passed reproached me with the hundred occasions on which I had not 'worked' something; never a day late returning from leave, scarcely ever dodged the march up to the leave camp, never managed an extension of leave. I was one of those for whom things did not wang. So I called the sergeant and handed him all the papers relating to the draft, and told him to entrain the men without waiting for me.

LIVING ARE THE DEAD

I had stopped at the southern end of the Pont Neuf and walked towards the old city. The first sirens let loose a call to the ships on the river. One after another their whistles quivered in the air. But I did not believe. Then from the Citadel a gun began to fire, one, two, three, four . . . each rapid punch of sound following upon the other's heels. The people on the bridge stopped and then went mad as it seemed, hurrying faster, running with their hats in their hands, under the bright, cool sun. Some were kissing each other, and laughing, with tears in their eyes, and some sang. But the crowd went faster and ever faster before my eyes, dizzily, and the streets became filled by processions moving under swaying banners. Rows of soldiers and sailors, English, French, and Belgian linked arms with Waacs, nurses, French shopgirls, civilians, waiters, and swayed across the streets. I stood at the end of the bridge looking at the rushing crowd and felt numb, as though a mirage had lifted itself before my eyes. I wanted some friend to make me feel something and I wanted to eat and drink, particularly to drink, so that I should forget everything but the hour. In my wallet there was not enough money.

There were two French soldiers in the first-class compartment of the Paris express. One of them was very drunk and waved a tricolore in our faces. He sang the 'Marseillaise' constantly. The train travelled into the night. The soldier's arm, enlivened by his bottle, became more menacing. I suggested he should stick the flag out of the window so that everyone should see it. We lowered the window a little and jammed the stick in the crack. Soon the wind blew it away. The Frenchman began to cry. I promised him a dozen flags at le Havre. I went up the corridor and in my abstraction walked right through a plate-glass door. The peak of my cap touched it first but I noticed nothing until the glass fell harmlessly at my feet. The drunken soldier was awakened by the noise and came out. The sight made him more cheerful. We got to le Havre about 7 o'clock.

The streets of the town were full of people following the torchlight processions. I dined alone at the Club and went back into the streets feeling incredibly lonely among all the people, and all night long, as 1 walked about, the thought of the unappeasable Front lay upon my mind and beat upon it with physical pain.

Apology

The war was over. But across my dark landscape the rain swept with steeply diagonal strokes, obscuring the splintered trees. What light remained fell upon the streaming helmets of men struggling through mud up to the front line. The craters in the foreground were filled with the carcases of mules, mingled with the bodies of men. Nearby a gun with a broken wheel lay on its side, and a train of pack mules carrying ammunition went towards the crest with nervous, stilted strides. The bombardment fell with macerating fury on the front, hastening its speed, and still the burdened figures went on, interminably, by the edge of the wood.

This recurrent vision, familiar by night and by day, accompanied me for some years. It was only one of several evidences that war was not over. Perpetually I turned landscapes into battlefields, choosing OPs, gun positions and wagon lines. Almost every night as I went to sleep I heard my 18-pounders firing overhead, and three or four years after the armistice I was visited by a strange conviction that the life that was left in me had sunk to so low an ebb that I could have emptied it by the mere act of will. I should be extinguished by volition, as I stood there, washing my hands, and I found that the act of willing to exist was painful and arduous. All sorts of nightmares came to me from the war, and occasionally still return, but the hopeless picture of the Somme near High Wood is constant, as an image of the war, and determined the composition of this book.

The thought was a sort of conviction that the violence of the war in certain places was so great that it must have fastened to the earth those who died upon it. The great army of souls was carrying on in ghostly sectors; carrying on without one single hope that there could be anything better on this earth than peace. With no other expectation whatever. Moreover, among them I seemed to see the shapes of many who had survived the war as living men. Our shades, I thought, still walk those fields. Some part of us is still doing duty over there. Perhaps something was spilled which can never be recovered. At times it has appeared as though all the vivid quality of life had been spent there and had left only sufficient consciousness to allow one to grow old and remember. All this is no more than to say that old soldiers never die, they only fade away. Fear, terror, anguish, can give one a dreadful intimacy with a few clods of earth now broken by the plough, with a dugout whose constituents were long since parted. But the spiritual shape perhaps remains.

Such losses, I believe, can never be appeased. But those who survived, made, I think, a sort of vow to the others, to those who went mad and to those who were killed, that they would never forget. The feeling was that one must try to carry home the conviction that quite ordinary people had to endure extraordinary hardships for no sufficient reason. They died, perhaps in pain of mind and body, with no consoling thought except that death would be relief. Nothing was further from their mind than that they were different from their fellows. In their bones they disbelieved the sentimental doctrine of heroism and the childish doctrine of the survival of the fittest. They thought perhaps that all fighting men deserved well of their country, and I believe they passionately desired that their country should understand it all, without mistake and without sentiment. I believe also that they feared, and feared truly, that these hopes would be disappointed.

But no one can express the opinions of the rest. Here I have attempted only to set down what I saw, in the detail and proportion which would have presented themselves to anyone who was in my place. Though I am conscious that it leaves out many important things, and perhaps the most important of all, I offer it in fulfilment of my promise.